JOHN WESLEY
His Puritan Heritage

A STUDY OF THE CHRISTIAN LIFE

JOHN WESLEY
HIS PURITAN HERITAGE

Robert C. Monk

EPWORTH PRESS   LONDON

JOHN WESLEY: HIS PURITAN HERITAGE

Copyright © 1966 by Abingdon Press

All rights in this book are reserved.

First published in Great Britain by
Epworth Press 1966

Book Steward
Frank H. Cumbers

Printed in the United States of America

To my Mother
and the memory
of my Father

ACKNOWLEDGMENTS

Grateful acknowledgment is due many persons for their contribution to this book. My sincere appreciation is expressed to the faculty of the department of religion of Princeton University who accepted the original form of this work as a Ph.D. dissertation. The illuminating instruction patiently offered not only contributed much to my knowledge but taught me the joy of research. I am especially indebted, however, to Professor Horton Davies, whose constant guidance and wise counsel carried me through my years of graduate study and whose sustained interest and persistent encouragement from then until now has contributed immeasurably to the preparation of this book. My appreciation is also due Professor Gordon Harland of Drew University who, through a lecture delivered on the subject, first stirred my interest in Wesley's relationship to the English Puritans.

The Danforth Foundation, the Lilly Foundation, the Board of Education of The Methodist Church, and the Woodrow Wilson Foundation generously provided the financial assistance through grants and fellowships which made the study possible.

The untiring efforts of Lawrence Kline, Methodist Librarian at Drew University; Frederick Arnold, Reference Librarian at Princeton University; and Mrs. John Warnick, Curator of the Methodist Historical Collection, Southern Methodist University, contributed greatly to the research for this work.

I want to extend special thanks to my colleague, Dr. Walter Hofheinz, whose meticulous review and helpful suggestion, which extended far beyond what might be expected or anticipated, has made it possible to bring the work to publication.

The debt to my wife Carolyn, who has sustained me through her care, assistance, and encouragement, cannot be calculated but is gratefully acknowledged.

ROBERT C. MONK

McMurry College, May, 1966

CONTENTS

ABBREVIATIONS

Bibliography	*The Works of John and Charles Wesley: A Bibliography,* Richard Green
CL	*A Christian Library*
DNB	*The Dictionary of National Biography*
Journal	*The Journal of the Rev. John Wesley, A. M.,* ed. Nehemiah Curnock
Letters	*The Letters of the Rev. John Wesley, A. M.,* ed. John Telford
LQHR	*London Quarterly and Holborn Review*
MMC	*Minutes of Methodist Conferences, 1744 to 1798*
Sermons	*Wesley's Standard Sermons,* ed. Edward Sugden
WHSP	*Wesley Historical Society Proceedings*
Works	*The Works of the Rev. John Wesley,* ed. Thomas Jackson

INTRODUCTION

John Wesley, in the more than a century and a half since his death, has been the object of immense scholarly inquiry as a leader of the evangelical revival, as the founder of Methodism, and as one who profoundly influenced the fabric of religious and social life in England and America during the eighteenth and nineteenth centuries. In recent years, prompted at least in part by the rising tide of ecumenical interest and endeavor, there has been a renaissance of Wesley studies. This new inquiry has been concentrated on Wesley's theology but has also led to reevaluation of his teachings and practice.

Wesley's eclecticism has long been recognized and has contributed to multifactoral treatment of this quite complex individual. From what have normally been considered widely diverse religious traditions, he selected those doctrines, principles, and practices which most suited his own purposes without regard to the labels which they might bear.

The selection was far from random but conformed to the central concerns and interests which guided all Wesley's work. An examination of each of the major traditions upon which Wesley was dependent would not necessarily explain the man Wesley, for each tradition was modified in accordance with his own dominant theological principles; the coalescence of all the traditions was produced by this unique religious figure. On the other hand, one can hardly hope to understand Wesley without examining the various traditions as they are reflected in his thought and practice.

John Wesley was a loyal son of the Church of England who, though buffeted in his relationship to her, was ever her defender. Both in thought and practice Wesley displayed a major dependence upon the tradition represented by this church. Reacting against the traditional nineteenth-century interpretation of Wesley as a leading representative of the Reformed sector of the English religious scene, Umphrey Lee, in his work *John Wesley and Modern Religion* (1936), attempted to define and emphasize the Anglican, or catholic, aspect of Wesley's thought. J. E. Rattenbury's works, *Wesley's Legacy to the World* and *The Eucharistic Hymns of John and Charles Wesley*, also contribute to the study of this catholic bent, particularly as it is reflected in sacramental practice. J. C. Bowmer, in *The Sacrament of the Lord's Supper in Early Methodism*, supports these studies. Carrying the catholic emphasis even further, Maximin Piette, in *John Wesley in the Evolution of Protestantism*, seeks to identify these tendencies in Wesley with those of the Roman Catholic tradition. That such interpretations are not confined to scholarship of a quarter of a century ago is attested by a recent publication by a Roman Catholic layman, John M. Todd, entitled *John Wesley and the Catholic Church*.

George C. Cell, on the other hand, in *The Rediscovery of John Wesley* (1935) sought to reemphasize the traditional interpretation of Wesley as more congenially related to the Reformation tradition. Many of the continental scholars supported such an interpretation, as did works such as William Cannon's *The Theology of John Wesley*.[1] Much recent scholarship has also supported this position: e.g., John Deschner, *Wes-*

[1] See Harald Lindström, *Wesley and Sanctification* (London: Epworth Press, 1950), pp. 1-14, for a thorough review of Wesley scholarship until the mid 1940's.

14

ley's Christology; Colin Williams, *John Wesley's Theology Today;* and
Martin Schmidt, *John Wesley: A Theological Biography.* Emphasizing
another dimension are works investigating the influence of the Moravian
pietists on Wesley, such as Clifford Towlson's *Moravian and Methodist*
and Franz Hildebrandt's *From Luther to Wesley.*

Professor Albert Outler's recent work, *John Wesley,* asserts that
Wesley's patristic study focused on the Eastern Fathers and was of primary significance in the molding of Wesley's theology, especially the
doctrine of holiness. Here then is yet another religious heritage which
influenced Wesley.

The majority of these studies, which are only representative titles
among many others, take note, to a greater or lesser degree, of the
similarity between Wesley and the English Puritan tradition. However,
even those which stress Wesley's relationship to the Reformed tradition
are normally concerned with showing Wesley's affinities with Calvin or
Luther and do not give sufficient attention to the fact that, for expression of this Reformed emphasis, Wesley depends upon the English
version of the tradition, Puritanism.

The resemblance between Wesley and the Puritan ethos has been
commonly recognized, especially the similarity of their teachings concerning the outward manifestations of the Christian life. During Wesley's evangelical career Bishop Warburton, in commenting on Methodism, identified the "true character of Methodism" with the "old Precisians, Puritans, and Independents." Wesley rejected the comment as
irrelevant to the question at hand, just as he rejected the attempted
identifications between his movement and the dissenting churches because of the organization of his societies.[2] Nevertheless, in the eyes of
many of his contemporaries he revived the spirit and practice of Puritanism. Late in Wesley's life one of his admirers indicated to him that,
though he presumed the name "Methodist" had not been used before
his own day, it had in fact been applied to certain of the Nonconform-

[2] John Wesley, *The Letters of the Rev. John Wesley, A.M.,* ed. John Telford (8 vols.;
London: Epworth Press, 1931), IV, 353. Cited hereafter as *Letters.* J. H. Overton, *The
Evangelical Revival in the Eighteenth Century* (London: Longmans, Green, and Co., 1886),
pp. 171-73, gives several other examples of the identification, including one by Horace Walpole.

ists, generally designating the disciplined, stringent, austere living of a Christian life.[3]

The identification of the Wesleyan movement with the Puritan movement on the basis of the Christian life has been used by friend and foe since Wesley's own day. Such was the connection which J. R. Green, in his *Short History of the English People,* saw between the two movements, at the same time crediting the Wesleyan movement with having "wrought out . . . the work of religious reform" which the Puritans had attempted the century before but failed to accomplish.[4] Leslie Stephen in his work, *History of English Thought in the Eighteenth Century,* criticized the Wesleyan movement by identifying the moral and ascetic austerities of the two, calling Methodism a "new Puritanism" but one which was really "a faint reflection of the grander Puritanism of the seventeenth century."[5] It is this ascetic temper of Wesley's ethic of life which George C. Cell identified with Puritanism.[6] J. H. Overton, though recognizing these similarities, also noted some of the theological interests common to the traditions, such as their contention "for the immediate and particular influence of the Holy Spirit, for the total degeneracy of man, for the vicarious nature of the Atonement."[7] Élie Halévy understood the Evangelical revival under Wesley to be the revival of the Puritan religious consciousness and to have made this consciousness, with its accompanying practice, a part of the very character of the Englishman, as well as significantly contributing to the fact that England did not experience a revolution such as the one in France in the eighteenth century.[8] J. Scott Lidgett's essay in *A New History of Methodism* asserts that the mission of Methodism

[3] See Curnock's note on the subject in *The Journal of the Rev. John Wesley, A.M.,* ed. Nehemiah Curnock (8 vols.; London: Epworth Press, 1909), V, 42 n. Cited hereafter as *Journal.* See also Luke Tyerman, *The Life and Times of the Rev. John Wesley, A.M.* (3 vols.; New York: Harper & Brothers, 1872), I, 67.

[4] J. R. Green, *Short History of the English People* (New York: Harper and Brothers, 1898), pp. 604, 739.

[5] Leslie Stephen, *History of the English Thought in the Eighteenth Century* (2 vols.; London: Smith, Elder and Co., 1881), II, 433.

[6] *The Rediscovery of John Wesley* (New York: Henry Holt and Co., 1935), p. vii.

[7] Overton, *The Evangelical Revival in the Eighteenth Century,* pp. 44-45.

[8] Élie Halévy, "La Naissance du Methodisme en Angleterre," *La Revue De Paris,* IV (1906), 521-22; *A History of the English People in 1815,* tran. E. I. Watkin and D. A. Barker (London: T. Fisher Unwin, 1924), p. 371.

was to "make the universal Christianity witnessed to by the Established Church real and the real Christianity of the Nonconformists universal." [9] Stressing the motivation, or spirit, of the movement, Professor Horton Davies credits Wesley and Methodism with reviving the "evangelical passion and experiential religion" of Puritanism.[10] Professor Outler recognizes the relationship by pointing out Wesley's "borrowing" his doctrine of Christian life from the Puritans.[11] It is not necessary to extend the list of examples to illustrate the widespread recognition of significant relationship between the work of Wesley and that of the Puritan divines. It is considered an established fact.

Another link between Wesley and the Puritans which was investigated at length by nineteenth-century biographers, and is still a topic of interest and research, was Wesley's Puritan ancestry.[12] A survey of this family background and its influence on Wesley may be useful for our consideration of his relationship with Puritanism.

The Puritan family lineage of John Wesley begins at least as early as two of his great-grandfathers and perhaps earlier. Bartholomew Westley, grandfather of Samuel Wesley, and John White, grandfather of Susanna Wesley, were recognized Puritans active during the period of the Commonwealth. Biographical information for Bartholomew Westley is far from adequate. George Stevenson's sketch of the various branches of the Wesley family indicates an ancient origin for the family with the name being spelled variously as Wellesley, Westley, and Wesley. Bartholomew was the third son of Sir Herbert Westley of Wesleigh County, Devon, and Elizabeth Wellesley, who had been a member of the Irish branch of the family.[13] While little is known of Bartholomew's early life,

[9] J. Scott Lidgett, "Fundamental Unity," *A New History of Methodism*, ed. W. J. Townsend, H. B. Workman, George Eayrs (2 vols.; London: Hodder and Stoughton, 1909), II, 438.

[10] Horton Davies, *The English Free Churches* (London: Oxford University Press, 1952), p. 141.

[11] Albert Outler, "Towards a Re-Appraisal of John Wesley as a Theologian," *The Perkins School of Theology Journal*, XIV (1961), 7.

[12] See John Whitehead, *The Life of the Rev. John Wesley, A.M.* (2 vols.; London: Printed by Stephen Couchman, 1793); Adam Clarke, *Memoirs of the Wesley Family* (London: Printed by J. and T. Clarke, 1823); George Stevenson, *Memorials of the Wesley Family* (London: S. W. Partridge and Co., 1876); and William Beal, *The Fathers of the Wesley Family* (London: J. Mason, 1833). For a recent treatment see Frank Baker, "Wesley's Puritan Ancestry," *London Quarterly and Holborn Review*, 187 (1962), 180-86; cited hereafter as *LQHR*.

[13] George Stevenson, *Memorials of the Wesley Family*, pp. xi ff.

Edmund Calamy indicates that he received a university education study-ing both theology and "physic." [14] He is listed as the rector of the parishes of Charmouth and Catherston in Dorset County in 1650 when a commission of inquiry investigated the parishes to determine their income and incumbents.[15] Bartholomew evidently had been called to Charmouth by the congregation after the removal of the rector in 1640. When he moved to the parish at Allington is not known, but he was here when the Act of Uniformity was enforced in 1662.[16] This act, imposed after the restoration of Charles II, required that all clergy of the Church of England accept without question "all and everything contained and prescribed" in the revised *Book of Common Prayer*, mak-ing it the standard of belief and worship. Bartholomew Westley along with some eighteen hundred to two thousand of his clerical colleagues who were Puritan in sympathy could not accept these requirements and so were ejected from their churches and livings on St. Bartholomew's Day, August 24, 1662. Forced to make his living by the practice of medicine, Bartholomew Westley was also required to move from his parish by the Five Mile Act.[17] He continued to preach occasionally but never resumed an active ministry before his death in 1670.

Bartholomew's son, John Westley, was perhaps better known in Puritan circles than his father. Born in 1636, he attended New Inn Hall, Oxford, during John Owen's vice-chancellorship of the university. Other renowned Puritans were in Oxford at the time as fellows and students; e.g., Thomas Goodwin, Stephen Charnock, John Howe, Philip Henry, and Joseph Alleine.[18] Young John Westley received special attention from John Owen and became known as a diligent student of Oriental languages in the course of attaining his B.A. and M.A. de-grees. On leaving the university he became associated with a "gathered

[14] Edmund Calamy, *The Nonconformist's Memorial*, ed. Samuel Palmer (2 vols.; London: Printed for W. Harris, 1775), I, 442.

[15] William Beal, *The Fathers of the Wesley Family*, pp. 26-27.

[16] Beal, pp. 22 ff., argues that Bartholomew Westley was ejected from Charmouth rather than Allington, but Baker, p. 186, points out that deed records would indicate that he was at Allington.

[17] The Act of Uniformity was followed by the Five Mile Act prohibiting those who would not conform from residing within five miles of an incorporated town or any parish they had formerly served.

[18] Luke Tyerman, *The Life and Times of the Rev. Samuel Wesley, A.M.* (London: Simpkin, Marshall, and Co., 1866), p. 34.

church" at Melcombe Regis preaching in the area and serving as a port chaplain. He accepted the call of the combined parish of Winterbourne Whitchurch, Dorset, as a minister on probation, and after receiving the approval of the Triers he was awarded the living by the Trustees in 1658.[19] During this period he appears to have organized a private school in order to supplement his income. In 1661 charges were brought against him for his unwillingness to use the Prayer Book; Calamy, using Westley's diary, recorded an account of the resulting interview with Bishop Gilbert Ironsides. The interview reveals that he had not been episcopally ordained and, indeed, felt that his call and commission to preach by the gathered congregation at Melcombe was quite sufficient.[20] He explained his refusal to accept ordination by commenting that he was called to the "work" of the ministry but not to the "office," which some interpreters have understood to be an anticipation of John Wesley's distinction between lay helpers and the ordained clergy.[21] Since he accepted the full responsibility of the parish as well as the living at Winterbourne Whitchurch, this supposition is questionable. Westley's strongest defense of his ministry was, however, on the basis of the "fruits" of his work evident in those persons converted "to the power of Godliness" or "the reality of religion" under his preaching at "Radipole, Melcombe, Turnworth, Whitchurch, and at sea." Similar arguments from the fruits of a ministry were to be used by his grandson, John Wesley, as justification for the work of the Methodists. Although John Westley swore allegiance and loyalty to Charles II upon the restoration, he, like his father, could not accept the requirements of the Act of Uniformity and was ejected from Winterbourne Whitchurch in 1662. Forced to wander for some time before finding permanent residence, he associated himself with the ministries of Joseph Alleine and others preaching to several semi-clandestine Presbyterian, Baptist, and Independent congregations. Given the use of a house by a friend in Preston, he served several congregations in the area, for which action he served

[19] The Triers and Trustees had been set up by the Commonwealth to examine, license, and appoint ministers for service in the Church.

[20] Edmund Calamy, *The NonConformist's Memorial*, I, 478 ff.; Tyerman, *The Life and Times of the Rev. Samuel Wesley, A.M.*, pp. 34 ff.

[21] Adam Clarke, *Memoirs of the Wesley Family*, pp. 36-37; Tyerman, *The Life and Times of the Rev. Samuel Wesley, A.M.*, p. 43.

at least four short prison terms. At his death in 1670 he was the pastor of a "gathered church" in Poole. To judge from his interview with Bishop Ironsides and his subsequent action, Westley was an Independent in his understanding of church order. In any case, he was a respected Puritan whose convictions would not allow him the comfort and security of service in the Church of England.[22]

Samuel Wesley, John Westley's son, was only a child at the time of his father's death, having been born in the year of his father's ejectment. Although the family suffered from the restrictions placed on them, Samuel was given a thorough education in several London dissenting academies. Forsaking nonconformity in his teens he entered Exeter College, Oxford, as a servitor and upon graduating in 1688 was ordained in the Church of England.[23] That year Samuel Wesley married Susanna Annesley, the bearer of an even more renowned Puritan heritage.

John White, Susanna's maternal grandfather, was a Puritan from his youth. His service to the Puritan cause as a barrister was extensive even before his election to Parliament in 1640. In the Long Parliament his position as chairman of the "committee for Scandalous Ministers" gave him an active role in the examination and ejection of many Anglican clergymen during the Puritan regime. He was also a leader in the movement to remove episcopacy as the form of church government. Active in the organization of the Massachusetts colony, he may have drafted its charter. The service of this layman, marked by intense piety, testifies to his devotion to the Puritan cause.[24]

Samuel Annesley, Susanna's father, was "one of the most eminent of the later Puritan Nonconformists."[25] According to Calamy "he was so early under serious impressions, that he declared he knew not the time when he was not converted."[26] Earning his B.A. and M.A. degrees at

[22] Edmund Calamy, *The Nonconformist's Memorial*, I, 478-86; cf. Frank Baker, "Wesley's Puritan Ancestry," *LQHR*, 187 (1962), 182-83.

[23] It was evidently at Oxford that Samuel dropped the "t" from the name, understanding Wesley to be the ancient and correct spelling.

[24] *Dictionary of National Biography*, ed. Leslie Stephen (59 vols., London: Smith, Elder, and Co., 1885), LX, 260. Cited hereafter as *DNB*. John Wesley mistakenly identified his great-grandfather with Dr. John White who was one of the chairmen of the Westminster Assembly, *Letters*, V, 76; cf. Frank Baker, "Wesley's Puritan Ancestry," *LQHR*, 187 (1962), 184.

[25] *DNB*, II, 7.

[26] Edmund Calamy, *The Nonconformist's Memorial*, I, 104-5.

Queens College, Oxford, in 1644, he was honored with a Doctor of Laws degree in 1648. Samuel Annesley was evidently episcopally ordained a deacon and in 1644 received Presbyterian ordination. He began his career as a naval chaplain; his first parish was in Kent. In 1652 he received a parish in London and in 1658 became the vicar of St. Giles, Cripplegate, from which position he was ejected when he refused to conform in 1662. Forced into retirement he continued to preach and, with others, established a meeting house at Little St. Helens which became a center of London Nonconformity. Because he was descended from the minor nobility and had sufficient private income, he supported and educated several of the young Nonconformists. It was at Little St. Helens in 1694 that Annesley and others conducted the first Presbyterian ordination to be held publicly after 1662.[27]

Susanna Annesley, the twenty-fifth child of Dr. Annesley, was born in 1669. The Annesley home was an outstanding example of a Puritan household where demanding educational standards accompanied disciplined devotional and moral training. In addition, since this was a center of Nonconformity, the children were exposed to intense theological discussion and debate. Susanna gained here such an appreciation and knowledge of Scripture and theology that, in Frank Baker's phrase, she later "proved a valuable source of theological reference for her sons." [28] At an early age she appears to have been familiar with the distinctions and arguments between the Established Church and Dissent and sometime before her marriage in 1688 she made her decision to leave Dissent and join the Church of England.

Whatever the reasons which led Samuel and Susanna Wesley to abandon the ranks of Nonconformity and join the Church of England, the move initiated significant shifts in their thought as well as practice. Samuel Wesley embraced the emphasis of his day on the early church and became a staunch supporter of a "high church" interpretation of the sacraments. Susanna appears to have concurred with most of the changes and never questioned her decision to join the Church of England.

However, to change one's religious affiliation out of honest convic-

[27] *DNB*, II, 7-8; Frank Baker, "Wesley's Puritan Ancestry," *LQHR*, 187 (1962), 183.
[28] Frank Baker, "Wesley's Puritan Ancestry," *LQHR*, 187 (1962), 184.

tion does not mean necessarily to escape from or to reject completely one's heritage and background. While Samuel Wesley could write a devastating critique of dissenting academies, he carried with him into the Church of England many of the virtues of Puritan training and education. Martin Schmidt has suggested that Samuel Wesley's great interest in biblical scholarship and instruction was greatly dependent on the legacy of his Puritan background.[29] Certainly, like the Puritans, Samuel Wesley displayed a devoted love for the Scriptures and his major scholarly endeavors were biblical. As Maldwyn Edwards points out, by precept and example he set a pattern of disciplined daily scholarship that was to greatly influence his sons.[30] Perhaps this discipline had its origins in the Puritan training of his own childhood. In a statement from his deathbed he reflected another Puritan emphasis and at the same time anticipated John Wesley's doctrine of assurance: "The inward witness, son, the inward witness; that is the proof, the strongest proof of Christianity." [31] Unlike many of his contemporaries he had not relinquished his conviction of the importance of vital personal religious experience—a conviction to which he would have been thoroughly exposed in his Puritan home. Samuel, no doubt unconsciously, passed along to his children the vestiges of Puritan influence and emphasis evident in his own life.

Susanna's contribution to this legacy is at least as great and perhaps exceeds Samuel's. A. W. Harrison comments: "The Epworth parsonage had a High Church atmosphere, yet it was essentially a Puritan home." [32] John Newton, attempting to document this statement and assuming that Susanna was the formative figure of the home, asserts that the Puritan piety and training of her own childhood molded the character of her household. "Her careful ordered timetable, her regular times set apart for meditation and self-examination before God, her keeping of a spiritual journal or day-book, her observance of the strict Puritan

[29] Martin Schmidt, *John Wesley, A Theological Biography* (Nashville: Abingdon Press, 1962), p. 40. Schmidt also asserts that Wesley "owed a great deal to the Puritan emphasis upon the importance of repentance, conversion, and rebirth," but it is difficult to substantiate this type of influence.

[30] Maldwyn Edwards, *Family Circle* (London: Epworth Press, 1949), p. 30.

[31] *Letters*, II, 135.

[32] Quoted by John A. Newton, *Methodism and the Puritans* (London: Dr. William's Trust, 1964), p. 4.

Sabbath—these were all part of her 'method' of life, to use the Puritan key-word." [33] Her pastoral care over the souls of her children to bring each to a "personal appropriation of God's grace" also reflects Puritan patterns. To these can be added Puritan emphases reflected in her theological advice to her sons and finally her total Christian personality.[34] Newton's statements are in danger of overstressing the Puritan nature of Susanna's personality and teachings and that of the household. Nevertheless, the general character of the home with its emphasis on genuine piety, biblical training, and rigid discipline which left no time for "light" diversions is strikingly similar to Puritan prototypes.

Whatever Puritan influence may be noted in the Epworth household and parental heritage must have been largely unconscious so far as Samuel and Susanna were concerned. Frank Baker comments that since they were both converts from Dissent "it is not surprising that they did not fill their children's heads with stirring tales of their predominantly Puritan forefathers." [35] John Wesley came to a genuine appreciation of the Puritans and their teachings after Aldersgate, and only in later life did he take an interest in his Puritan ancestry. Intrigued by the idea that one of Charles's sons might become a minister he wrote: "It is highly probable one of the three will stand before the Lord. But, so far as I can learn, such a thing has scarce been for these three thousand years before, as a son, father, grandfather, *atavus*, *tritavus*, preaching the gospel, nay, and the genuine gospel in a line." [36] The emphasis placed here on the "genuine gospel" indicates his sympathies at that time with these forebears.

Investigation into Wesley's Puritan heritage other than the obvious points of contact in his ancestry, while not extensive, has revealed significant areas of relationship. Several general articles and monographs are suggestive in their comments on the topic. An essay by George Eayrs entitled "Links Between the Ejected Clergy of 1662, The Wesleys, and Methodism," while primarily a survey of Wesley's Nonconformist an-

[33] *Ibid.*, p. 5.
[34] *Ibid.*, pp. 6-7. Newton makes an interesting case for the essential Puritan cast of Susanna's character and thought in his comments in "Letter from Susanna Wesley to her Son John," *Wesley Chapel Magazine*, January, 1965, pp. 8-12.
[35] "Wesley's Puritan Ancestry," LQHR, 187 (1962), 181.
[36] *Letters*, V, 36.

cestry, indicates Wesley's appreciation for the Puritan tradition and comments on Wesley's church policy.[37] Duncan Coomer's article, "The Influence of Puritanism and Dissent on Methodism," pointing out some of the major areas of relationship, comments briefly on the similarity in teachings relative to the Christian life, Wesley's use of Puritan authors in *A Christian Library,* and his dependence upon this tradition for the covenant service.[38] A recent and more comprehensive monograph is John Newton's *Methodism and the Puritans.* Newton's stress on the Puritan nature of Susanna Wesley's character, thought, and household has been noted. Newton comments on the Puritan writers in *A Christian Library,* and he goes on to delineate some of Wesley's indebtedness to the Puritans in the areas of "Theology, Liturgy, Pastoralia, Family Piety, and Ethics." In addition, he suggests that many of Wesley's lieutenants were substantially influenced by Puritanism.

The most intensive investigations of the subject have been in Wesley's liturgical indebtedness to the Puritan tradition. John Bishop in his work *Methodist Worship in Relation to Free Church Worship,* which is primarily an analysis of Methodist worship itself, has drawn together much of the information concerning Wesley's incorporation into Methodism of Puritan forms and modes of worship.[39] Horton Davies has delineated Wesley's dependence upon Puritan liturgical practices in his chapter, "The Methodist Union of Formal and Free Worship," in *Worship and Theology in England.*[40] Specialized investigation in this area has been done in the work of Frederick Hunter and Frank Baker on the covenant service, which is a direct incorporation of a Puritan form, though used in a special way by Wesley.[41] Frederick Hunter has also

[37] George Eayrs, "Links Between the Ejected Clergy of 1662, The Wesleys, and Methodism," *The Ejectment of 1662 and the Free Churches,* ed. Alexander Maclaren (London: The National Council of Evangelical Free Churches, n.d.), pp. 99-119.

[38] Duncan Coomer, "The Influence of Puritanism and Dissent on Methodism," *LQHR,* 175 (1950), 346-50.

[39] John Bishop, *Methodist Worship in Relation to Free Church Worship* (London: Epworth Press, 1950).

[40] Horton Davies, *Worship and Theology in England: From Watts and Wesley to Maurice, 1690-1850* (Princeton: Princeton University Press, 1961), pp. 184 ff.

[41] Frederick Hunter, "The Origins of Wesley's Covenant Service," *Wesley Historical Society Proceedings* XXII (1940), 126-30. Cited hereafter as *WHSP.* Frank Baker, "The Beginnings of the Methodist Covenant Service," *LQHR,* 180 (1955), 215-20.

attempted to show that Wesley's changes in *The Book of Common Prayer* for use by the American Methodists carried out the suggested changes in that book offered by the Presbyterians at the Savoy Conference in 1661, and that Wesley consciously followed the summary of these suggestions as found in Edmund Calamy's *Abridgment of Mr. Baxter's History of His Life and Times.*[42] A. Kingsley Lloyd has shown that in at least some of his hymns Charles Wesley was directly dependent upon the biblical expositions of Matthew Henry.[43] More attention might well be given to this important area, for both John and Charles Wesley seem highly appreciative of the work of Matthew Henry. Wesley's appreciation and use of Isaac Watts might also be fruitfully investigated since Wesley's first venture into hymnody, *A Collection of Psalms and Hymns,* was largely dependent upon Watts. Gordon Wakefield also comments on the general relationship between Wesley and the Puritans in this important area.[44] Although these investigations clearly indicate a real dependence by Wesley upon the Puritan tradition in terms of liturgical innovations, none of them sufficiently studies Wesley's use of two principal Puritan practices—extemporaneous preaching and "free" prayers. Obviously, in the eyes of his contemporaries, these practices must have identified him with the Puritan tradition.

Another area of relationship is investigated by F. C. Pritchard in *Methodist Secondary Education.* Pritchard places Wesley's organization and curriculum of Kingswood School in the heritage of the dissenting academies and shows the close similarity of these respective educational institutions.[45]

Wesley and the Puritans display a striking similarity in their concern for the practical application of the Christian gospel to the daily life of

[42] Frederick Hunter, "Sources of Wesley's Revision of the Prayer Book in 1784-88," *WHSP,* XXIII (1941-42), 123-33. It should be noted that other Wesley scholars, such as Wesley Swift and J. E. Rattenbury, question the emphasis Hunter gives to Calamy's influence on Wesley, but there is little question that the revisions *are* those suggested by the Presbyterians, whether or not Wesley was dependent upon Calamy for these suggestions. (Swift, "Methodism and the Prayer Book" and "The Sunday Service of the Methodists," *WHSP,* XXVII [1949-50], 33-41; XXIX [1953-54], 12-20; Rattenbury, "Note on Article on 'Sources of Wesley's Revision of the Prayer Book of 1784-88,'" *WHSP,* XXIII [1941-42], 173-75.)

[43] A. K. Lloyd, "Charles Wesley's Debt to Matthew Henry," *LQHR,* 171 (1946), 330-37.

[44] Gordon Wakefield, *Puritan Devotion: Its Place in the Development of Christian Piety* (London: Epworth Press, 1957), *passim.*

[45] F. C. Pritchard, *Methodist Secondary Education* (London: Epworth Press, 1949), pp. 59-73.

the believer. The present study takes as its central focus the relationship of this common concern in the two traditions. In order to establish the nature of this relationship, be it that of similarity, affinity, or dependence, investigation is made of Wesley's use, recommendation, and abridgment of Puritan literature. On the basis of these source materials, a discussion of the theological foundations of the Christian life forms the background for the study of the specific teachings, practices, and emphases which connect Wesley to the Puritan divines. This methodology is intended to reveal those areas in which Wesley himself most closely related his own understanding of the Christian life to that of the Puritans, rather than depending in any large measure upon the outward manifestations in which similarities may seem evident but where the actual relationship may be tenuous.

The term "Puritan" has a wide variety of associations and applications. It may refer to any person concerned with the renovation of religious thought and practice from the earliest centuries to the present. In late sixteenth-century England it referred to those who sought to continue the Protestant Reformation by establishing what they understood to be "pure" forms of doctrine, worship, and church polity. The political implications and consequences of these endeavors identified the seventeenth-century Puritans with the struggle for liberty and constitutional rights. For purposes of our study the term designates Englishmen in these centuries who were unified in their desire to purify and renew Christian thought and life. They were also united by their conviction that Christianity based on a vibrant faith involves man in an experiential relationship with the God revealed in Christ. Religious authority is also based on the Scriptures, which become the primary rule and guide of thought and action. As John Wilkinson has pointed out, their theological concentration is on the "sovereignty and righteousness of God and the all-pervading character of human sinfulness" buttressed by a deep concern for salvation. Their ethical idealism as a corollary of these convictions, wherein no action is free from the moral demands and considerations, resulted in a serious, circumspect and disciplined daily life.[46]

[46] John T. Wilkinson, "The Mind of the Puritan," *LQHR*, 187 (1962), 35-38.

However, within the bounds of this unity of belief and concern there was great freedom of opinion. The Puritan movement, therefore, included persons representing a wide variety of theological emphases, ecclesiastical policies, and political positions. The term includes some who remained loyal to the Established Church, the Separatists such as the Baptists, some Independents who separated from the Established Church, and those Presbyterians and Independents who were finally forced out through the Act of Uniformity of 1662. As Geoffrey Nuttall indicates, these were "all spiritually nearer to one another than is any of them to the Roman Catholic Church or to the Laudian party within the Church of England. They have their own internal differences . . . but in a large sense they have much in common, and for this faith and experience which they share . . . there is no other name than Puritan." [47]

[47] Geoffrey F. Nuttall, *The Holy Spirit in Puritan Faith and Experience* (Oxford: Basil Blackwell, 1947), p. 9.

Part I: JOHN WESLEY
and PURITAN LITERATURE

I

Puritan Authors in Wesley's Publications

John Wesley's emergence in the early 1740's as a principal leader of the Evangelical Revival coincided with his recognition of the "power of the press" as an instrument of evangelization. The importance of the press in spreading the Christian message had long been recognized, and by Wesley's time the number of religious works was myriad. Much of this material, however, was economically unavailable to large portions of the society. Wesley's firm conviction that "reading Christians will be knowing Christians" [1] led him to attempt to provide this literature to the poorer and less educated element of the population through the publication of tracts and small books. To accomplish this purpose, Wesley was obliged to abridge material of other authors, in

[1] *Letters*, VI, 201.

addition to writing many tracts, pamphlets, and books himself.[2] Such work provided quality religious instruction for his followers and also gave him an opportunity to supervise more closely what they were reading.

Among his abridgments Wesley included many items of Puritan literature. This material helps to determine Wesley's relationship to the Puritan tradition and thus clarifies the extent of his familiarity with the Puritans, his evaluation of them, and indicates the areas of life and thought of that tradition which he found most congenial.

The productive years of Wesley's literary life span the exceptionally long period from 1733 until his death in 1791. Hardly a year passed in which a major work was not produced by his pen. During the years 1749-55, in the midst of many other tasks, Wesley edited *A Christian Library*, his largest single literary venture, consisting of fifty duodecimo volumes. This work provides invaluable information relative to Wesley's purposes and methods in abridging the works of other authors and, more important, is a principal source for examining and evaluating his use of Puritan materials.

1. A Christian Library

In August, 1748, the father of Methodism, in a letter to a friend, outlined his objectives in publishing *A Christian Library*:

I have often thought of mentioning to you and a few others a design I have had for some years of printing a little library, perhaps of fourscore or one hundred volumes, for the use of those that fear God. My purpose was to select whatever I had seen most valuable in the English language, and either abridge or take the whole tracts, only a little corrected or explained, as occasion should require. Of these I could print ten or twelve, more or less, every year, on a fine paper, and large letter, which should be cast for the purpose. As soon as I am able to purchase a printing press and types, I think of entering on this design. I have several books now ready and a printer who desires nothing more

---

[2] These amounted to more than 370 publications. (T. W. Herbert, *John Wesley as Editor and Author* [Princeton: Princeton University Press, 1940,] p. 2). James Joy sets the figure at over four hundred. ("Wesley: Man of a Thousand Books and a Book," *Religion in Life*, VIII [1939], 73.)

than food and raiment. In three or four weeks I hope to be in London, and if God permits, to begin without delay.[3]

As Wesley intimates, the idea for such a library did not originate in 1748. On June 18, 1746, Dr. Philip Doddridge, principal of a Dissenting academy in Northampton, addressed a letter to Wesley in which he gives Wesley his thoughts "on that little Collection of Books, which you seem desirous to make for some young preachers."[4] Anxious to publish the best literature available, Wesley evidently had not only been collecting lists of books which might be used but also may have done some of the abridging long before publication.[5]

Wesley's avowed purpose in *A Christian Library* was to publish the "choicest Pieces of Practical Divinity." Such works, in the thought of seventeenth- and eighteenth-century England, applied the truths of the Christian gospel to the daily lives of the believer or, in Wesley's words, constituted "Christianity reduced to *practice*."[6] Wesley's introduction to Macarius' commentary on the Scriptures states the position quite well: "That his acquaintance with those Sacred Writings was not merely *literal or speculative*, but that *it was a true and practical knowledge*."[7] While practical divinity might, and usually did, incorporate biblical commentary and exegesis, that was not its primary object. The distinction between "speculative" theological inquiry and practical instruction is, however, of more consequence. Wesley did not deprecate theological endeavors to explicate the intricacies of doctrine; neverthe-

[3] *Letters*, II, 152. Although the finished work did not consist of as many volumes as Wesley here anticipated, the plan was materially realized. However, there were no "whole tracts" included without abridgments, and very few explanatory notes were added.

[4] Philip Doddridge, "Letter to Mr. Wesley: A Scheme of Study for a Clergyman," *The Arminian Magazine*, I (1778), 419.

[5] Curnock suggests that some of this work was done as early as Wesley's sojourn in Georgia but gives no supporting evidence for his statement (*Journal*, I, 425). Wesley may have gained his original idea for such a publication from an early work by his father. As a leading member of the "Athenian Society," Samuel Wesley was a major contributor to one of their publications entitled *A Young Student's Library*, a work of extracts and abridgments "of the most valuable books" on general knowledge (Luke Tyerman, *The Life and Times of the Rev. Samuel Wesley, A.M.*, p. 150; E. Martin, "The Christian Library," *WHSP*, II [1899-1900], 191).

[6] John Wesley, *A Christian Library* (2nd ed.; 30 vols.; London: Printed by T. Cordeux, for T. Blanshard, 1819-26), II, 3. Cited hereafter as *CL*.

[7] *CL*, I, 69 (italics mine). Professor Outler has pointed out that this work was credited in the eighteenth century to "Macarius the Egyptian" but in actual fact was written by a fifth-century Syrian monk greatly dependent on Gregory of Nyssa (Albert Outler, ed., *John Wesley* [New York: Oxford University Press, 1964], p. 9).

less, he understood practical divinity to be more significant for the common man. His endeavor was, then, to make the gospel "intelligible to plain men."

To accomplish this, he sought carefully to select, from among the variety of available writings, those most edifying. Even these selections required clarification through the elimination and revision of technical language and theological argumentation, for, as Wesley was acutely aware, the ordinary man of his day was often uneducated in anything more than the rudiments of reading and writing, if, indeed, he was not entirely illiterate. Clarification was also required because of the constant controversy that found its way into the writings of the scholars, the inconsistency of instruction, and the "mystical attempts to find hidden meanings in plain truths." Wesley was anxious to "separate the pure, genuine Divinity, out of this huge mingled mass." [8]

His approach to the task of abridgment is clearly delineated:

I have also particularly endeavoured to preserve a consistency throughout, that no part might contradict any other; but all conspire together, "to make the man of God perfect, thoroughly furnished unto every good word and work."

But in order to do this, I have been obliged, not only to omit the far greater part of several eminent authors, but also to add what was needful, either to clear their sense, or to correct their mistakes. And in a design of this nature, I apprehend myself to be at full liberty so to do. I therefore take no author for better, for worse; (as indeed I dare not call any man Rabbi,) but endeavour to follow each so far as he follows Christ. And not (knowingly) one step farther.[9]

Such liberties with the materials of other authors, while questionable by modern standards, were quite common before the days of copyright laws. Nevertheless, it is only natural that such a work would be the object

---

[8] *CL*, I, viii. Wesley's concern to express the teachings of the gospel in the language of the people is best stated in the introduction to his sermons: "I design plain truth for plain people: Therefore, . . . I abstain from all nice and philosophical speculations; from all perplexed and intricate reasonings. . . . I labour to avoid all words which are not easy to be understood, all which are not used in common life; and, in particular, those kinds of technical terms that so frequently occur in Bodies of Divinity; those modes of speaking which men of reading are intimately acquainted with, but which to common people are an unknown tongue" (*The Works of the Reverend John Wesley*, ed. Thomas Jackson [14 vols.; London: Wesleyan Conference Office, 1872], V, 2. Cited hereafter as *Works*).

[9] *CL*, I, ix; cf. IV, 106.

of much critical comment. Under the pressure of criticism raised, on one hand, by persons in the Church of England attempting to show that Wesley was a dissenter[10] and, on the other hand, by his Calvinistic opponents anxious to find an inconsistency in his theological position,[11] Wesley was forced to make public defense of the *Library*.

He readily admitted mistakes caused by preparing the works only as he could "snatch time in traveling, not transcribing them," and, more importantly, by trusting the ability of his printer to decipher his own markings and not checking the final copy. He further admitted that "it is probable too, I myself might overlook some sentences which were not suitable to my own principles."

After making these concessions, Wesley was ready to defend himself against any attempt to make him responsible for all of the doctrines and views expressed in the *Library*. "I did believe and I do believe, every tract therein to be true, and agreeable to the oracles of God. But I do not roundly affirm this of every sentence contained in the fifty volumes." [12] He was willing to be counted as editor, not author, of these treatises. Nevertheless, these publications help clarify Wesley's relationship to the authors whose works he edited.

The willingness to "mind not who speaks but what is spoken" is the genius of the *Library* and, for that matter, of all the abridging Wesley attempted.[13] Although Wesley could reject the predestinarianism of a Goodwin or an Owen, he saw no valid reason for rejecting the truths that they might teach concerning the living of the Christian life and

[10] Stephen Church, "Letter to the Rev. Mr. Wesley," *The London Magazine*, XXIX (1760), 587.

[11] Wesley recognized, after some debate, that a tract entitled *The Scripture Doctrine of Imputed Righteousness asserted and maintained by The Rev. Mr. John Wesley, author of the Preservative Against Unsettled Notions in Religion. Extracted from His Own Publications* had, in fact, been taken largely from *A Christian Library* and could on occasion be quoted in opposition to his own theological statements (*Works*, X, 374 ff.; *Letters*, IV, 207).

[12] *Works*, X, 381-82. Due to these criticisms, Wesley was convinced of the necessity for correcting the mistakes in the *Library* (*Letters*, V, 241). He corrected his own copy, and it is this hand-corrected copy that forms the basis of the second edition, issued under the editorship of Thomas Jackson in 1819-26. The present study uses this second edition of the *Library* as its source. For comment on the second edition see Richard Green, *The Works of John and Charles Wesley: A Bibliography* (London: Methodist Publishing House, 1906), p. 95, cited hereafter as *Bibliography*; Didymus ("pseud."), "Mr. Wesley's *Christian Library*," *The Wesleyan-Methodist Magazine*, VI (1827), 313.

[13] *Letters*, IV, 121.

other congenial doctrines. Openness to truth wherever he found it is the clue to his accepting so much from the Puritan divines, who were certainly outside the scope of his formal education. This discriminating eclecticism calls for a detailed analysis of the contents of *A Christian Library* in order to determine to what extent he actually used Puritan sources.[14]

Puritan Authors Included in A Christian Library

Wesley provided few prefaces or introductions to the works included in *A Christian Library* and consequently, seldom gave the reader his valuable and incisive evaluation of their contents. Fortunately, one of the exceptions to this general practice is his preface to the Puritan materials. Here is found Wesley's most extensive comment on the Puritans. Immediately following martyrological accounts of the lives of exemplary Christians he commented:

After an account of the lives, sufferings, and deaths of those holy men, who sealed the ancient religion with their blood, I believe nothing would either be more agreeable or more profitable to the serious reader, than some extracts from the writings of those who sprung up, as it were, out of their ashes. These breathe the same spirit, and were, in a lower degree, partakers of the same sufferings. Many of them took joyfully the spoiling of their goods, and all had their names cast out as evil; being branded with the nickname of Puritans, and thereby made a byeword and a proverb of reproach.

I have endeavoured to rescue from obscurity a few of the most eminent of these: I say a few; for there is a multitude of them, which it would be tedious even to name. Nor have I attempted to abridge all the works of these few; for some of them are immensely voluminous. The Works of Dr. Goodwin alone would have sufficed to fill fifty volumes. I have therefore selected what I conceived would be of most general use, and most proper to form a complete body of Practical Divinity.[15]

---

[14] With all Wesley's fine plans and diligent work on *A Christian Library*, one might expect it to share the phenomenal success that most of his abridgments enjoyed; unfortunately, this was not the case. It is a melancholy entry in the *Journal*, dated November 6, 1752, which notes that Wesley had lost money on the venture. The entry closes with the revealing statement: "Perhaps the next generation may know the value of it" (*Journal*, IV, 48). In spite of this, he never ceased to insist that his preachers study it for their own instruction and share it with the societies (*Journal*, IV, 94, 189; *Letters*, IV, 272; VII, 64, 83).

[15] *CL*, IV, 105.

These comments indicate not only Wesley's esteem for the Puritans,[16] but also his reason for incorporating their works in the *Library*.

The presence of these works, however, brought criticism from Wesley's colleagues in the Church of England. The November, 1760, issue of *The London Magazine* carried a letter to John Wesley questioning his orthodoxy as a clergyman of the Church of England, inquiring whether *A Christian Library* was not simply an "odd collection of mutilated writings of dissenters of all sorts." [17] Wesley responded to this question in the next issue of the magazine: "No. In the first ten volumes there is not a line from any dissenter of any sort. And the greatest part of the other forty is extracted from Archbishop Leighton, Bishops Taylor, Patrick, Kenn, Reynolds, Sanderson; and other ornaments of the Church of England." [18]

This unequivocal answer is typical of Wesley, but it is doubtful that it was very satisfactory to his questioner. The problem arises in the different definitions of the term "dissenter." This term was first applied to the "dissenting brethren" of the Westminster Assembly—that is, to the Independents and Congregationalists—who were not in agreement with the majority opinion of that predominantly Presbyterian body.[19] After the Act of Uniformity of 1662, the term became the popular designation for all those persons who would not conform to the Prayer Book and remained outside the Church of England, which included most Presbyterians, Independents, Baptists, and others of Puritan inclination. Wesley, however, appears to have held a rather clear distinction between "Dissenters" who voluntarily removed themselves from the church, such as the Baptists and some Independents, and those persons "forced out" by the Act of Uniformity, whom he termed Nonconformists or Puritans.[20] If Wesley intended such a distinction, he

[16] Since Thomas Goodwin, a renowned leader of the Nonconformists in the latter half of the seventeenth century, is specifically mentioned in this preface, it is safe to assume that Wesley intended to include in his comments the heroes of Nonconformity, as well as the early Puritans whose work is prefaced by this introduction.

[17] Stephen Church, "Letter to the Rev. Mr. Wesley," *London Magazine*, XXIX (1760), 587.

[18] "Letter to Mr. T. H., alias Philodemus, alias Somebody, alias Stephen Church, alias, R. W.," *Ibid.*, p. 651.

[19] William Haller, *The Rise of Puritanism* (New York: Harper & Row, 1957), p. 16.

[20] *Works*, I, 262; II, 49; VIII, 114; *Journal*, IV, 93. R. Butterworth suggests that Wesley used the term to refer to Independents as distinguished from Presbyterians ("Wesley and the Dissenters," *WHSP*, VIII [1911-12] 27).

may have justly claimed that the first ten volumes contained no Dissenters; nevertheless, these volumes do include a few Puritan authors.[21]

Thorough investigation of the remaining forty volumes will show that authors of the Puritan tradition in actual fact constitute the "greatest part" of the total, even though few were voluntary Dissenters. Applying a broad definition of the term "Puritan" (including the Dissenters) to the list of English authors in the *Library* reveals that thirty-two [22] are Puritans while twenty-eight are from the Church of England.[23] In terms of bulk of material, or the actual space occupied by the writings of various authors, Puritan materials make up an even larger proportion of the *Library*.[24]

It should be noted that among those listed in this study as Church of England men there are some who display Puritan sympathies, even though they conformed to the Church of England in 1662. Archbishop Robert Leighton (d. 1684), the Scottish divine, would have qualified under Richard Baxter's classification as an "old Presbyterian" who accepted reordination while privately and knowingly understanding it in terms different from those of the officiating bishop.[25] Bishop Edward Reynolds (d. 1676) was a participant in both the Westminster Assembly

---

[21] Joseph Hall, Robert Bolton, John Preston, Richard Sibbes, Samuel Clarke, and John Foxe.

[22] To this number should be added the major work of joint Puritan authorship, *An Extract from the Assembly's Shorter Catechism.*

[23] A complete list of the authors included appears in Appendix I of the present study. Classification of the authors has been possible through the use of the *Dictionary of National Biography*, Edmund Calamy's three lists of ministers ejected in 1662, A. G. Matthew's *Calamy Revised*, Benjamin Brooks's *Lives of the Puritans*, Daniel Neal's *History of the Puritans*, Samuel Clarke's various *Lives* and martyrologies, and the standard bibliographical reference works. For purposes of this calculation those persons from the early period when Puritanism constituted a "party" within the Church of England have been counted as Puritans; and those who conformed in 1662, even though some may have had Puritan sympathies, have been counted among the Church of England authors.

[24] According to a cursory count of the pages of the second edition of the *Library*, Puritan materials constitute some 7,200 pages, whereas the Church of England materials make up only 3,900.

[25] *DNB*, XXXIII, 5. Baxter distinguishes three kinds of conformists: the conformists proper, some of the old ministers formerly called Presbtyerians, and the Latitudinarians. The Presbyterians in this group conformed and subscribed to the Act of Uniformity with the understanding that the bishop bade them "do it in their own sense." The Latitudinarians were mostly Cambridge men and included the Cambridge Platonists. According to Baxter, these were "ingenious Men and Scholars, and of Universal Principles and free, abhorring at first the *Imposition* of these little things, but thinking them not great enough to stick at when *Imposed*" (*Reliquiae Baxterianae, or Mr. Richard Baxter's Narrative of His Life and Times* [London: by Matthew Sylvester, 1696] Part II, p. 386).

and the Savoy Conference. He conformed, evidently thinking others would join him, and took a bishopric only after consulting with Baxter, Calamy, and other Puritan leaders.[26] Most of the Cambridge Platonists, trained at Emmanuel College when it was largely Puritan and in general sympathy with the political aspirations of the Commonwealth, were judged by the Westminster Assembly as "fitt to be fellows." [27] They differed at several major points with orthodox Puritan theology, but they shared the Puritan concern for vital personal religion displayed in everyday life. Of this group Wesley uses Ralph Cudworth (d. 1688), Nathanael Culverwel (d. 1651), John Smith (d. 1652), John Worthington (d. 1671), and Henry More (d. 1687).

An analysis of the list of Puritan authors included in *A Christian Library* reveals that Wesley's selection is principally confined to authors who were active in the latter half of the seventeenth century, or more correctly, in the period after 1640. Only five of those who were leaders in the movement during its earlier days are included. Bishop Joseph Hall (d. 1656) was considered by Wesley to be one of this number, although he noted that there may be some question about this.[28] The others are Robert Bolton (d. 1631), John Preston (d. 1628), William Whateley (d. 1639), and Richard Sibbes (d. 1635). John Foxe may also be counted among this number, even though his massive work, *Acts and Monuments*, carried its influence far beyond the confines of party and theological loyalties.[29] Wesley failed to use works of his own period in

[26] *DNB*, XLVIII, 40. Henry Scougal (d. 1678), another Scottish divine with opinions close to those of Leighton, was reverenced among the Puritans as one of their own (*DNB*, XXXIII, 5). George Whitefield attributes his conversion to Scougal's *The Life of God in the Soul of Men*, which had been given to him by Charles Wesley (G. Whitefield, *Journal* [London: Banner of Truth Trust, 1960], pp. 46-47.)

[27] *DNB*, XIII, 271, LIII, 74. Baxter judges them, along with the "old Presbyterians," to be the "honour of the Conformists" whose "profitable Preaching is used, by God's Providence, to keep up the Public Interest of Religion, and refresh the discerning sort of Auditors" (*Reliquiae Baxterianae*, Part II, p. 386).

[28] *CL*, I, 106; cf. *DNB*, XXIV, 77. See Douglas Bush, *English Literature in the Earlier Seventeenth Century: 1600-1660* (Oxford: Clarendon Press, 1945), p. 323, for one who does not consider Hall to be a Puritan.

[29] John Foxe, *Acts and Monuments of the Christian Martyrs, and Matters Ecclesiasticall passed in the Church of Christ, from the Primitive beginnings, to these our daies* (4 vols.; London: Printed for the Company of Stationers, 1641). Foxe is listed as a Puritan by Benjamin Brook, *The Lives of the Puritans* (3 vols.; London: Printed for James Black, 1813), I, 326; Daniel Neal, *History of the Puritans* (4 vols.; Dublin: Printed for Brice Edmond [1755]), I, 146-47; *DNB*, XX, 142-48.

the *Library*, as had been suggested by Doddridge. Only John Howe (d. 1705) and Thomas Crane (d. 1714) lived in Wesley's century. Had Wesley's original idea of making the *Library* about a hundred volumes been carried out, he might well have included works of his contemporaries, such as Doddridge, Isaac Watts, and others.

The wide range of Puritan theological and ecclesiastical opinion, so detrimental to their cause during the Commonwealth, was clearly evident in the works produced in the period from which Wesley selected the major portion of his material. Representatives of the variant views are included in the *Library*, although Wesley's biases are evident in the selection. Of the twenty-seven Puritans from this period only five are Independents or Congregationalists. This number includes the leaders, such as Thomas Goodwin (d. 1680), John Owen (d. 1683), and John Flavel (d. 1691), with Lewis Stuckley (d. 1687) and the layman Francis Rous (d. 1659) being lesser known members of the group. In addition to these, the more radical wing of Puritanism is also represented by a lone Baptist, John Bunyan (d. 1688).

The remainder of the Puritan authors are drawn from the ranks of the Presbyterians, including the major leaders of the church during the period of the Commonwealth; consequently, the leaders of the two thousand ministers ejected by the Act of Uniformity in 1662 are represented: Richard Baxter (d. 1691), Samuel Clarke (d. 1683),[30] Edmund Calamy (d. 1666), Isaac Ambrose (d. 1663), Joseph Alleine (d. 1668), Richard Alleine (d. 1681), Samuel Annesley (d. 1696), and John Howe (d. 1705). Other Presbyterians included are Sir Matthew Hale (d. 1676), John Kitchin (d. 1662?), Matthew Pool (d. 1679), Thomas Crane (d. 1714), Samuel Charnock (d. 1680), William Dell (d. 1664), Thomas Manton (d. 1677), Herbert Palmer (d. 1647), and Samuel Shaw (d. 1696). The Scottish Presbyterians are represented by such men as Samuel Rutherford (d. 1661), Hugh Binning (d. 1653), and John Brown (d. 1679).[31]

[30] Samuel Clarke (1599-1683), the Puritan divine, is not to be confused with the famous metaphysician of the same name, Samuel Clarke (1675-1729). The latter was the chaplain to the Bishop of Norwick, whose theories on the Trinity caused him to be accused of Arianism (*DNB*, X, 441-42).

[31] For comparative lists of Puritans in *A Christian Library* see Duncan Coomer, "The Influence of Puritanism and Dissent on Methodism," *LQHR*, 175 (1950), 347, and John Newton, *Methodism and the Puritans*, p. 8.

Numerical comparisons of the denominational or party affiliations of the Puritans as given here should be used, at best, with caution. Wesley undoubtedly would have been surprised at such a calculation (he obviously never made one) and would have claimed that here, as elsewhere, he looked to what was said and not to who said it. Nevertheless, Puritans with Presbyterian sympathies were by far the largest group included, which would seem to indicate Wesley's preference for the more moderate wing of Puritanism.

Exemplary Lives in A Christian Library

A large section of the *Library* is made up of "accounts" of exemplary Christian living. The popularity of diaries and biographical history was a common feature of the period, finding some of its most eloquent expression in the hagiography and martyrology of Christians.[32] Samuel Clarke, patterning his work on John Foxe's *Acts and Monuments,* was the major biographer of the Puritans. Although Wesley added some material from other Puritan sources, he was principally dependent on Clarke for most of the lives included in the *Library.* He was critical of Clarke's selections in that they did not give adequate place to some of the "most eminent men" of the Church of England and corrected this through some additions.[33] Even with these additions, however, of the lives found in the *Library,* the Puritans number more than twice those of the Church of England.[34] Just as the Puritan authors were the major source for Wesley's treatment of "practical divinity" in the *Library,* they also provided the majority of the examples that he gave of how the teachings of this divinity were to be applied in an individual's life.

[32] John Foxe's *Acts and Monuments,* Thomas Fuller's *The History of the Worthies of England,* and Samuel Clarke's *A General Martyrology* and *The Lives of Sundry Eminent Persons in this Later Age* are some of the more renowned works of this type. See William Haller, *The Rise of Puritanism,* p. 101, for Richard Baxter's comment on the importance of the spiritual character of such works.

[33] "I have therefore been obliged to vary from my first design, both by omitting many lives which Mr. Clarke has inserted, . . . and by inserting those of some whom he has omitted, but who were men famous in their generations, and highly esteemed by all who love the image of God, in whomsoever it may be found" (*CL,* XV, 3). These additions are the lives of Richard Hooker (d. 1600), Sir Henry Wooton (d. 1639), John Donne (d. 1631), George Herbert (d. 1633), Bishop William Bedell (d. 1642), Archbishop Ussher (d. 1613), and Henry Hammond (d. 1660).

[34] A complete list of the exemplary lives is found in Appendix II.

Wesley's appreciation of this type material is seen in his extensive use of "accounts" of the lives of his followers, in addition to those he gathered from other sources. Such lives became a tradition and hallmark of the Methodist societies, where, as among the Puritans, they were a major source of inspiration and proof of the working of the Holy Spirit.[35]

2. Writings of Puritan Divines in Wesley's General Publications

Although *A Christian Library* was the most extensive project of abridgment attempted by Wesley and is the principal example of his use of Puritan literature, he published many other abridgments during his career. As might be expected from the distribution found in the *Library*, works of Puritan divines constitute a large portion of these publications.

Of the approximately fifty abridgments and abstracts printed as separate volumes, more than a third are from the Puritan tradition.[36] While there is no set pattern in the types of writings, selected writings on practical divinity, not unexpectedly, predominate; e.g., Joseph Alleine's *Christian Letters* and *An Alarm to the Unconverted Sinner,* John Janeway's *Token for Children,* Richard Baxter's *A Call to the Unconverted* and *The Saint's Everlasting Rest,* and William Whateley's *Directions for Married Persons.*[37] Jonathan Edwards' three accounts of the revival in New England and abridgments of Milton's *Paradise Lost* and Bunyan's *Pilgrim's Progress* may be classified as practical divinity, since they were understood by Wesley as instructive pieces.[38] To these should be added

---

[35] An examination of the first few issues of *The Arminian Magazine,* begun by Wesley in 1778, reveals a number of hagiographies drawn from the ranks of Methodist societies. Wesley's *Journal* is filled with what he usually terms a "remarkable account," that is, an account of the work of the gospel in the life of a sinner (*Journal,* IV, 268-69, 381-87). See also, e.g., Richard Green's items 89, 188, 215, in *Bibliography;* Thomas Herbert, *John Wesley as Editor and Author,* pp. 12-13.

[36] Richard Green's comprehensive *Bibliography,* with the corrections and additions to it found in the *Wesley Historical Society Proceedings,* is the basis of this survey (*WHSP,* III [1901-02], 123-30; XXI [1937-38], 132-33). Collections of hymns and psalms are not considered in this calculation, although Clifford Towlson points out that Wesley's early (1737) *Collection of Psalms and Hymns* is largely dependent upon those of Isaac Watts (*Moravian and Methodist* [London: Epworth Press, 1957], pp. 196-98).

[37] Several of these are also found in *A Christian Library,* although some are new abridgments.

[38] Wesley, quite wisely, seldom attempted the abridgment of such renowned literary pieces as these works of Milton and Bunyan, and the general opinion of such attempts is negative. (See *Bibliography,* p. 28; Thomas Herbert, *John Wesley as Editor and Author,* pp. 85-88.)

Isaac Watts's *Treatise on the Passions,* abridged by Wesley for *The Arminian Magazine.*[39]

Exemplary lives were often published by Wesley as separate tracts for easy distribution. Puritan lives printed in this manner include Jonathan Edwards' account of *The Life of the Late Rev. Mr. David Brainerd, Missionary to the Indians,* an extract from *The Life and Death of Mr. John Janeway,* and *The Life and Death of the Reverend Learned and Pious Mr. Thomas Halyburton.*[40]

Theological interests other than practical divinity are represented in such works as an abridgment of Jonathan Edwards' treatises *On the Religious Affections*[41] and *The Distinguishing Marks of a Work of God.*[42] Of more importance in terms of Wesley's own theological formulations are Richard Baxter's *Aphorisms of Justification* and John Goodwin's *Treatise on Justification* and *Exposition of the Ninth chapter of the Epistle to the Romans.*[43] Both of these authors were somewhat suspect in conservative Puritan circles because of their "Arminian" tendencies, which was no doubt their attraction for Wesley. From Wesley's contemporaries is drawn Dr. Watts's *Serious Consideration Concerning the Doctrines of Election and Reprobation.*

The preface to Wesley's *Explanatory Notes upon the New Testament* discloses his primary dependence on the *Gnomon Novi Testamenti* by Johann Albrecht Bengel, the Württemberg Pietist. In addition, Wesley acknowledges his indebtedness to three English works, among them Philip Doddridge's *Family Expositor* and the "work of Dr. Guyse" (pre-

[39] This is most likely the abridgment referred to in Wesley's *Journal,* III, 353, in which his opinion of himself and Watts is forcefully and revealingly stated: "I abridged Dr. Watts's pretty 'Treatise on the Passions.' His hundred and seventy-seven pages will make a useful tract of four-and-twenty. Why do persons who treat the same subjects with me, write so much larger books? Of many reasons, is not this the chief,—We do not write with the same view? Their *principal end* is to get money; my *only one* is to do good."

[40] This work was one of Wesley's earliest publications (1739). He read the work and was greatly impressed by it while in Georgia (*Journal,* I, 308, 437).

[41] Edwards' work is characterized by Wesley's preface as a "dangerous heap wherein much wholesome food is mixed with much deadly poison." The poison, i.e., Calvinism, is naturally eliminated in the abridgment. (*Bibliography,* p. 170). Wesley, in his treatise, "Thoughts upon Necessities," closely examines Edwards' famous *Freedom of the Will* and argues against its teachings (*Works,* X, 460, 463, 475).

[42] Albert Outler understands Edwards to have been a major source of Wesley's evangelical theology, particularly in the doctrine of the Spirit. (*John Wesley,* pp. 15-16.)

[43] The latter work was published in successive issues of Volume III (1780) of *The Arminian Magazine.*

sumedly this is *An Exposition of the New Testament*).[44] The companion volume, *Explanatory Notes on the Old Testament,* is likewise dependent on Puritan biblical scholarship since it uses as a major source Matthew Henry's *Exposition of the Old and New Testaments.*

The Arminian Magazine provided Wesley with an excellent vehicle in which to publish many brief tracts and exemplary lives, as well as such curious articles as *An Extract from Mr. Baxter's Certainty of the World of Spirits fully evinced by Unquestionable Histories of Apparitions and Witchcraft.*[45]

This cursory look at Wesley's general publications reveals essentially the same patterns in the use of Puritan materials as found in *A Christian Library.* A broad range of authors is represented, drawn largely from the latter half of the seventeenth century, although—to be sure—more of his contemporaries are represented. The most significant amplification is in his acknowledged indebtedness to Puritan scholarship in the area of biblical commentary.

Examination of Wesley's use of Puritan literature delineates many interesting and instructive features of Wesley's relationship to the Puritan tradition. However, the major contribution is demonstration of Wesley's thorough acquaintance with the wide range of Puritan literature. He was not only acquainted with the leaders of the Puritan tradition but knew the writings of some of the lesser known men of this persuasion.

This familiarity with the Puritans is surprising for a person of Wesley's education and vocation, and it must have raised some questions among his co-workers in the Church of England. The comment of the Presbyterian Philip Doddridge in his letter to Wesley is instructive at this point: "I will not presume, Sir, to mention to you the Divines of the Established Church though to my Pupils I have given a larger enumeration of the principal of them, . . . But, as I may reasonably conclude, the Puritans, and the Divines of the Separation, less known to the Generality of those with whom you, Sir, may be concerned, you will pardon me,

[44] John Wesley, *Explanatory Notes upon the New Testament* (London: The Epworth Press, 1958), pp. 7-8. John Guyse (1680-1761) was an Independent minister well known as a defender of orthodoxy against the Arian theories popular in his day (*DNB*, XXIII, 394). For comment on Wesley's dependence on these sources, see *Bibliography*, pp. 91-92; *Journal*, IV, 92.
[45] *The Arminian Magazine*, VI (1785).

that I mention a few of them, and of the chief Pieces." [46] Doddridge's apologetic mention of the Puritans assumes that one of Wesley's station would normally have little familiarity with, or interest in, the Puritans. Church of England men were usually loath to study or acquaint themselves with anyone under the stigma of separation. While Wesley may have gained an appreciation for some writers of the Puritan tradition in his home, the prejudices of his formal education would have discouraged pursuit of these writings. The breadth of his reading in these writers is, therefore, even more amazing since most of these endeavors must have been undertaken after his formal education.

Like Doddridge, who did not allow party label to deter him from familiarity with the "valuable writings of the Established Church," Wesley, in contrast to most of his contemporaries, overlooked the points of separation to view the universal truths contained in the Puritan writings. In doing so he gave expression to the catholicity of his religious viewpoint.

Where or when Wesley gained an acquaintance with these works is largely a matter of conjecture. V. H. H. Green's listing of Wesley's readings in the period 1725-34 notes only a few of the more renowned materials: Milton's *Paradise Lost*, Bishop Hall's *Contemplation of the New Testament*, Isaac Watt's *On Predestination*, and the *Works* of Richard Baxter, Edmund Calamy and Samuel Clarke.[47] Wesley's Georgia diaries indicate that in the winter and spring of 1737 he was reading such Puritan works as Bishop Hall's *Meditation on Heaven,* Clarke's *Lives,* the *Works* of John Owen, Milton's *Paradise Regained, The Life of Thomas Halyburton,* and the *Catechism of the Assembly* (presumably this is the Westminster Assembly).[48] In the autumn after Aldersgate (1738) he read Edwards' "truly surprising narrative of the conversions lately wrought in and about the town of Northampton, in New England." [49] May, 1739, found him reading Daniel Neal's *History of the Puritans,*[50] and in October of that year he mentioned reading *Bunyan's*

[46] "Letter to Mr. Wesley: A Scheme of Study For a Clergyman," *The Arminian Magazine,* I (1778), 421.

[47] V. H. H. Green, *The Young Mr. Wesley* (New York: St. Martin's Press, 1961), pp. 305-19.

[48] *Journal,* I, 309, 319, 336, 351-52, 357.

[49] *Journal,* II, 83.

[50] *Journal,* II, 205

Life, as well as some of Bunyan's works and, once again, Milton's *Paradise Lost.*[51] Further study of the titles referred to in his journals and letters until the publication of *A Christian Library* fails to reveal any broad knowledge of these writings.[52] Those mentioned represent some of the more important and commonly read of the Puritan materials but give no indication of Wesley's knowledge of the far wider range of Puritan authors represented in *A Christian Library.* Doddridge's advice no doubt gave Wesley some direction in reading these authors, but comparison of Wesley's selection with Doddridge's list shows that these suggestions constitute only a small part of the writings finally included.[53]

The most plausible explanation for this familiarity is that, once Wesley was willing to drop the prejudices of education and background, he was open to materials explicating the "Christian life," no matter what their source. This concern must have led him to the writings with a heavy emphasis on practical divinity, which, of course, included the Puritan writers. His insatiable habits of reading could well account for the wide range of authors. On the other hand, as we shall see, Wesley was willing to credit the Puritans with preeminence in this area, and, recognizing this, he may well have made a thorough and exhaustive examination of their writings. However their inclusion may be explained, Wesley clearly was not only familiar with the tradition, but he was also willing to permit their insights concerning the Christian faith and life to play a dominant role in the instruction of his own people.

[51] *Journal,* II, 288, 312-13.
[52] "A Bibliographical Catalog of Books Mentioned in John Wesley's Journals," *WHSP,* IV (1903-04), 17-19, 47-51, 74-81, 107-11.
[53] See Appendix I for such a comparison.

II

WESLEY'S ABRIDGMENT OF PURITAN LITERATURE

Commendable and beneficial abridgment is a work of art; John Wesley was a master of the medium. His methodology may be regarded as anticipating that of the modern-day digests although his accomplishments as the entire editorial staff of his projects have not been equaled in modern publications. The range and variety of his abridging work among the Puritans is evident, but this would have to be measurably expanded if his total endeavors were considered. Almost any printed material in the field of religion was "fair game," as is appropriately noted in Osborn's reported comment, "It is a wonder Mr. Wesley did not abridge the Gospel according to St. John." [1]

Wesley's primary methodologies of abridgment, as stated in the pref-

---

[1] As quoted by Green, *Bibliography,* p. 171.

ace to *A Christian Library,* have been noted.[2] Many of these are technical in nature; e.g., deletion of illustrations, modernization of language, etc. However, Wesley goes beyond such technical changes when he attempts to "preserve a consistency throughout" the writings. Modifications of this type are made according to the theological biases of the editor. Both forms of abridgment may be seen in a comparison of the original unexpurgated treatises with Wesley's editions of these works. Based on such comparisons, the present chapter examines Wesley's abridgments of Puritan literature.

Because of the large number of treatises handled by Wesley and the fruitlessness of extended comparisons, selection of those treatises to be studied has been somewhat arbitrary. Detailed comparison has been made of four works. Basic theological differences are vividly crystallized in Wesley's abridgment of the Westminster *Shorter Catechism.*[3] John Preston's *New Covenant,* discussing one of Wesley's major teachings, Christian perfection, comes from the early period when the Puritan cause constituted one "party" within the Church of England.[4] An example of a substantial theological treatment of the doctrine of the Holy Spirit is a work of John Owen, *On Communion with God the Father, Son, and Holy Ghost.*[5] Richard Alleine's *Vindiciae Pietatis: or A Vindication of Godliness* (1664) represents later Puritan instruction and a defense of an unpopular religious movement.[6]

There is no way to be certain what editions of the original materials Wesley used for purposes of abridgment. Most of the Puritan works used by Wesley would have been available in early editions during his own

[2] *CL,* I, ix.

[3] *The Shorter Catechism of the Westminster Divines: Being a facsimile of the First Edition "with the Proofs thereof out of the Scriptures;" which was ordered to be printed by the House of Commons, 14th April, 1648,* ed. J. H. Cotton and J. C. Pears, Jr. (Nashville: Printed for Presbyterian Theological Seminary, Chicago, 1943); cited hereafter as *The Shorter Catechism.*

[4] John Preston, *The New Covenant or The Saint's Portion* (London: Printed by I. D. for Nicholas Bourne, 1630), cited hereafter as *New Covenant.*

[5] John Owen, *On Communion with God the Father, Son, and Holy Ghost,* Vol. X in *Works* (28 vols.; London: Printed for Richard Baynes, 1826); cited hereafter as *On Communion.* Owen was the most distinguished pneumatologist among the seventeenth-century Puritans.

[6] Richard Alleine, *Vindiciae Pietatis: or A Vindication of Godliness* (London: 1664), cited hereafter as *Vindiciae Pietatis.*

time. From his comments concerning their preparation for the printer, it can be assumed that he had copies which he could mark freely,[7] thus, the editions he used were current enough to have been in plentiful supply.

1. Methods of Abridgment

Wesley's basic objectives in abridging any material were clarity of presentation, brevity within the bounds of conveying essential meaning, and readability for the common man. Omission is the primary means by which these objectives may be attained.

Brevity as an essential element in abridgment needs little explanation or comment; however, the general procedure used by Wesley in accomplishing this is instructive. Brevity may be obtained in two ways; either by the omission of large sections or sentences or by the omission of words and clauses. Wesley preferred the latter method although he certainly used both. Of those treatises examined, Preston's *New Covenant* is reduced most radically through extensive deletions.[8] This is, nevertheless, the exception rather than the rule. Because of his general practice of eliminating words and clauses, Wesley's editing pen is evident in almost every sentence of every treatise that he abridged.[9] Such thorough treatment witnesses to the meticulous care with which Wesley approached his task.

Preston's work furnishes a good example of Wesley's tendency to conflate what in the original may be separate chapters into one continuous narrative. *The New Covenant* is composed of fourteen separate sermons,

---

[7] *Works*, X, 381.

[8] In its original form the treatise constituted 486 pages and is reduced by Wesley to a mere 45 pages. When allowances are made for smaller type and a somewhat larger printed page used in Wesley's edition, the reduction is still extraordinary.

[9] *Vindiciae Pietatis*, p. 11 [CL, XVIII, 11], p. 59 [CL, XVIII, 42]; *New Covenant*, pp. 87-100 [CL, VI, 15]. In order to provide adequate information, wherever a comparison is made between Wesley's abridgment and the original material two page references are provided: the first refers to the page of the original treatise and the second, in brackets, indicates the page of Wesley's abridged version. In addition, Wesley's changes in the original text are indicated thus: The original words of the text which Wesley omitted are set in small capital letters; Wesley's additions are in brackets; text used by both the original author and Wesley is set in boldface type.

but in Wesley's edition, divested of introductory and summary materials, it becomes one continuous treatise with no chapter or sermon divisions.

Wesley commonly deleted strictly illustrative, explanatory, or embellishing statements.[10] Because the majority of Puritan literature consists of published sermons, this type of expurgation is common. Hortatory passages, so prevalent in sermon material, undergo the same fate.[11]

The concern for brevity sometimes led Wesley into creating passages which are either confusing or which change the sense of the original. The deletion of a question while retaining its explanation is, at best, confusing. Wesley's failure to eliminate or change pronouns occasionally allows them to refer to completely different antecedents than those to which they originally referred.[12] With no indication of this, meanings are often changed, albeit unintentionally. Such examples might be more readily excused if Wesley had intended to "correct" or amend the text, as he allowed himself the liberty to do, but where they are evidently only the consequence of expurgation which does not carefully reorient the context, they might well have been avoided.

With the common reader in mind, Wesley often eliminated foreign words and phrases, retaining the English translations which were often given in the original treatise.[13] Extended discussions of the meaning and etymology of Greek and Latin words were also dropped.[14] This does not mean that all foreign references were omitted, for Wesley carefully retained those which were essential to the meaning of a passage.

---

[10] The following example from Alleine's treatise is typical of Wesley's elimination of repetitious and superfluous words and clauses: "Fleshly Wisdom, A CARNAL [or] Policy; which consist in an understanding where the interest of the flesh lies, and in the ordering AND MANAGING of ourselves and our affairs so, that we may advance and secure this interest. By the interest in the flesh, I mean, all those things which please and gratify [nature] THE FLESH, AND WHEREWITH THE FLESHLY MINDS OF MEN ARE MOST DELIGHTED, AND PLACE THEIR CONTENT AND HAPPINESS IN, as outward peace and quiet, OUTWARD EASE AND SECURITY, OUTWARD plenty and prosperity, OUTWARD credit and reputation." (*Vindiciae Pietatis*, p. 52 [*CL*, XVIII, 38].)

[11] *Vindiciae Pietatis*, pp. 98-100 [*CL*, XVIII, 69], p. 109 [*CL*, XVIII, 77].

[12] *On Communion*, p. 285 [*CL*, XI, 89]; cf. pp. 315-16 [*CL*, XI, 105]: *New Covenant*, p. 295 [*CL*, VI, 29].

[13] "And hath a great zeal about THE MINIMA LEGES, the lower or more circumstantial matters." *Vindiciae Pietatis*, p .3 [*CL*, XVIII, 7], cf. p. 29 [*CL*, XVIII, 24]; *On Communion*, p. 275 [*CL*, XI, 83], p. 300 [*CL*, XI, 97-98].

[14] *On Communion*, pp. 275-76 [*CL*, XI, 83-84], cf. p. 307 [*CL*, XI, 100]; *Vindiciae Pietatis*, p. 14 [*CL*, XVIII, 14].

Antiquated words are modernized; Alleine's "phanatic" [sic] becomes Wesley's "enthusiast," a word denoting the same type of emphasis and behavior but more common in Wesley's own day.[15] Crude expressions of an earlier age are changed to their more acceptable equivalents.[16]

The substitution of one word for another occasionally changes the emphasis of a statement, giving it added significance: "your" becomes "our," broadening the scope of the passage; "soul" becomes "person" to give emphasis to the total man rather than to indicate only a "part" of him; "saint" becomes "Christian," changing the nuance slightly but significantly.[17] Grammatical changes or corrections are commonplace and are usually in the interest of rectifying antiquated practices.

Wesley, still pursuing the interests of the common reader, takes philosophical arguments which are supported by technical and scholastic presentation as prime targets of his editorial pen. Not all philosophical arguments are eliminated since, in many cases, they form an integral part of the treatises and can only be omitted to the detriment of the whole work. Owen, for example, could hardly make a point without stating it philosophically; therefore Wesley retains much of this but tempers it. Where possible, he expurgates without hesitancy strictly philosophical arguments and explanations which only play a supporting role.[18] This pattern is seen when arguments from proportionality and a detailed discussion concerning the nature of God as simple, perfect without mixture, composition, number, etc., are omitted from Preston's work.[19] Wesley, in most cases, as in this one, is satisfied simply to retain the statements concerning the nature of God, without including the philosophical argument. The technicalities of an involved theological statement are often reduced or omitted when they contain nothing particularly instructive for Wesley's reader: **"The business of sending the Holy**

[15] *Vindiciae Pietatis*, p. 95 [*CL*, XVIII, 67], p. 108 [*CL*, XVIII, 76].

[16] **"Lusts are** BIG BELLIED, **[prolific], a world of monstrous births are continually springing forth from them."** (*Vindiciae Pietatis*, p. 105 [*CL*, XVIII, 73], cf. p. 204 [*CL*, XVIII, 144].)

[17] *Vindiciae Pietatis*, p. 214 [*CL*, XVIII, 149], p. 88 [*CL*, XVIII, 62]; *On Communion*, p. 295 [*CL*, XI, 94]. It may well be that in this latter case more than change in nuance is implied. For Wesley the word "saint" may have had a sectarian stigma since in some Puritan usages it implied "the gathered church" rather than the national church.

[18] *On Communion*, pp. 278-79 [*CL*, XI, 86], p. 330 [*CL*, XI, 115].

[19] *New Covenant*, pp. 37-42 [*CL*, VI, 8], p. 73 [*CL*, VI, 14], p. 365 [*CL*, VI, 41].

Ghost by Christ, WHICH ARGUES HIS PERSONAL PROCESSION ALSO FROM HIM, THE SON, **was a deep mystery which at once they could not bear; and therefore he thus instructs them in it by degrees."** [20]

True to his principle of deleting those items that were controversial, especially those referring to the burning controversial issues of the time in which the treatises were written, Wesley omits Alleine's derogatory reference to a "zealous Advocate for the lawfulness of sports on the Lord's Day." [21] In a similar vein, Wesley omits Owen's statements decrying the practice of ejecting from the Church of England those ministers who insisted upon free forms of worship.[22] Wesley could accept the sentiment of Owen's objection but hesitated to raise the issue in his own time. Not all controversial comments were eliminated however, since some, written in the heat of earlier conflict, still had relevance to problems of Wesley's own time. Alleine's insistence on the significance and meaning of the outward forms of worship is retained, probably for instruction of Wesley's readers who were raising the question of the reliability of such forms.

Wesley clarifies confusing and repetitious points by omission and where necessary adds transitional comments. Preston's tract is oftentimes confusing, since, when he is moving from one point to another in the general outline, no indication is given of a new departure; and conversely, so many points are numbered serially that it is difficult to retain a clear understanding of that to which the numbers refer. Wesley corrects this by clarifying the transitions and eliminating some of the unnecessary references to series.[23]

Similarly, in Preston's comments on man's part in the covenant with God, he gives no indication that this is what he is discussing. No such ambiguity is present in Wesley's edition in which he prefaces the passage with this statement: "But here consider what is the condition of this

[20] *On Communion*, p. 277 [*CL*, XI, 85].
[21] *Vindiciae Pietatis*, p. 120 [*CL*, XVIII, 83]. James I promulgated the *Book of Sports*, allowing certain sports on Sunday—a rude offense to Puritan sentiments which reverenced the Sabbath as a holy day to be observed without frivolity. The statement could also have been understood by Tory Wesley to be anti-Royalist and thereby repugnant, but it is doubtful that Alleine intended it to be so. The offense to Alleine was not political but religious.
[22] *On Communion*, pp. 313-14 [*CL*, XI, 104].
[23] *New Covenant*, p. 390 [*CL*, VI, 42].

covenant of grace on man's part." [24] On the whole, the additions are few and generally of this type, although simple explanatory sentences or phrases are occasionally interpolated.[25] A few summary sections may be noted where the full text has been replaced by Wesley's comments, but this is also the exception rather than the rule.[26]

Paraphrasing and rearrangement are among the most effective means of obtaining clarity and brevity. In addition, they provide opportunity for Wesley to make changes which he thinks "improve" or correct the thought of the treatise. The following is a representative example:

THE THIRD THING TO BE EXPRESSED, IS THE MANNER OF WRITING IT; THE APOSTLE HERE COMPARES HIMSELF AND ALL OTHER MINISTERS TO THE PEN, BUT IT IS CHRIST THAT WRITES THE EPISTLE, THE EPISTLE IS HIS, FORE THESE WORKS HE DOTH IN IT, IT IS HE THAT TAKES THE PEN, IT IS HE THAT HANDLES IT, AND USETH IT, IT IS HE THAT PUTS INKE INTO THE PEN, IT IS HE THAT APPLIES IT, SO THAT THOUGH THE MINISTER BE THE IMMEDIATE WRITER OF THESE LAWES IN THE HEART, YET THE INKE IS THE HOLY GHOST, AND IT COMES ORIGINALLY FROM CHRIST, AND BESIDES THEY [Now you must observe that it is Christ that thus writes the law of God in the heart of man, which he doth ordinarily, by means of the minister (who is, as it were, the pen), through the power of the Holy Ghost (which is, as it were, the ink;) for the means] are not left to themselves, but the Lord must concurre with them immediately; WE [the ministers] are but co-workers with him, he holds OUR [their] hands, as it were, when WE [they] write the Epistle in any man's heart, it is he that guides the PENNE, [pen] as it is he that puts Inke into it, IT COMES ORIGINALLY FROM HIM, and therefore the Epistle is his.[27]

Wesley's addition of the word "ordinarily" to the sentence, explaining Christ's working through the minister, leaves no question about there being other means by which the Holy Spirit may effect a change in the hearts of men, a point Preston would have readily admitted but which is not clear in his statement.[28]

[24] *Ibid.*, p. 360 [*CL*, VI, 40].
[25] *Vindiciae Pietatis*, p. 300 [*CL*, XVIII, 176].
[26] *New Covenant*, p. 317 [*CL*, VI, 31].
[27] *Ibid.*, p. 324 [*CL*, VI, 33-34], cf. p. 107 [*CL*, VI, 15-16].
[28] Wesley would always want to leave open the possibility of God's working through lay "instruments" of conversion, through preachers and teachers.

Each of the foregoing methods of abridgment, when joined to the next, produces an instructive image of how Wesley edited the works of others. Nevertheless, only in abstraction is one able to separate these from the preponderate influence of theological considerations in the actual abridgment.

2. Theological Considerations in Abridgment

A theologian's own allegiances—his interests and interpretations—serve to concentrate his attention on those elements of another man's writings which he considers important and to eliminate those aspects which he may consider erroneous or extraneous. An analysis of deletions, changes, and embellishments in abridged materials may indicate, therefore, specific areas of theological affinities and differences. The comparative method used in this study attempts to determine the theological criteria applied by Wesley to the Puritan materials he edited.

Criteria may fall into either positive or negative categories. Affinities of theological position are most clearly revealed in the selection of particular doctrines and teachings for publication. In addition, the retention of comments intact and the numerous changes which do not modify the theological positions of the original treatises substantiate the areas of agreement. Consideration of examples of positive agreement and affinity between Wesley and the Puritans is reserved until the extended discussions found in Parts II and III of this study.

Differences of theological opinion are most often indicated through consistent omission of certain doctrines or concepts and through modifications of theological positions in certain statements retained. Such omissions and modifications are now considered to determine the negative theological criteria Wesley applied to the Puritan materials.[29]

If it is allowed that the Westminster *Shorter Catechism,* within the limits imposed upon it by its purpose, generally incorporates the major theological precepts of the Puritan tradition, it may be taken as a guide to the theological divergencies between Wesley and that tradition.

---

[29] The difficulty of distinguishing between what is omitted because of basic theological disagreement and what is omitted merely for the sake of brevity calls for caution against overemphasis in the use of this methodology but does not eliminate the significant insights to be gained by it.

Wesley's major deletions from the catechism are the questions dealing with election and predestination,[30] effectual calling,[31] and the decrees.[32] These statements, formulated on the basis of a Calvinistic interpretation of predestination, meant that God had chosen some men for eternal salvation, while rejecting others; that is to say, God's grace is not universally offered. Wesley was not willing to let these statements remain since in his own understanding God's saving grace is offered to all men.[33] Other references to election or predestination are similarly modified; e.g., "God's elect" becomes "mankind," [34] and "they that are effectually called" becomes "they that truly believe." [35]

Since Puritan writers were normally Calvinistic, Wesley constantly deletes and corrects predestinarian references throughout the works he abridges.[36] Comments incorporating such assumptions are altered: "Even men, THEY do us not (without his COMMISSION [permission]) the least good, nor the least hurt." [37] Passages which depend upon

[30] "Q. Did God leave all mankinde to perish in the estate of sin and misery? A. God, having out of his meere good pleasure from all eternity elected some to everlasting life, did enter into a Covenant of grace to deliver them out of the estate of sin and misery, and to bring them into an estate of Salvation by a Redeemer." (*The Shorter Catechism*, p. 8.)

[31] "Q. What is Effectual Calling? A. Effectual Calling is the work of God's Spirit, whereby, convincing us of our sin and misery, inlightening our mindes in the knowledge of Christ, and renewing our wills, he doth perswade and inable us to imbrace Jesus Christ freely offered to us in the Gospel." (*Ibid.*, p. 10.)

[32] "Q. What are the Decrees of God? A. The Decrees of God are, his eternal purpose according to the counsel of his will, whereby for his own glory, he hath fore-ordained whatsoever comes to pass. Q. How doth God execute his Decrees? A. God executeth his Decrees in the Works of Creation and Providence." (*Ibid.*, p. 6.)

[33] The incessant struggle between Wesley and the Calvinistic wing of the Evangelical Revival was over this very point of election. As Wesley points out, his adversaries followed the interpretation of the Confession of the Westminster Assembly which makes it clear that "some men and angels are predestined unto everlasting life, and others fore-ordained to everlasting death." (*Works*, X, 206.) The latter half of this statement is most offensive to Wesley. The classic statement of his own position is found in his sermon entitled "Free Grace": "The grace or love of God, whence cometh our salvation, is *Free in All* and *Free for All*." (*Works*, VII, 373.) Wesley understood all men to have an opportunity through "prevenient grace" to accept or reject God's offer of "saving grace." For a discussion of this doctrine see below, p. 101.

[34] *The Shorter Catechism*, p. 8 [*CL*, XIV, 393].

[35] *Ibid.*, p. 10 [*CL*, XIV, 398].

[36] "Carnal men often come before the Lord with mock praises, give thanks for their ELECTION, justification, sanctification." (*Vindiciae Pietatis*, p. 155 [*CL*, XVIII, 108], cf. pp. 134-36 [*CL*, XVIII, 94].) "Now the Holy Spirit is promised under a two-fold consideration. 1st. as spirit of sanctification TO THE ELECT, to convert THEM [us] and make THEM [us] believers." (*On Communion*, p. 278 [*CL*, XI, 85], cf. p. 294 [*CL*, XI, 93-94].)

[37] *New Covenant*, p. 3 [*CL*, VI, 6].

predestinarian concepts are omitted, such as Preston's argument that every act of man is directed by God.

A corollary to predestinarianism is the doctrine of perseverence; i.e., if a man is one of the elect chosen by God's irresistible grace he may never completely lose his "reward"—eternal life—since to turn completely away from God is not possible. Wesley recognized that such a doctrine ultimately jeopardizes man's responsible moral action, since salvation, under this scheme, is never threatened by man's own acts; antinomianism is a logical outgrowth of such teaching.[38] Accordingly, passages dealing with perseverance are generally dropped.[39]

The next major omission in *The Shorter Catechism* is the question concerning perfection: "Q. Is any man able perfectly to keep the commandments of God? A. No mere man since the fall is able in this life perfectly to keep the commandments of God, but doth daily break them in thought, word and deed." [40] The Westminster divines, acknowledging the nature of sinfulness even in the elect, reject the possibility of perfection. Wesley also acknowledged sinfulness in believers; nevertheless, he propounded a doctrine of perfection. "If love is the sole principle of action" and if the believer has "the mind that was in Christ," all things are done in love.[41] The perfected believer may make "mistakes" because of infirmities, ignorance, misjudgment, etc., which are in fact morally imperfect; yet, since these are not contrary to perfect love, they are not "sins." [42] For Wesley this meant that perfection was a possibility, through God's grace, for every believer, although he never claimed to have received "perfection" himself. Wesley no doubt felt that the statement in the catechism unduly limited the possibilities of perfection.

[38] For Wesley's criticism of the doctrine, see his tract, *Serious Thoughts upon the Perseverance of the Saints*, in *Works*, X, 284-98; cf. 241-54.

[39] This passage is such an example: "But for the Elect, that can never fall quite away, this diligence is required, and is proper to them; they still look to themselves, lest they lose that which they have wrought, lest they should not receive a full reward; for, though they cannot lose their reward altogether, yet they may lose a part of their reward." (*New Covenant*, pp. 264-65 [*CL*, VI, 29].) Preston is here attempting to retain responsibility by establishing degrees within the reward—a position Wesley would have to reject. (Cf. *On Communion*, p. 298 [*CL*, XI, 97].)

[40] *The Shorter Catechism*, p. 17.

[41] *A Plain Account of Christian Perfection*, in *Works*, XI, 383-85.

[42] *Ibid.*, pp. 395-96. For a discussion of the doctrine of perfection see below, pp. 111 ff.

His doctrine of perfection also led to other alterations: "Q. What benefits do Believers receive from Christ at [their] death? A. The souls of Believers ARE at their death MADE PERFECT IN HOLINESS, AND DO IMMEDIATELY pass into glory; and their bodies, BEING STILL UNITED TO CHRIST, DO rest in their graves till the Resurrection." [43] Perfection is allowed, in this statement, at the moment of death but no earlier. Wesley, believing that perfection was an ever-present possibility, deletes those phrases which are contrary to his own opinion.[44]

Similarly, the question and answer which define sanctification demand a slight but significant omission. "Sanctification is the work of God's free grace, whereby we are renewed in the whole man after the image of God, and are enabled MORE AND MORE to dye unto sin, and to live unto righteousness." [45] To retain the phrase "more and more" would threaten the possibility of "entire sanctification" or perfection in this life.[46] "More and more" assumes that man is never completely dead unto sin, an assumption Wesley is not willing to make. It should be noted, however, that Wesley understood the sanctification present in most believers, those who had not been blessed with perfection, to be a gradual process.

The only other significant omission in the catechism is the question on the nature of adoption and references to the doctrine in other questions.[47] This is a perplexing deletion since Wesley evidently held the traditional interpretation that believers are received into sonship through adoption. Romans 8:14-16, the classic scripture text for the doctrine, is the basis for his sermon "The Spirit of Bondage and Adoption." [48]

[43] *The Shorter Catechism*, p. 11 [*CL*, XIV, 400].

[44] "As to the time, I believe this instant [of perfection] generally is the instant of death, the moment before the soul leaves the body. But I believe it may be ten, twenty or forty years before." (*Works*, XI, 466. Cf. *Sermons*, I, 168; II, 173.) Although Wesley in this passage seems to accept the traditional Reformed formulation, his whole doctrine of perfection depended on perfectibility in life, not at death.

[45] *The Shorter Catechism*, p. 10 [*CL*, XIV, 399].

[46] *Works*, VIII, 294.

[47] "Q. What is Adoption? A. Adoption is an act of God's free grace, wherebye we are received into the number, and have a right to all the privileges of the Sons of God." (*The Shorter Catechism*, p. 10.)

[48] *Sermons*, I, 179-98. "You have not received the spirit of bondage again unto fear; but you have received the Spirit of Adoption, whereby we cry, Abba, Father." (Rom. 8:15 Cf. *Sermons*, I, 233, 207, 367.)

The doctrine is also a part of his understanding of the order of salvation. James MacDonald has suggested that the question is omitted for brevity and "in order to throw into bolder relief two great cardinal crises of the believer's experience, commonly called justification and sanctification." [49] MacDonald may be correct, for justification and sanctification are normally the poles around which other elements in the order of salvation are concentrated. In the catechism, the order is "justification, adoption, sanctification," apparently giving equal recognition to sonship provided through adoption. Wesley may have sought through this deletion to place justification and sanctification in "bolder relief" with no intention of objecting to adoption. Another plausible explanation for deletion is its close connection in the catechism to the decrees and election.[50]

The remaining changes in the catechism are generally in the interest of clarity or brevity. One which should be noted is in the definition of the Lord's Supper. In the phrase "according to Christ's appointment" Wesley changes "Christ's" to "God's," making the sacrament rest on the authority of the Godhead instead of on the Son.[51] A similar change is made in one of Preston's statements.[52] Wesley clearly wanted to avoid any chance of misrepresentation or misinterpretation.

A few omissions which hinge on theological presuppositions other than those evident in *The Shorter Catechism* may be noted in the selected examples studied. Wesley is always conscious of the distinction to be drawn between the life lived by the believer and that by the unbeliever, but he constantly guards against a believer interpreting this distinction as a

[49] James A. MacDonald, *Wesley's Revision of the Shorter Catechism* (Edinburgh: George A. Morton, 1906), p. 57. MacDonald provides a useful comparison of Wesley's abridgment of *The Shorter Catechism* with the original and occasionally gives some interesting notes on this abridgment. His purpose is to show "the connection of Methodist Doctrine with that of the Reformed Church, the Ancient faith, and the word of God," which leads him into a good deal of hortatory presentation.

[50] Wesley also omits one of Owen's sections dealing with the "Spirit of Adoption," but there is no consistent pattern of elimination of this doctrine. (*On Communion*, p. 305 [CL, XI, 99].)

[51] *The Shorter Catechism*, p. 20 [CL, XIV, 411].

[52] "JESUS CHRIST, AS HE IS A PROPHET OF GOD [God] hath sent HIM [his Son Jesus Christ] to teach thee all things belonging to Salvation." (*New Covenant*, p. 376 [CL, VI, 37].) Also in the interest of clarity, "heart" is changed to "thought" in the question on the seventh commandment, in which it speaks of "the preservation of our own and our neighbor's chastity, in heart, speech, and behavior." (*The Shorter Catechism*, p. 16 [CL, XIV, 405].)

cause for pride. Alleine, especially, is not always careful at this point, and Wesley consistently deletes such passages.[53] The same is true for passages pointing to the personal profit, either spiritual or material, which may accrue to one because he is a Christian.[54]

In any attempted comparison of an abridgment with the original, it is an artificial and false procedure to force every omitted passage (or for that matter every passage retained) into a reconstructed logical framework. No doubt, if questioned, the abridger could produce a reason for each deletion he makes but inevitably some of these are matters of personal preference, interest, and prejudice. As a consequence, some passages must remain puzzling to the investigator. At times, points which seem particularly cogent to the argument or to Wesley's general viewpoint are omitted, while repetitious material is occasionally retained. A partial explanation lies in the fact that the examiner of an abridgment and the abridger himself will inevitably have differing interests, and, therefore, what appears important to one may not seem so to the other. Because of this, it is impossible to provide a valid logical reason for some of these "puzzling" omissions; however, a few may be noted.

The last eighty pages of John Preston's work, *The New Covenant*, are omitted by Wesley, although this section might well have supported Wesley's own views on how we know that we are "within the fold" of the Christian community—in Preston's words, "if we have the Covenant." [55] Included are the witnesses of faith, the Holy Spirit, our own spirit, the fruits of the spirit, and our readiness to live a Christian life. All these Wesley used in his own treatises and sermons, and it would appear that he might well have retained at least the salient points.[56]

[53] *Vindiciae Pietatis*, p. 219 [*CL*, XVIII, 152], p. 239 [*CL*, XVIII, 165].

[54] Wesley omits: "He bids a man *deny himself, and take up his cross.* Is it for him? No, my Beloved, it is for ourselves, and therefore when a man denies himself in his profit, in his credit, when he denies himself in the satisfying of his lusts; all this is for his owne profit; as you have it clearly set down in Isay 48:17. *I am the Lord that teacheth thee to profit;* therefore *harken to my commandments.*" (*New Covenant*, p. 106 [*CL*, VI, 15].) "He hath promised outward riches, wee are heyres of all the world; so that it is likewise a part of his *Covenant*, when a Man wants any outward comfort, any outward helpe, any blessings, or deliverance, he may goe to Christ." (*New Covenant*, p. 381 [*CL*, VI, 38]; *Vindiciae Pietatis*, p. 395 [*CL*, XVIII, 195].)

[55] *New Covenant*, pp. 403-86.

[56] See Wesley's sermons "The Spirit of Bondage and the Spirit of Adoption," "The Witness of the Spirit," "The Witness of our Own Spirit," *Sermons*, I. The marks of the "truly saved" are also omitted from *Vindiciae Pietatis*, pp. 274-86 [*CL*, XVIII, 166].

One of Owen's most instructive illustrations relative to the necessity of the witness of the Holy Spirit is curiously omitted by Wesley. Using a court case as an illustration, Owen shows that an issue may finally turn on the appearance of a single but essential witness. So it is in the life of a believer; the case is finally decided when he receives the Spirit in his own life. The illustration is not only cogent to the context in which it is used but clarifies in commonly understood terms a significant point. It would appear that for Wesley's readers the illustration might have been particularly helpful. Perhaps the concept of the Holy Ghost as Advocate seemed too legalistic for the Spirit of Love.[57]

The doctrine of perfection affirmed that in this life one could be totally committed to God, through his grace, and this may have kept Wesley from including Alleine's "provisions" for those who could not successfully hold themselves to the rigors of the covenant pattern of life.[58] Alleine had outlined a definite pattern of disciplined study, questioning, prayer, etc., which is entered into in a covenant with God. In addition, he had provided a shorter formula for those without the strength to follow the full course and a special "short-term" vow for those who could not hold themselves to the more demanding obligations. Wesley omitted all these provisions even though he must have recognized that few would be able to abide completely in the covenant relationship, since, in his revision of the covenant service taken from that given here by Alleine, he provided that it be renewed at least annually. Omissions such as these remain outside any strict logical or categorical theological principles which may be discerned through the comparative method.

Investigation of these selected examples of Wesley's abridgments has made it clear that the major theological omissions center around the doctrine of election and related concepts which would unduly limit sanctification within this life. While other differences of theological opinion between Wesley and the Puritan tradition are perhaps discernible, those revealed in this comparative study are central among the theological criteria used in Wesley's editing.

Criteria of abridgment dependent on technical methods and theological considerations of a negative nature are interesting and instructive

[57] On Communion, p. 296 [CL, XI, 96].
[58] Vindiciae Pietatis, pp. 270-71 [CL, XVIII, 166], p. 306 [CL, XVIII, 180].

in discovering certain features of Wesley's relationship to the Puritan tradition. However, because they concentrate on areas of divergence, their contribution, while important, does not give a balanced representation of the relationship. To these criteria must be added consideration of the large areas of concord between the two traditions in teaching, practice, and thought.

SUMMARY OF PART I
JOHN WESLEY AND PURITAN LITERATURE

The investigation of Wesley's use of Puritan literature offers several suggestions as to the nature of Wesley's relationship to the Puritan heritage. First, Wesley is far better acquainted with the writings of the Puritans than might be expected of one with his training and loyalties in the early eighteenth century. His acquaintance with the numerous individual works of recognized and reliable authorities as well as lesser-known writers is extensive.

Second, the area of practical divinity forms the closest link between Wesley and the Puritan tradition, as is evident not only from the analysis of *A Christian Library* but also from the survey of his general publications.

Third, Wesley is not only familiar with the writings of the Puritans, but he had a very high estimation of their value. His recognition of Puritan abilities and their contribution to an adequate understanding of the Christian life is the principal basis for their inclusion in his publications, where they become a major, though certainly not an exclusive, source of instruction.

Fourth, the inclusion of martyrologies and hagiographies in the *Library* is an extension of a well-recognized and vital tradition within the Puritan community. Although Wesley modified it somewhat by broadening its base, his emphasis upon this tradition served to make such spiritual histories a part of his own movement.

Fifth, selection of these authors out of the multitude from which he might have chosen is, for Wesley, guided by three principal considerations: (1) the availability of source materials which he was free to prepare for the printer; (2) selection of materials which were specifically related to his own concerns and interests, i.e., practical divinity (this must have eliminated much of the available material); and (3) the simple matter of Wesley's personal preference even among these materials —in his words, he selected what he conceived would be "of most general use."

Sixth, using technical methods of abridgment Wesley is usually able, while freely modifying the treatises, to retain their original meaning and intent. Brevity is accomplished by eliminating illustrative, controversial, and irrelevant materials. Paraphrasing, modernization of words, and rearrangement contribute to the clarity of the statements. Improved readability of the treatises is provided by the omission of foreign phrases and theological and philosophical arguments.

Seventh, the theological considerations which guided Wesley's omissions and modifications indicate several areas of divergent opinion. These are primarily in their respective understandings of God's election of the believer, man's active role in salvation, the perseverance of the saints, and the extent of man's perfectibility.

Part II: THEOLOGICAL FOUNDATIONS
of the CHRISTIAN LIFE

III

THEOLOGICAL FOUNDATIONS: EXPERIENCE, JUSTIFICATION, ASSURANCE, COVENANT

Wesley's preface to the Puritan materials incorporated in *A Christian Library* contains instructive comment as to his attraction to these authors. Although he indicates their faults such as poor style, verbosity, repetitiousness, and propensity to controversy, he calls special attention to their "excellencies." Earnestness, strength of judgment, clear and just sentiment, comprehensiveness, and, of particular importance, earnestness of spirit concerning the importance and greatness of their subject are a few examples. To these are added their exaltation of Christ, whom they make the fountain and sum of all things, their dependence upon the Scriptures, which they honor next to God himself, and their use of the Scriptures as the basis of all authoritative decisions.[1]

[1] *CL*, IV, 105-6.

Other emphases, however, had an immediate relevance for Wesley: "That they are continually tearing up the very roots of Antinomianism, by shewing at large, from the oracles of God, the absolute necessity, as of that legal repentance which is previous to faith, so of that evangelical repentance which follows it, and which is essential to that holiness, without which we cannot see the Lord." [2] This Puritan cognizance of a believer's sin after justification and the consequent necessity of repentance in a believer provides Wesley with support in his own battle against antinomianism.

Their ability to teach receives the strongest commendation:

But the peculiar excellency of these writers seems to be, the building us up in our most holy faith. It is frequently observed, that after the first joy of faith, wherein the young believer rides as upon the wings of the wind, he either suddenly, or gradually, sinks down, and meets as it were a vast vacuity. He knows not what to do with his faith, or how to exercise himself unto godliness. There appears a great gulph, an huge chasm between the first and the perfect love. Now this Mr. Bolton, Dr. Preston, Dr. Sibs, and their contemporaries, above all others, instruct us how to pass through: how to use the faith which God has given, and to go from strength to strength. They lead us by the hand in the paths of righteousness, and shew us how, in the various circumstances of life, we may most surely and swiftly grow in grace, and in the knowledge of our Lord Jesus Christ.[3]

Here is the emphasis on practice and belief leading to mature Christian life and faith which Wesley finds to be congenial to his own interests.

One theological inadequacy is noted: "They generally give a low and imperfect view of sanctification or holiness." This comment may seem incongruous with his praise of their instruction in the Christian

[2] *Ibid.*, p. 107. Wesley's distinction between the repentance before entering into faith and "evangelical repentance" is seen in this passage from his sermon entitled "The Repentance of Believers": "There is also a repentance and a faith (taking the words in another sense, a sense not quite the same, nor yet entirely different) which are requisite after we have 'believed the gospel'; yea, and in every subsequent stage of our Christian course, or we cannot 'run the race which is set before us.' And this repentance and faith are full as necessary, in order to our *continuance* and *growth* in grace, as the former faith and repentance were, in order to our *entering* into the kingdom of God." (John Wesley, *Wesley's Standard Sermons*, ed. Edward H. Sugden [2 vols.; London: Epworth Press, 1921], II, 380, cited hereafter as *Sermons*.)

[3] *CL*, IV, 107-8.

life, but it most likely refers to the Puritan failure, in Wesley's opinion, to carry the doctrine of sanctification to its culmination, i.e., perfection.

The dominant concern for practical divinity expressed by Wesley in these prefatory comments, as well as his selection of materials, suggests not only the teaching and practices most cogent to this study but also theological doctrines related to these teachings.

To be sure, Methodism has often been known, particularly in America, as a movement which emphasizes the life that a Christian leads without too much interest in the beliefs which undergird this Christian life.[4] Recent theological renewal among Methodists may perhaps be modifying such an opinion.[5] In any case, it certainly was not true of Wesley himself.[6] Behind his interests in the Christian life lay the doctrines which make this life relevant. Like the Puritans, most of his own expression of these doctrines was hammered out in the course of theological controversy with his contemporaries. Such controversy, though often arising from practice and teaching, was concerned with the theological assumptions which accompany these practices. Theology in this setting is always related to practice, therefore never disconnected from life. Nevertheless, since practice is motivated by conviction, the theological principles are of primary importance and are logically to be considered before the practices of the Christian life are examined.

[4] Colin W. Williams, *John Wesley's Theology Today* (Nashville: Abingdon Press, 1960), p. 5; *Life Magazine*, November 10, 1947, p. 113. "They [Methodists] are primarily concerned with developing among their members a personal commitment to the gospel and to the life of moral perfection which they see implied in it. They regard Christianity as a social movement which through its organization endeavors to bring about a Christian transformation of the whole of human life. They are not hostile to theology but they relegate theological responsibility to a minor place in the life of both the Church and the individual Christian." (Wilhelm Pauck, "Theology in the Life of Contemporary American Protestantism," *Religion and Culture: Essays in Honor of Paul Tillich*, ed. Walter Leibrecht [New York: Harper & Brothers, 1959], p. 273.)

[5] An interesting and noteworthy example of the effect that the renewed interest in theology has had in America is the publication of S. Paul Shilling's work, *Methodism and Society in Theological Perspective* (Nashville: Abingdon Press, 1960). Published under the auspices of the Board of Christian Social Concerns of The Methodist Church as one volume of a series studying the social interests and teachings of Methodism, it devotes the first chapter to an examination of the criticisms of Methodism's apparent lack of interest in theology.

[6] Statements such as Albert Outler's presidential address to the American Theological Society ("Towards a Re-Appraisal of John Wesley as a Theologian," *The Perkins School of Theology Journal*, XIV, 5-15) and his recent book, *John Wesley*, make a substantial case for new consideration of the depth and significance of Wesley's theological formulations.

Most of these relate directly to the "order of salvation" which serves as the pattern for their consideration. Many other theological concerns, e.g., the doctrine of man, the doctrine of God, etc., are relevant and are occasionally discussed in the explication of practical divinity but do not receive primary consideration.

1. Experience

A central element in the theology of the Christian life for both Wesley and the Puritans was the experiential nature of religion. Religion is neither mental assent nor formal worship alone but also the experience of a uniquely personal relationship between God and man. The believer perceives the presence of God in his own being. Wesley, speaking of a friend, comments, "Our conversation turned . . . upon *experimental religion* . . . . The theory of religion he certainly has. May God give him the living experience of it!" [7] Religion in this context is a dynamic, energizing force, arising from experiential contact with God. However, experiential religion has a second element in that it expresses itself in the life that the believer lives. Daily actions, concerns, and patterns are transformed because of the reality of the relationship established with God.

Religion must be more than mere intellectual assent to doctrine or the formality of attending church services; it also will express itself in application of honesty, justice, and mercy in daily life.[8] To be significant religion must have the vitality of personal experience.

One need only read Baxter's description of a "true" minister and Bishop Joseph Hall's comment relative to his own faith to appreciate the experiential emphasis among the Puritans.

One can say more from the feeling and experience of his soul, than another can in a long time gather from his Books. And that which he saith will come

---

[7] *Letters*, VII, 47 (italics mine); cf. *Sermons*, I, 81.

[8] "On the one hand, are those who have not so much as the form of godliness; on the other, those who have the form only: there stands the *open*, there the *painted*, sepulchre. . . . The one having almost as little concern about religion, as if there were 'no resurrection, neither angel nor spirit'; and the other making it a mere lifeless form, a dull round of external performances, without either true faith, or the love of God, or joy in the Holy Ghost!" (*Sermons*, I, 85; cf. *Letters*, II, 72-73.)

warm to the hearers in a more lively experimental manner, than usual carnal Preachers speak.[9]

There is nothing more easy, than to say divinity by rote; . . . but to hear God speak it to the soul, and to feel the power of religion in ourselves, and to express it out of the truth of experience within, is both rare and hard. . . . It will never be well with me . . . till sound experience have really catechized my heart, and made me know God and my Saviour otherwise than by words.[10]

George C. Cell connects Wesley's own emphasis upon experience with that of Nonconformity through Wesley's mother, Susanna Wesley.

Evidently Wesley's mother, . . . was not wholly in the dark about the essential revelational and experiential nature of the Christian Faith. Both of Wesley's parents had become strongly Anglican in their attachments. But the conviction that experience is the stronghold of the Christian apologetic points unmistakably to their Nonconformist antecedents where in the nature of the case, external authority being reduced to a minimum, the higher significance of inner experience of necessity was pushed into the foreground of Christian doctrine. It was in the Nonconformist branches of English Christianity that the appeal to experience had its strongest and richest, though not exclusive, development.[11]

Perhaps this statement dangerously minimizes the significant emphasis upon experience Wesley gained through the Moravians, but it correctly points to the English antecedents of Wesley's own emphasis. Horton Davies expresses it succinctly when he comments that Methodism's

[9] Richard Baxter, A Christian Directory: or, A Summ of Practical Theologie, And Cases of Conscience (London: by R. White, for N. Simmons, 1673), p. 918. Jerald Brauer notes this emphasis in his comment on the distinctive nature of Puritanism, "Now, what was so distinctive about this religious experience that it differentiated Puritanism from Anglicanism? Above all it was what the Puritan called 'experiential' or 'experimental.'" (J. Brauer, "Reflections on the Nature of English Puritanism," Church History, XXIII [1954], 101.) Geoffrey Nuttall understands this experiential emphasis to be a characteristic of the Congregationalists, differentiating them from the Presbyterians, yet the emphasis is present throughout all parties of the classical Puritan tradition. (G. Nuttall, Visible Saints: The Congregational Way, 1640-1660 [Oxford: Basil Blackwell, 1957], p. 112.)

[10] Joseph Hall, Meditations and Vows, in The Works of Joseph Hall, ed. Josiah Pratt (10 vols.; London: C. Whittingham, 1808), VI, 43. Richard Alleine brands as a "Phanatick" the person who imagines he is a true Christian merely because he carries out the forms of religion in every detail (Vindiciae Pietatis, p. 152).

[11] Cell, The Rediscovery of John Wesley, p. 90.

"evangelical passion and *experimental religion* were a revival of Puritan religion." [12]

This emphasis upon the experimental nature of religion, particularly the stress upon the personal, inner relationship with God, carries with it the danger of undercutting the authority of external form, practice, or tradition. Wesley recognized this danger, and with the insistence upon experiencing religion went the insistence that there be checks and balances which test the authority of the experience itself. The truths about God taught in Scripture, the well-tried doctrines formulated through tradition, the form of the Christian life as exemplified in other believers, all stand along with experience as authoritative criteria for the Christian faith. These authoritative elements in fact become a believer's own, through experience, since it keeps them from being only irrelevant externals.[13] In Colin William's phrase, "Experience . . . is the appropriation of authority." [14]

The Puritan understanding of the place and importance of experience closely parallels Wesley's in its insistence upon "checks and balances" in this phase of Christian life, even though it must be admitted that the more radical branches, particularly the Quakers, cast off the "external" authorities. John Owen's defense of his exposition of the doctrine of the Holy Spirit, although written in another context, correctly expresses his recognition of various "authorities": "In the substance of what it delivered, I have the plain testimonies of the Scripture, the suffrage of

[12] Horton Davies, *The English Free Churches* (London: Oxford University Press, 1952), p. 141 (italics mine). David Shipley compares the Methodist emphasis upon experience with the British "sect" movement, such as the Anabaptists, early Independents, and Quakers, but he could have found evidence for such in the more conservative of Puritans as well. (Shipley, "Methodist Arminianism in the Theology of John Fletcher" [Unpublished Ph.D. dissertation, Yale University, 1942], pp. 135-36.)

[13] Wesley is clear in his concept of the relation between experience and doctrine: "Experience is not sufficient to prove a doctrine unsupported by Scripture," for this is only enthusiasm but "experience is sufficient to *confirm* a doctrine which is grounded on Scripture." (*Sermons*, II, 357-58.) Colin Williams, *John Wesley's Theology Today*, pp. 33-34, is correct in criticizing Rattenbury for tending to make all doctrines and all authority for the Wesleys dependent upon experience even to the point of commenting, "There was, of course, much in their teaching that did not come out of their experience, but that is the commonplace and, to some extent, misleading part of it." (J. E. Rattenbury, *Wesley's Legacy to the World* [London: Epworth Press, 1928], p. 84.)

[14] *John Wesley's Theology Today*, p. 33.

the ancient church, and the experience of them who do sincerely believe, to rest upon." [15] As will be seen, the Puritans had been as anxious as Wesley to guard against the dangers of "experimental religion" without losing the thing itself—the real experience of God's love in the heart of the believer.

The relationship between this experiential nature of religion and its theological formulations needs to be understood. For Wesley the primary value of theological doctrine was neither in its formulation, its adequate dealing with all intellectual questions, nor its speculative nature, but in its relevance to life. The theological discussion and investigation of a particular doctrine, e.g., the Holy Spirit, is of real interest for Wesley and truly speaks of what lies behind Christian practice; at the same time discussion, comment, and formulation must lead to practice, to experience. Theology cannot be separated from life.

The Puritan emphasis upon experience reveals a similar understanding of the nature and importance of theology. In Owen's words, his treatise on the Holy Spirit is an attempt to "accommodate the doctrines treated of unto practice" and therefore, it has a "continual intermixture of practical applications which runs along in them all." [16] This emphasis is summarized in Geoffrey Nuttall's comments on the Puritan doctrine of the Holy Spirit:

Richard Baxter . . . declares the doctrine to be "a most practical article of our belief"; and the Puritan approach throughout the century is with practice clearly in view . . . . What is new . . . is the place given in Puritan exposition to experience, and its acceptance as a primary authority. . . . The interest is primarily not dogmatic, at least not in any theoretic sense, it is experimental. There is theology, but, in a way which has hardly been known since St. Augustine, it is a *theologia pectoris*.[17]

The experiential concept of religion concentrates upon the present reality of the relationship between God and man, but its ultimate ob-

[15] John Owen, *Concerning the Holy Spirit*, in Owen, *Works*, II, xiii. It should be noted that such external authorities as the *Westminster Confession* were also of particular consequence for most Puritans. This is a point George Cell apparently discounts in the statement quoted above.

[16] *Concerning the Holy Spirit*, p. xii.

[17] Nuttall, *The Holy Spirit in Puritan Faith and Experience*, pp. 6-7.

ject is salvation—both present and future. Wesley and the Puritans
followed in general the traditional understanding of the "order of salvation,"[18] but it is instructive to note Wesley's formulation of this salvation process. His sermon "The Scripture Way of Salvation" (1765)
gives this outline of salvation: (1) The work of prevenient grace in
natural man; (2) repentance before justification; (3) justification or
forgiveness with its effects: peace, joy, and hope—assurance; (4) new
birth which brings a sense of God's love through the gift of the Holy
Spirit and is the beginning of the real change in man—sanctification;
(5) repentance after justification; (6) the gradual work of sanctification; and (7) entire sanctification—perfect love.[19] Some of these
"states" are not as neatly separated in actual fact as they would appear
here, but the general order is evident. Certain of the stages in this order
of salvation, particularly three, four, five, and six, are of special interest
in an attempt to relate Wesley's theology to that of the Puritan tradition.

Before entering into discussion of the specific areas of theological
affinity evident in Wesleyan and Puritan presentations of the doctrine
of salvation, it should be noted that their respective doctrines of original
sin (the condition of man which calls for an "order of salvation") are
substantially the same. Wesley's treatise on this subject was, at least in
part, a defense of Isaac Watts's formulation of the doctrine.[20] Quotations from John Howe's Living Temple are used extensively in the
treatise.[21] With the Puritans, Wesley affirmed the original sinfulness of
man and uses their literature as a support of his own position, even

[18] Chapters X-XIII of The Westminster Confession of Faith give the order as Effectual
Calling, Justification, Adoption, and Sanctification. This order was normative for most of the
Puritan tradition. The Confession of Faith of the Assembly of Divines at Westminster, ed.
S. W. Carruthers (London: Presbyterian Church of England, 1946); cited hereafter as West-
minster Confession.

[19] Sermons, II, 444-48. For another formulation of the order which gives fuller treatment
to the bondage of man to sin and the necessity of the revelation of God through the gospel
before repentance and justification, see Wesley's comments on Rom. 6:18 in Explanatory Notes,
pp. 541-42; cf. Sermons, I, 94-98; Works, VI, 509.

[20] Works, IX, 327, 345-97.

[21] Ibid., pp. 286-88. Many of the treatises included in the Library comment extensively on
the doctrine; e.g., Joseph Alleine's An Alarm to Unconverted Sinners (London: Printed by
Nevil Simmons, 1672); Thomas Goodwin's A Child of Light Walking in Darkness (London:
Printed by F. G. for R. Dawlman, 1659); and John Flavel's Navigation Spiritualized.

though his corollary doctrine of prevenient grace would have been rejected by most of them.

2. Justification by Faith

Wesley's consistent exposition of faith as the one necessary condition of salvation placed him squarely within the heritage of the Reformers and distinguished him, as he himself recognized, from many of his Church of England contemporaries, who had accepted at least a modified form of the Catholic interpretation of the salvation process.[22] Scholars have spent much energy in the past quarter century attempting to determine the relationship of justification and sanctification in Wesley's theology. Those favoring a Catholic (or Anglican) interpretation, such as Maximin Piette and Umphrey Lee, have insisted upon the dominant role of sanctification.[23] At the other extreme is William Cannon's statement, "Wesley's doctrine of justification was the measure and determinant of all else." [24] Perhaps Colin Williams expresses the consensus of much of recent scholarship when he affirms the Reformation orientation of Wesley's doctrine of salvation, in which justification *and* sanctification are by faith through grace alone.[25]

Most of these studies, while stressing Wesley's understanding of the role of faith and its obvious Reformation orientation, do not consider the English writers which Wesley himself recommends as legitimate and exemplary interpreters of the doctrine. Chapter II noted that among

[22] In 1739 Wesley lists five differences between himself and many of the other clergymen of the Church of England, all of which stem from his insistence upon a justification distinguished from, and antecedent to, sanctification which is based solely on God's grace. (*Journal*, II, 275.) Wesley's exposition of the doctrine is most clearly seen in his sermons, particularly "Justification by Faith," "The Righteousness of Faith," and "The Scriptural Way of Salvation" in *Sermons*, II, 441-60; I, 112-46.

[23] Maximin Piette, *John Wesley in the Evolution of Protestantism*, trans. by J. B. Howard (New York: Sheed and Ward, 1937); Umphrey Lee, *John Wesley and Modern Religion* (Nashville: Cokesbury Press, 1936).

[24] William R. Cannon, *The Theology of John Wesley* (Nashville: Abingdon Press, 1946), p. 14.

[25] For comments supporting this understanding of Wesley's theology see Richard M. Cameron, "John Wesley's Aldersgate Street Experience," *The Drew Gateway*, XXV (1955), 210-19; Robert E. Chiles, "Methodist Apostasy: From Free Grace to Free Will," *Religion in Life*, XXVII (1957), 438-49; Robert E. Cushman, "Theological Landmarks in the Revival Under Wesley," *Religion in Life*, XXVII (1957), 105-18; David C. Shipley, "Wesley and Some Calvinistic Controversies," *The Drew Gateway*, XXV (1955), 195-210.

Wesley's abridgments were two which dealt specifically with the doctrine of justification, Richard Baxter's *Aphorisms of Justification* and John Goodwin's *Treatise on Justification*.[26]

Wesley's publication of Baxter's work was relatively early (1745); in that year this treatise served as the "study material" for the second annual Methodist conference, which dealt specifically with justification.

Q. 4. Shall we read over together Mr. Baxter's "Aphorisms concerning Justification?"

A.   By all means. Which were accordingly read. And it was desired, that each person present would in the afternoon consult the scriptures cited therein, and bring what objections might occur the next morning.[27]

Green quotes Wesley as recommending it as a "powerful antidote against the spreading poison of antinomianism." [28] The treatise continued to be a favorite of the Methodists judging from the fact that Wesley's abridgment of it went through four editions by 1797.

John Goodwin's treatise was abridged and published twenty years later (1765) in the midst of Wesley's controversy with the extreme Calvinists.[29] In his preface to the work Wesley comments:

Perhaps I should not have submitted, at least not so soon, to the importunity of my friends, who have long been soliciting me to abridge and publish the ensuing treatise, had not some warm people published a tract, entitled, "The Scripture Doctrine of Imputed Righteousness Defended." I then judged it absolutely incumbent upon me to publish the real Scripture doctrine. And this I believed I could not either draw up or defend better than I found it done to my hands by one who, at the time he wrote this book, was a firm and zealous Calvinist. This enabled him to confirm what he advanced by such authorities,

[26] At this point in our study, only Wesley's relationship to these Puritan writers as exemplified in his use of their treatises is discussed, but the major reasons for his attraction to these treatises will appear in the section on "final justification," which in the "order of salvation" fits more logically at the end of Part II, pp. 122-32.

[27] *Minutes* (1745) in *Works*, VIII, 282.

[28] *Bibliography*, p. 37.

[29] Wesley's chief defender in the controversy with the Calvinists in the decade of the 1760's, John Fletcher, draws extensively on the works of Baxter, Goodwin, Flavel, Matthew Henry, and even John Owen to serve as witnesses to the Methodist interpretation of justification, particularly as to the necessity of works following justification. (*Checks to Antinomianism* [4 vols.; New York: J. Soule & T. Mason, 1820], I, 66, 92, 276-85; *Works of John Fletcher* [4 vols.; New York: Carlton and Lanahan, n.d.], I, 576, 578.) See below, p. 128.

as well from Calvin himself, as from his most eminent followers, as I could not have done, nor any who had not been long and critically versed in their writings.[30]

The last sentence makes it clear that Wesley identified his own interpretation with that of the Reformers; in order to do this he looked to the English expositors of the doctrine who were closest, in his opinion, to the "real Scripture doctrine."

Wesley's publication of John Goodwin's treatise met with somewhat the same reaction the *Treatise on Justification* had received from the "orthodox" Calvinists when it was published more than a century earlier. John Erskine, using the treatise as authority, charged Wesley with teaching justification by works. Wesley vehemently denied the charge and in defense of the treatise commented: "I desire no one will condemn that treatise before he has carefully read it over; and that seriously and carefully; for it can hardly be understood by a slight and cursory reading. And let whoever has read it declare, whether he has not proved every article he asserts, not only by plain express Scripture, but by the authority of the most eminent Reformers." [31] The objections to the treatise principally focused on Goodwin's essentially Arminian interpretation of the doctrine, which closely coincided with Wesley's own understanding.[32] The same charges were made against Baxter's treatise, although it had not been the center of as much controversy as Goodwin's.

Is it legitimate to use these treatises to demonstrate Wesley's affinity with Puritan theology when they represent such an obvious divergence from the "mainline" Calvinistic Puritan interpretation? This question may be answered affirmatively if Baxter and Goodwin are allowed to be legitimate members of the Puritan tradition; this is hardly to be denied,

---

[30] "Preface to a Treatise on Justification," *Works*, X, 316. See also Wesley's letter to Thomas Rankin concerning the publication of the treatise. (*Letters*, IV, 274.) Rankin was evidently interested enough in the publication to attempt to find subscribers to finance its immediate publication. (*Letters*, IV, 279.)

[31] *Remarks on a Defense of Aspasio Vindicated* in *Works*, X, 349.

[32] John Goodwin did not consider himself an Arminian and did not appeal to the Arminian tradition for support but, as Wesley notes in the preface, he always supports his argument through Calvin and his followers. (See A. G. Matthews, *Calamy Revised* [Oxford: Clarendon Press, 1934], p. 227.)

even if they were criticized for their views by others within that tradition.[33] More important, is it not possible to see in Richard Baxter and John Goodwin a development, within the Puritan tradition itself, of an interpretation of the doctrine which freed it from the straitjacket of rigid Calvinism? If this is true these men can be understood as the precursors of a more adequate understanding of justification, while preserving the truth of the Reformers' emphasis on faith. If so, they saved the doctrine of faith from the inadequacies of the "double decree" while guarding against the semi-Pelagian doctrines present in many of their Anglican contemporaries—and those of Wesley. In these men may be seen the breadth of the Puritan tradition which allowed for development in theological formulation while retaining the central truths of a Reformed tradition.

3. Assurance—The Witness of the Spirit

The experiential religious life has as its center an awareness of being accepted by God through the grace offered in the gospel—a knowledge that what the gospel says and promises is actually true for *me*. Such a personal awareness not only is a rational deduction from these promises but also, of far greater significance, springs from contact with God in which he makes known to the believer the reality of this acceptance.[34] This consciousness of being accepted is part of the doctrine of assurance, a seminal doctrine in the theology of Wesley and the Puritans.[35] To serve as a basis of comparison between Wesleyan and Puritan formulations of the doctrine, the general features of Wesley's interpretation are outlined here.

Perhaps the appropriate point to begin is Wesley's own record of his Aldersgate experience: "I felt I did trust in Christ, Christ alone for sal-

---

[33] Baxter has historically been accepted as a leading exponent of the mature Puritan tradition (see Geoffrey Nuttall, *The Holy Spirit*, p. 10; *DNB*, III, 429-37). Goodwin must also be placed in the tradition, for his general sympathies lay here even though some of his ideas certainly brought him into conflict with others of the same tradition. (See *DNB*, XXII, 145-47; A. G. Matthews, *Calamy Revised*, p. 227; Gordon Wakefield, *Puritan Devotion* [London: Epworth Press, 1957], p. 4.) Perhaps both men should be called Arminian Puritans.

[34] The integral relation between experience and assurance in Wesley's thought is indicated when he refers to an "experimental assurance." (*Explanatory Notes*, p. 622 [I Cor. 12:3].)

[35] Lycurgus M. Starkey, *The Work of the Holy Spirit* (Nashville: Abingdon Press, 1962), p. 128, notes the similarity in the concern for experiential religion evident in the witness of the spirit present in both Wesley and the seventeenth-century Nonconformists.

vation; and an *assurance* [italics mine] was given me that He had taken away *my* sins, even *mine*, and saved *me* from the law of sin and death." [36] The same sentiment is present in Wesley's sermon on "The Witness of the Spirit" (1746), in which, with appropriate hesitancy but convincing clarity, he defines the witness:

> But what is that testimony of God's Spirit . . . . It is hard to find words in the language of men to explain "the deep things of God." Indeed, there are none that will adequately express what the children of God experience. But perhaps one might say (desiring any who are taught of God to correct, to soften, or strengthen the expression), the testimony of the Spirit is an inward impression on the soul, whereby the Spirit of God directly witnesses to my spirit, that I am a child of God; that Jesus Christ hath loved me, and given Himself for me; and that all my sins are blotted out, and I, even I, am reconciled to God.[37]

Wesley's hesitancy in attempting a definition is justified, for any definition must be tempered by the realization that for each person the ex-

[36] *Journal*, I, 476. Arthur Yates, in *The Doctrine of Assurance* (London: Epworth Press, 1952), pp. 3-11, interprets Wesley's Aldersgate experience as having its essential meaning in assurance. Here it was that Wesley knew assurance from God, so that rather than calling this a conversion experience it is best understood as the time when Wesley became fully aware of his own acceptance. Colin Williams (*John Wesley's Theology Today*, pp. 102-105) correctly emphasizes that if Aldersgate is to be understood as the point at which assurance becomes true for Wesley it is actually the full "realization" of a doctrine which Wesley had long taught: "The experience was the confirmation of a doctrine already accepted." In two early sermons (1733) on the Holy Spirit, "The Circumcision of the Heart" and "On Grieving the Holy Spirit," assurance is expressed in much the same language as after 1738. Assurance is "a divine evidence or conviction of His love, His free unmerited love to me a sinner; . . . a confidence whereby every true believer is enabled to bear witness, 'I know that my Redeemer liveth,' that . . . He hath reconciled me, even me, to God; and I 'have redemption through His blood, even the forgiveness of sins.'" (*Sermons*, I, 270-71.) In his sermon "On Grieving the Holy Spirit" assurance is affirmed largely in terms of the "earnest of final salvation"—a foretaste of what is to come (*Works*, VII, 485-92). Wesley in these sermons certainly had a doctrine of assurance but somehow a "conviction" or "confidence" does not quite express the same thing as an "assurance" that it is so for me. The difference between confidence that Christ died for me and has reconciled me to God and assurance or testimony that He has actually accepted me *now* lies in a true experience in which this becomes a reality for me. Aldersgate in this sense is Wesley's appropriation of a doctrine taught but not experienced before this time.

[37] *Sermons*, I, 207-8. Wesley comments on this definition in his second sermon on this topic (1767): "After twenty years' further consideration, I see no cause to retract any part of this. Neither do I conceive how any of these expressions may be altered, so as to make them more intelligible." (*Ibid.*, II, 345.) He is true to his willingness to be corrected or instructed, for he comments to Joseph Benson in 1781, "I do not insist on the term 'Impression!' I say again, I will thank anyone that will find a better; be it 'discovery,' 'manifestation,' 'deep sense,' or whatever it may." (*Letters*, VII, 61.)

perience is different. More important, any definition is an attempt to put into intellectual terms an event which is not simply rational and therefore must be defined and explained with an openness to more cogent avenues of expression. However, Wesley was convinced of the reality or the "fact" of assurance and of the necessity to preach and teach the doctrine.[38]

It is the more necessary to explain and defend this truth, because there is a danger on the right hand and on the left. If we deny it, there is a danger lest our religion degenerate into mere formality; lest, having 'a form of godliness,' we neglect, if not 'deny the power of it.' If we allow it but do not understand what we allow, we are liable to run into all the wildness of enthusiasm. It is therefore needful, in the highest degree, to guard those who fear God from both these dangers, by a scriptural and rational illustration and confirmation of this momentous truth.[39]

This conviction that the doctrine is of particular consequence for the ordinary believer, and should therefore be preached, brought Wesley into conflict with many of his contemporaries, for in it they saw only the dangers of "enthusiasm." [40]

In a letter dated 1768 he distinguished between the various concepts of assurance and made other remarks indicative of the nature of his own teaching:

I believe a few, but very few, Christians have an assurance from God of everlasting salvation; and that is the thing which the Apostle terms the plerophory or full assurance of hope.

[38] "The manner how the *divine* testimony is manifested to the heart, I do not take upon me to explain. Such knowledge is too wonderful and excellent for me: I cannot attain unto it. . . . But the fact we know; namely, that the Spirit of God does give a believer such a testimony of his adoption, that while it is present to the soul, he can no more doubt the reality of his sonship, than he can doubt of the shining of the sun, while he stands in the full blaze of his beams." (*Sermons*, I, 210.)

[39] *Sermons*, II, 343.

[40] In the early period of his ministry he is willing to call assurance the "main doctrine of the Methodists." (*Letters*, II, 64.) Later he affirms, "It is one grand part of the testimony which God has given them [the Methodists] to bear to all mankind. It is by His peculiar blessing upon them . . . that this great evangelical truth has been recovered, which had been for many years wellnigh lost and forgotten." (*Sermons*, II, 343-44.)

I believe more have such an assurance of being now in the favour of God as excludes all doubt and fear. And this, if I do not mistake, the Apostle means by the plerophory or full assurance of faith.

I believe a consciousness of being in the favour of God (which I do not term plerophory, or full assurance, since it is frequently weakened, nay perhaps interrupted, by returns of doubt or fear) is the common privilege of Christians fearing God and working righteousness.

Yet I do not affirm there are no exceptions to this general rule. Possibly some may be in the favour of God, and yet go mourning all the day long . . . .

Therefore I have not for many years thought a consciousness of acceptance to be essential to justifying faith.[41]

Several important features of Wesley's position become evident in this passage. First, the "assurance of faith" is a present reality; there is an immediacy about it which makes it a present event. In Wesley's words to his brother Samuel, "It is an assurance of present salvation only . . . and can, therefore, be weakened and lost." [42] Second, it is a "common privilege" of the Christian believer but not necessary for salvation—a position on which Wesley had changed through the years, in that he originally insisted that it was necessary for salvation.[43] Third, the distinction between "assurance of faith" and "assurance of hope" indicates Wesley's affirmation of "degrees" of assurance—that is, assurance may be stronger or weaker in individual believers or within the same believer at different times.[44] Even so, assurance of final salvation is a rare event. Fourth, assurance eradicates doubt and fear in the believer.

As has been seen, the doctrine is grounded in the teachings relative to the "witness of the spirit." Wesley asserts that the real difference between himself and those who oppose his position is over the reality of a direct witness from God. All will admit some witness—usually understood as the indirect witness of the "fruits of the spirit"—but is there a direct witness? [45] Wesley insists that there is, and that this is the essential

[41] *Letters*, V, 358; cf. I, 255, 290; III, 305.
[42] *Ibid.*, I, 308.
[43] *Journal*, II, 333-34; *Works*, VIII, 276, 291; *Letters*, II, 108; V, 358. See Arthur Yates, *The Doctrine of Assurance*, pp. 61-71, for a full exposition of the changes evident in the doctrine as taught by Wesley.
[44] *Letters*, I, 255, 279; III, 161; II, 46; *Works*, IX, 380.
[45] *Sermons*, II, 346, 357.

meaning of the doctrine. As David Shipley indicates, the Wesleyans always understood the important element in man's relationship to God to be that "God comes to man in this experience." [46] The godward side of the relationship is preeminently important, for to stress only the response of man as manifest in the fruits of the spirit comes dangerously close to justification by works.[47]

This direct testimony to the believer is, however, accompanied by his own awareness of it and by its "fruits" within his own life. The testimony of our own spirits affirm the direct testimony. Wesley calls this the "indirect" testimony.

"Strictly speaking, it is a conclusion drawn partly from the Word of God, and partly from our own experience. The Word of God says, everyone who has the fruit of the Spirit is a child of God; experience, or inward consciousness, tells me, that I have the fruit of the Spirit; and hence I rationally conclude, 'Therefore I am a child of God.' " [48] This syllogistic statement of the "witness of our own spirits" points to the intimate connection between our own consciousness of assurance and the objective evidence of it found in the fruits of the spirit. These fruits of the spirit are the result of the witness of God that the believer is accepted. They are of two kinds: the inward, immediate fruits of "love, joy, peace, long-suffering, gentleness, goodness," and the outward fruits which come from this inward witness and which are the "doing good to all men"—good works.[49] Naturally, these outward fruits are not separate from the inward, and together they are the basis of the testimony of our own spirits.[50] If the believer can consciously affirm that in his own life there is evidence of love, joy, peace, gentleness, and good works, then these witnesses substantiate the assurance given through the immediate testimony of God the Holy Spirit.

[46] Shipley, "Methodist Arminianism in the Theology of John Fletcher," p. 151.

[47] "One of our preachers that was (I mean Hampson) has lately made a discovery that there is no such thing in any believer as a *direct, immediate* testimony of the Spirit that he is a child of God, that the Spirit testifies this *only* by the fruits, and consequently that the witness and the fruits are *all one*. Let me have your deliberate thoughts on this head. It seems to me to be a point of no small importance. I am afraid lest we should get back again unawares into justification by works." (*Letters*, V, 8.)

[48] *Sermons*, II, 346.

[49] *Ibid.*, I, 217; *Letters*, V, 364; II, 105.

[50] *Sermons*, II, 348; I, 151-55.

The witness of a "good conscience to God" and of a fruitful life serves as the objective test by which one distinguishes the true witness of God's Spirit from that of self-deception. Both of these are, of course, drawn from scripture, and when pressed as to how assurance is known to be true, since it is essentially personal and therefore unknowable by others, Wesley refers to the scriptural marks which precede, accompany, and follow the gift.[51] These duplicate to some extent the outline of the fruits of the spirit but they are noted here in order to show the scriptural references to the objective witnesses: (1) conviction of sin and repentance, Mark 3:2, Acts 3:19; (2) new birth or "a vast and mighty change; a change 'from darkness to light,' " Acts 2:5-6; (3) a humble joy—"a meekness, patience, gentleness, long-suffering. There is a soft, yielding spirit; a mildness and sweetness, a tenderness of soul, which words cannot express"; (4) keeping the Lord's commandments, I John 5:3; John 14:21.[52] All these, combined with the witness of the believer's own conscience that he has these marks, constitute the test of the spirit.

Wesley assumes that the witness of God's spirit must be antecedent to the testimony of our own spirit:

We must be holy of heart, and holy in life, before we can be conscious that we are so; before we can have the testimony of our spirit, that we are inwardly and outwardly holy. But we must love God, before we can be holy at all; this being the root of all holiness. Now we cannot love God, till we know he loves us . . . . And we cannot know His pardoning love to us, till His Spirit witnesses it to our spirit. Since, therefore, this testimony of His Spirit must precede the love of God and all holiness, of consequence it must precede our inward consciousness thereof, or the testimony of our spirit concerning them.[53]

In speaking of the tests of the spirit and the generative force by which the fruits of the spirit are produced in the believer, no doubt this order is correct,[54] but Sugden is correct in criticizing Wesley for attempting to distinguish temporally between the two witnesses.[55] Obviously, the

[51] *Ibid.*, I, 211; cf. 207.
[52] *Ibid.*, I, 211-15, 151-55.
[53] *Ibid.*, I, 208; II, 349.
[54] See Colin Williams, *John Wesley's Theology Today*, pp. 109-10.
[55] *Sermons*, I, 208 n.; II, 349 n.

immediate fruits of the spirit—joy, peace, and love—while the result of God's witness, are still a real part of the assurance itself since they take the place of or "drive out" doubt and fear. Although the two witnesses may therefore be logically distinguished, with God's witness preceding that of the believer, in actual fact the event is simultaneous. The consciousness of joy, peace, and love comes with, and is a part of, the consciousness of acceptance. A temporal separation or antecedent is quite correct in terms of the outward fruits—the good works of men—but both God's witness and man's awareness of this witness come in the same event, forming a joint witness of the Holy Spirit and our own spirits.[56]

Wesley's attempt to retain the truth of the gift of the Spirit without falling into the extremes of either formalism or enthusiasm is further guarded by his admonition at the close of the 1769 sermon—both the witness and its fruits are to be tested by each other.

Let none ever presume to rest in any supposed testimony of the Spirit, which is separate from the fruit of it. If the Spirit of God does really testify that we are the children of God, the immediate consequence will be the fruit of the Spirit. . . .

Let none rest in any supposed fruit of the Spirit without the witness. There may be foretastes of joy, of peace, of love, and those not delusive, but really from God, long before we have the witness in ourselves, . . . but it is by no means advisable to rest here; it is at the peril of our souls if we do. If we are wise, we shall be continually crying to God until His Spirit cries in our heart, "Abba Father!" This is the privilege of all the children of God, and without this we can never be assured that we are His children. Without this we cannot retain a steady peace, nor avoid perplexing doubts and fears.[57]

These two, the witness and its fruits, are then to be joined together and, as such, offer a reality of vital contact and relationship between God and the believer while serving as tests of each other. While these two are held together as tests of each other, the fruit is nevertheless recognized as finally dependent upon the witness, so that the whole relationship affirms God's initiative and man's dependence.

[56] See Arthur Yates, *The Doctrine of Assurance*, p. 77; cf. *Works*, XI, 420. Richard Baxter clearly understands this to be the case. (Baxter, *The Saints' Everlasting Rest*, in *The Practical Works of Richard Baxter* [23 vols.; London: James Duncan, 1830], XXII, 493-94.)
[57] *Sermons*, II, 358-59.

It has been noted that Wesley taught a doctrine of assurance before 1738, drawing his early interpretation of this doctrine from his own training in the Established Church. In fact, as the following passage indicates, he had been taught to reject any understanding of the doctrine as a dynamic reality to be expected in the present life of the believer.

When Peter Bohler, as soon as I came to London, affirmed of true faith in Christ, (which is but one,) that it had these two fruits inseparably attending it, "dominion over sin, and constant peace from a sense of forgiveness," I was quite amazed, and looked upon it as a new gospel. If it was so, it was clear I had no faith. But I was not willing to be convinced of this. Therefore I disputed with all my might, and laboured to prove that true faith might be where these were not; especially, where that sense of forgiveness was not; for, all the scriptures relating to this I had been long since taught to construe away, and *to call all Presbyterians who spoke otherwise.*[58]

This passage reveals that Wesley was quite aware that a doctrine of assurance conveying a real consciousness of forgiveness and acceptance had been an integral part of the Puritan tradition in England.[59] Moreover, he was familiar with specific expositions of it by the Puritan writers. In a letter to the editor of *Lloyd's Evening Post*, December 20, 1760, in answer to criticism by "Mr. T. H. alias E. L.," Wesley observes:

You say: "No Protestant divine ever taught your doctrine of Assurance." I hope you know no better; but it is strange you should not. Did you never see Bishop Hall's Works? Was not he a Protestant divine? Was not Mr. Perkins, Bolton, Dr. Sibbs, Dr. Preston, Archbishop Leighton? Inquire a little farther; and do not run thus hand over head, asserting you know not what. By assurance (if we must use the expression) I mean "a confidence which a man hath in

[58] *Principles of a Methodist*, in *Works*, VIII, 366 (italics mine). Wesley, of course, later modified his opinion that this "sense of forgiveness" was *necessary* or inseparable from justifying faith but he never ceased to insist upon the reality of the experience and its nature as a "common privilege" of believers.

[59] Gordon Wakefield (*Puritan Devotion: Its Place in the Development of Christian Piety*, pp. 124-26) declares the doctrine of assurance to be a "distinctively Puritan and evangelical contribution" and goes on to show that William Perkins calls it "A Case of Conscience the Greatest that ever was." Commenting that they often state it in syllogistic form, he points out that Wesley does the same. Compare Wesley's statement in *Sermons*, I, 210, and his abridgment of Bolton's *General Directions for a Comfortable Walking with God*, CL, IV, 406.

God that by the merits of Christ his sins are forgiven and he reconciled to the favour of God." [60]

If this statement is taken at face value, Wesley quite obviously felt that the doctrine of assurance he propounded was the same doctrine as had been taught by leading representatives of the Puritan element of the English church. In fact, he pushed the doctrine further back, asserting that "Luther, Melanchthon, and many other (if not all) of the Reformers frequently and strongly assert that every believer is conscious of his own acceptance with God, and that by a supernatural evidence." [61]

It is true that Wesley, in his more elaborate defenses of the doctrine against the charge of enthusiasm, sought to show that assurance was a legitimate part of the heritage of the Established Church. In *A Farther Appeal to Men of Reason and Religion* (1745) and in his letters to Thomas Church (1746) and Bishop Warburton (1762) extensive sections are given to the task of showing that a doctrine of assurance of adoption and the real witness of the Spirit had been the teaching of some of the Church of England's most honored representatives, particularly Bishop Pearson, and of the offices and sermons—most significantly, the Homilies—of the Church. [62] Wesley was convinced that the doctrine was part of the teaching of both the Puritan and the "catholic" parties within the church and had been incorporated in the liturgy and tradition of English Christianity. [63] Even so, as his reference to the concept as a Presbyterian doctrine indicates, he was quite conscious of the particular strength the doctrine held in this tradition and of its forceful presentation there.

With the exception of William Perkins (d. 1602), all the "Protestant divines" listed by Wesley in the passage above are represented by works in *A Christian Library*. The authors mentioned are also, for the most part, major leaders and from the "early period." The materials of these

---

[60] *Letters*, IV, 126. Wesley came to suspect the term "assurance" not only because it was not scriptural but also because there was a tendency to understand it derogatorily, and it was identified most often with "assurance of perseverance" or final salvation. (*Letters*, III, 228.) See Howard Watkins-Jones, *The Holy Spirit from Arminius to Wesley* (London: Epworth Press, 1929), p. 318.

[61] *Letters*, III, 159.

[62] *Works*, VIII, 99-106; *Letters*, II, 233-35; IV, 376-81.

[63] An explanation of his appealing to these divergent authorities in various defenses may lie in his usual pattern of quoting the authorities most congenial to his opponent wherever possible.

authors, both those included in the *Library* and in other works, serve as a logical basis for an investigation of how closely Wesley's doctrine conforms to that found in early English Puritanism.

The most common Puritan statement relative to assurance itself defines it as an "assurance of eternal salvation" [64]—or to use Wesley's terminology, an assurance of hope. Assuming a traditional Calvinistic doctrine of predestination, this is the only logical formulation, for any assurance is an assurance of eternal salvation or election.[65] Wesley did not reject this understanding of assurance but thought it to be the privilege of a few and, with his Arminian concept of grace, stressed the assurance of "present salvation." [66] Herein lies the major distinction between Wesley's doctrine and that of the Puritans. However, the Puritan doctrine is much closer to what Wesley defines as "assurance of faith" than might be expected.

While the Puritan divines did not distinguish, as Wesley does, between assurance of faith and assurance of hope, the whole point in stressing the doctrine was to indicate the immediate reality of a present witness which affirms the salvation of the believer.

You will say, What is the seale or witness of the Spirit? MY BELOVED, **it is a thing that we cannot expresse, it is a certaine divine expression of light, a certaine inexpressible assurance that wee are the sonnes of God, a certaine secret manifestation, that God *hath received us*, and put away our sinnes.**[67]

The Spirit, if it cometh, it subdueth all doubts. . . . In this witness hee taketh in no other testimony to confirm it, but witnesseth by himself. And hence ariseth joy unspeakable, and glorious, and peace which passeth all understanding, for it is an extract of heaven when we see our being in the state

[64] William Perkins, *A Treatise of Conscience*, in *The Works of William Perkins* (3 vols.; London: John Legatt, 1616), I, 541; Robert Bolton, *General Directions for a Comfortable Walking with God* (London, 1641), p. 326 [*CL*, IV, 408]; cited hereafter as *Walking with God*.

[65] This is the concept of assurance which Wesley's brother Samuel so strenuously objected to —it obviously holds great dangers of presumptuous pride and antinominianism. (*Letters*, I, 308.)

[66] *Letters*, V, 358.

[67] John Preston, *The New Covenant*, p. 400 [*CL*, VI, 44] (italics mine). "A secret persuasion wrought in the heart whereby God assures you that he is yours, and you are his . . . . He hath said to your soul, 'I am your salvation.'" (John Preston, *The Breast Plate of Faith and Love* [London: Printed by W. I. for Nicholas Bourne, 1630], Part II, p. 85 [*CL*, V, 386-87].)

of grace, not in the effect only, but as in the breast and bosome of God.[68]

Here both Preston and Sibbes leave little doubt as to the importance of the assurance as a present reality. That this was true in the general seventeenth-century Puritan tradition is attested by Yates's comment, "The general tendency [among the Puritan and Nonconformist divines] is to interpret assurance as signifying an inner sense of *present* salvation, conveyed as a privilege to the Christian by the direct testimony of the Holy Spirit." [69] The certainty of salvation draws its meaning and purpose from the knowledge of present salvation—it is living in such a comforting, certain, and stable relationship *now* that is of primary importance. Doubts and fears are driven out by it and present life has a vitality which would be impossible otherwise.

This emphasis should not be allowed to overshadow the fact that, for the Puritans, assurance is of both present *and* future salvation. Sibbes comments, "Our assurance is not only for the present, but for the time to come." [70] Perkins, who was chiefly concerned to distinguish *true* Christianity from that of the "papists," normally interprets assurance as that of eternal salvation, yet even for him the present element is stressed since the whole question is whether a man may be "certaine of his own salvation" in this life.[71] In a predestinarian framework both elements must be held together, for consciousness of present salvation is consciousness of future salvation because of election and its correlate "perseverance of the saints." [72]

The Puritan emphasis upon the present nature of salvation must, therefore, be distinguished from that of Wesley since a present conscious-

---

[68] Richard Sibbes, *A Fountain Sealed* (London: L. Chapman, 1637), p. 167. Thomas Goodwin clearly understands the immediate nature of the witness: "First, the *immediate light of his countenance*, which is a clear evident beam and revelation of God's favour, immediately testifying that we are his; which is called the SEALING [testimony] of the Spirit, RECEIVED AFTER BELIEVING." (Goodwin, *A Child of Light Walking in Darkness* [London: Printed by F. G. for R. Dawlman, 1659], p. 14 [CL, VI, 235-36].)

[69] Arthur Yates, *The Doctrine of Assurance*, p. 172.

[70] *A Fountain Sealed*, p. 216.

[71] Perkins, *Works*, I, 540. He defines the assurance of the papists as "assurance by hope," which sounds much like Wesley's designation of what Perkins taught.

[72] Colin Williams, *John Wesley's Theology Today*, pp. 122-25, may be correct when he says Wesley freed the doctrine of assurance from the presumption of final salvation by "cutting away the doctrine of double predestination." However, he overlooks the fact that the Puritan stress on the reality and vitality of a present consciousness of salvation mitigates, and to some extent overcomes, the dangers in a doctrine of assurance of eternal salvation.

ness of eternal salvation is somewhat different from a present consciousness of present salvation only. In one sense this is only a matter of emphasis, for Wesley did not reject completely the possibility of an assurance of eternal salvation. However, this would minimize the real difference, which is, of course, based on the different concepts of the operation of grace used by Wesley and the majority of the Puritans. Wesley's Arminianism allowed no more than present knowledge for most believers, and the Calvinistic concept linked both present and future knowledge even where the present aspect is emphasized over that of the future. Recognition of the difference should not, however, obscure the vitality of the Puritan expression of the doctrine and emphasis upon a present consciousness of salvation.

The peculiarly personal aspect of this assurance—expressed by Wesley as "mine, even mine"—is also an emphasis of the Puritan interpretation. "Now the Spirit doth not only teach the truths of the gospel, but the applications of those truths, that they are ours: this truth of the gospel is mine . . . . It is a Spirit of application, to bring home those gracious promises to everyone in particular; to tell us the things that are given us of God; not only the PARTICULARS [things] that are given to the Church, but to us in particular." [73]

Experience taught these Puritan divines that however real and immediate the assuring witness of the Spirit might be at the moment, there were times when even the most faithful believer doubted his state of grace. Consequently, all the authors examined allow for periods of doubt and questioning when the assurance once seen so vividly may be "clouded over." There is a hesitancy to say that this assurance is "lost" during these times because of their concept of perseverance, but their answer is usually that given by John Owen—the witness or assurance is present but simply not realized or appropriated by the believer.[74] *The Westminster Confession,* as we shall see, allows that as-

[73] Richard Sibbes, *A Fountain Opened,* p. 27 [*CL,* VI, 65-66]; Sibbes, *The Nativity of Christ,* in *The Works of Richard Sibbes,* ed. A. B. Grossart (7 vols.; Edinburgh: James Nichol, 1863), VI, 353 [*CL,* VI, 125]; Robert Bolton, *On Walking with God,* p. 317 [*CL,* IV, 404].

[74] Owen, *On Communion,* pp. 285-86; John Preston, *The Breast Plate of Faith and Love,* Part I, pp. 126-27 [*CL,* V, 364-65]; Bolton, *On Walking with God,* p. 335 [*CL,* IV, 413]; Sibbes, *A Fountain Sealed,* p. 233. Bolton, on the basis of the degrees of assurance, could insist that assurance most often comes in times of prayer, special need, persecution, etc. Wesley consistently eliminated such passages. (Robert Bolton, *On Walking with God,* pp. 336 ff. [*CL,* IV, 414 ff.].)

surance may be "shaken, diminished and intermitted." Intermitted could be interpreted to mean that this assurance can be lost, but the confession goes on to assume that other supports of faith (love, sincerity of heart) would bear one up until the time assurance is "revived." [75] Although this allows some question as to whether or not it is possible for it to be really "lost," the general tone of the statement is more in terms of diminished than lost.

To admit the possibility of doubt is to affirm the fact of degrees of assurance. Some may have the witness to a stronger degree than others —those young in the faith are naturally understood to have more doubt mixed with their assurance than those more mature. Sibbes distinguishes three "ranks" of Christians in which assurance is progressively fuller and more complete: those who do believe but out of fear and who therefore have no real sense of acceptance; those who have some sense of assurance but are not completely free of fear; and those who are "fully assured." [76] These correspond roughly to Wesley's favorite designation of Christians as children, youth, and fathers.[77]

The Puritan divines examined display a divergence of opinion as to the necessity of assurance. For Preston the witness of the Spirit is "necessarily required" since man "shall not believe" until he knows that "God is thy Father." [78] Perkins also insists that "an infallible certainty of pardon of sin, and life everlasting, is the propertie of every renewed conscience." [79] This would seem to be the logical position for those following strict predestinarian categories, for if one is truly elected and has appropriated this election through faith, assurance of this election would seem a corollary and necessary element. Nevertheless, as Wesley saw in his mature years, to insist upon assurance or the witness of the Spirit as a prerequisite of salvation is to go beyond justification by faith alone. Richard Sibbes was quite aware of the dangers of confusing faith with assurance. "A man may be in the state of grace, by giving consent

[75] *Westminster Confession*, p. 15.
[76] *A Fountain Sealed*, pp. 209-10.
[77] *Sermons*, II, 157.
[78] *The Breast Plate of Faith and Love*, Part II, p. 53 [CL, V, 380]. This is true for Preston because he makes assurance in the believer a *reflex* action of faith which is strengthened or helped by the witness of the Holy Spirit. (*Ibid.*, Part I, p. 63 [CL, V, 349].)
[79] Perkins, *Works*, I, 547.

to Christ and relying on him for mercy, and yet want assurance of pardon and reconciliation." [80] "Wee must know that faith is one thing, assurance another." [81] He speaks of assurance as a gift, similar to Owen's contention that the comforting work of the Spirit is at the discretion of God and not necessarily present in all.[82] Bolton comments, "Assuredly that assurance which is ever secure, is but a dreame," which may be interpreted to mean that assurance can be lost and, therefore, cannot be necessary to salvation.[83]

Using Wesley's terminology to distinguish between the two types of witness, it may be affirmed that the Puritans insisted on the reality of both the "direct" and the "indirect" witnesses.[84] Preston's introduction to his comments upon the "witness of the spirit" is an example of the usual presentation.

Now follows the testimony of God's Spirit, which we shall see described. . . . When a man hath believed, and tooke *Jesus Christ;* secondly, when he hath washed and purified himselfe; that is, hee hath gone about his work, and so his own spirit gathers a testimony hence, that he is in a good estate; after hee hath thus believed, then saith hee, comes the *Holy Ghost,* and seales the same thing unto you.[85]

The testimony of the Spirit comes then as one which "secondeth and confirmeth" those evidences of faith already present. In this framework it

---

[80] *Salvation Applied,* in *The Works of Richard Sibbes,* V, 393. "For it is one thing to believe and cast myself upon Christ for pardon of sins, and another thing upon that act to feel assurance and pardon. . . . We ought to labour for both, for affiance and consent in the will, to cast ourselves upon Christ, for salvation; and then upon believing we ought to find and feel this assurance." (*Ibid.,* V, 393.)

[81] *A Fountain Sealed,* p. 211.

[82] John Owen, *On Communion,* pp. 297-98. "It is one thing to have holiness really thriving in any soul, another for that soul to know it, and to be satisfied in it; and these things may be separated." (*Concerning the Holy Spirit,* in Owen, *Works,* II, 470.)

[83] *On Walking With God,* p. 335 [*CL,* IV, 413]. Cf. Baxter, *Richard Baxter's Confession of His Faith* (London: Printed by R. W. for Thomas Underhil, 1655), p. 208.

[84] The witnesses were occasionally considered by the Puritans as only two tests, examples, or marks among others as to how one is to recognize the validity of the covenant relationship and the true faith. (Preston, *New Covenant,* pp. 390-400 [*CL,* VI, 42-44]; Owen, *On Communion,* pp. 294 ff.)

[85] *New Covenant,* p. 400 [*CL,* VI, 44]. Wesley omits this passage and inserts in its place this interesting phrase, "But above all these is the testimony of God's spirit," indicating his own understanding of the primary importance of the witness of the Spirit. Cf. Bolton, *On Walking with God,* pp. 317-27 [*CL,* IV, 404-8].

may appear that the good life and the accompanying testimony of the believer's spirit must precede the receiving of the direct witness. However, this was probably not the intention, for each of the witnesses was part of a whole; the order of presentation did not indicate a dependence of one witness upon the preceding one even if this were the normal course of events in a believer's own experience. Taken all together, they give a consentient witness. Wesley insisted upon the opposite order of direct witness before the indirect witness. Yet the Puritan order does not imply a denial of the witness of the Spirit as the primary element in the whole concept of assurance. Sibbes makes this quite plain:

This testimony of the Spirit containeth in it the force of all, word, promise, oath, seal, etc. This is greater than the promise, as a seal is more than our hand. . . . Our owne graces indeed, if we were watchful enough, would satisfye us. . . . Howsoever, the Spirit, if it cometh, it subdueth all doubts; . . . in this witness hee taketh in no other testimony to confirm it, but witnesseth by himself.[86]

This insistence upon the reality and priority of the direct witness distinguishes both the Puritans and Wesley from those who would confine assurance to the indirect witnesses alone.

It is Bolton who reminds the believer that the two witnesses are to be tested by each other:

Wherefore, if any man pretend to have this witness [the witness of the Spirit], and yet want the testimony of his conscience to the same purpose; the testimony of universal obedience; . . . I can give none but this cold comfort: he is miserably deceived by the devil's counterfeit glory of an angel . . . which in time of trial will vanish into nothing. . . .

But though this last manner of assurance be more immediately from the

[86] *A Fountain Sealed*, p. 167. "The Spirit worketh . . . it immediately by himself, without the imposition of any reasonings, or deductions and conclusions. . . . He immediately works the minds of men to a rejoicing and spiritual frame, filling them with exultation and gladness; not that this arises from our reflex consideration of the love of God, but rather gives occasion thereunto." (Owen, *On Communion*, p. 310 [*CL*, XI, 102]. Cf. Bolton, *On Walking with God*, p. 328 [*CL*, IV, 409].)

Spirit; yet the others are not effectual upon the heart, without the excitation, illumination, and assistance of the same blessed Spirit.[87]

Wesley's own admonition to rest in neither witness without the confirmation of the other is strikingly similar.[88] For both men, one without the other is delusion.

Wesley is following in the pathway of the Puritan tradition when he insists upon the Scriptures as the authority for the whole doctrine. As has been indicated, the central text is Romans 8:15-16, and no exposition of the doctrine is complete without building upon this. The fruits of the Spirit are, as in Wesley, the scriptural marks, and every mark or testimony is grounded in scriptural support.[89] One is to distinguish between true witness and delusion through the avenues of the scriptural marks—the fruits of love, peace, joy, good works—and the witness of conscience in affirming these.

One of the results of the witness of the Spirit, prayer, is emphasized by the Puritans but omitted by Wesley. Because the testimony of the Spirit allows one to cry "Abba, Father"—to recognize and know oneself as a child—prayer becomes more intimate and meaningful. "It may be thou hast prayed to God before, but not as to a Father." [90] "The testimony of the Spirit is ever attended with the spirit of prayer." [91] Geoffrey Nuttall declares that the very foundation of prayer for the Puritans was the "conviction of God's Fatherhood"—the witness of the Spirit.[92] Here is established a reverent familiarity of children with their father. Wesley's exposition misses this altogether, except as he retains the references in his abridgments of Puritan materials. This, in some sense,

[87] *On Walking with God*, pp. 328-29 [*CL*, IV, 408-9]; Preston, *The New Covenant*, p. 90. Richard Baxter's comment also joins the two witnesses: "And, if I am not mistaken, the testimony of the Spirit, and the testimony of conscience, are two concurrent testimonies, or causes, to produce one and the same effect, and to afford the premises to the same conclusion, and then to raise our joy thereupon, so that they may well be said to witness together." (*The Saints' Everlasting Rest*, in Baxter, *Works*, XXII, 439-94.)

[88] *Sermons*, II, 358.

[89] "A sound persuasion by the Spirit is ever answerable exactly to the word; . . . and therefore, if thy present state, wherein thou conceived thyself to be safe, be condemned by God's Word, thy confidence is vain." (Bolton, *Walking with God*, p. 329 [*CL*, IV, 410]; cf. Preston, *New Covenant*, p. 390 [*CL*, VI, 42].

[90] Preston, *The Breast Plate of Faith and Love*, Part II, p. 105 [*CL*, V, 390].

[91] Bolton, *Walking with God*, p. 336 [*CL*, IV, 414].

[92] *The Holy Spirit*, pp. 63 ff.

is a loss, for the concept expresses so well the personal relationship which makes the whole doctrine of assurance so appealing.

The treatises and authors examined here serve as a representative cross-section of the early period of Puritan thought. The doctrine found its way into the *Westminster Confession*, where its exposition provides a convenient summary.

Such as truly believe in the Lord Jesus, and love Him in sincerity, endeavouring to walk in all good conscience before Him, may, in this life, be certainly assured that they are in the state of grace, and may rejoice in the hope of the glory of God, which hope shall never make them ashamed.

This certainly is not a bare conjectural and probable persuasion grounded upon a fallible hope; but an infallible assurance of faith founded upon the divine truth of the promises of salvation, the inward evidence of those graces unto which these promises are made, the testimony of the spirit of adoption witnessing with our spirits that we are the children of God, which Spirit is the earnest of our inheritance, whereby we are sealed to the day of redemption.

This infallible assurance doth not so belong to the essence of faith, but that a true believer may wait longer, and conflict with many difficulties, before he be partaker of it; yet, being enabled by the Spirit to know the things which are freely given him of God, he may, without extraordinary revelation, in the right use of ordinary means, attain thereunto. . . .

True believers may have the assurance of their salvation divers ways shaken, diminished, and intermitted; . . . yet are they never utterly destitute of that seed of God, and life of faith, that love of Christ and the brethren, that sincerity of heart, and conscience of duty, out of which, by the operation of the Spirit, this assurance may, in due time, be revived; and by the which, in the meantime, they are supported from utter despair.[93]

In the Confession the treatment of assurance as an essential part of faith is ambiguous enough to indicate that some of the Assembly must have shared Sibbes's opinion of the relationship of faith and assurance. The statement, "Assurance doth not so belong to the essence of faith, but that a true believer may wait longer . . . before he be a partaker of it," allows the possibility that assurance is not of the "essence of faith" at all. If a "true believer" may be without assurance for any period,

---

[93] *Westminster Confession*, p. 15.

it is safe to assume that, should he die in this period, he would still be saved. Assurance is therefore not "of the essence of faith." On the other hand, to say that "assurance doth not so belong to the essence of faith, but that a true believer may wait longer" indicates that it does belong in some fashion. Obviously, a man of either opinion could be encompassed by this statement.

The doctrine remained a major emphasis in Puritan circles throughout the seventeenth century. Owen treats the fact of assurance in his discussion of the Comforter and discusses it again in his work, *Concerning the Holy Spirit*.[94] Baxter and a host of others support the reality of the fact of assurance through the witness of the Spirit,[95] but perhaps Bolton best expresses, in vivid imagery, the Puritan feeling for and appreciation of the witness.

A SOUND AND UNDECEIVING PERSUASION THAT THOU ARE EVERLASTINGLY LOCKT IN THE ARMS OF GOD'S MERCY AND LOVE, GROUNDED UPON THE WORD, SECONDED AND SET ON BY THE SPIRIT, [The real testimony of the Spirit] is a most rare and rich Jewell, which doth infinitely OUTSHINE AND OVERWEIGH IN SWEETNESS AND [outweigh in] worth any rocke of Diamond, CRISTELL MOUNTAINE, OR THIS GREAT CREATION, WERE IT ALL CONVERTED INTO ONE UNVALUABLE PEARLE.[96]

Was Wesley correct in implying that his doctrine of assurance was the same as that taught in the Puritan tradition? Unquestionably a large measure of similiarity is present between Wesley's presentation and that of the Puritan divines examined. In a sense, Wesley's exposition of the doctrine puts him midway between the Puritans, who insisted upon the reality of the witness of the Spirit which, as a corollary, implied assurance of eternal salvation, and the Church of England opinion of his day which rejected the reality of a witness because it might imply "enthusiasm" and an assurance of eternal salvation. Wesley, then, retained

[94] Owen, *Works*, II, 470 ff.

[95] See Geoffrey Nuttall, *The Holy Spirit*, pp. 48-61, for a detailed discussion of the witness of the Spirit in the Puritan tradition and Watkin-Jones, *The Holy Spirit from Arminius to Wesley*, pp. 306-9, for a similar discussion noting both the Puritan and Anglican formulations.

[96] *On Walking with God*, p. 333 [CL, IV, 412]; Wesley's abridgment indicated how occasionally his editorial pen, while retaining the meaning, loses the strength and vitality of the passage.

the important reality of the witness without necessarily implying eternal salvation. At the same time, with the Puritans, he guarded against enthusiasm and presumption through joining the necessity of "the witness of our own spirits," dependent upon fruits of the Spirit, with the witness of the Holy Spirit.

Identification does not entail exact correspondence, and Wesley's doctrine does diverge at some points from that of the Puritans; nevertheless, identification is perfectly valid. Wesley clearly saw that what he pointed to—personal consciousness of salvation which gives vitality and meaning to present life—was also what the Puritan tradition affirmed. This doctrine not only points toward additional areas of relationship between Wesley and the Puritans but also is a cornerstone of their affinity.

4. Covenant Theology

For a large segment of the Puritan tradition another ground for assurance is found in the covenant made with God. Man, through faithfully binding himself to God in a covenant, is assured that if he carries out the terms of the covenant he will enjoy a sure and saving relationship with God. This covenant concept is, of course, the common heritage of all Christians, stemming from the Old Testament covenants; yet, as L. J. Trinterud has shown, it came into prominence during the sixteenth century, about the time the contract theory of government began to be expounded, in the theologies of certain Rhineland Reformers (Zwingli, Oecolampadius, Bucer, Martyr, and others).[97] Its fullest exposition is in the seventeenth century in the work of Johannes Cocceius. In England this "covenant" or "federal" theology, based on continental precedents, became identified with the Puritans. For them, the whole of the Christian interpretation of salvation is encompassed in this covenant theology, particularly as it witnesses to both God's judgment and mercy.[98] Wesley does not stress the covenant idea as a means of assurance; nevertheless, he does use the basic tenets and terminology to express man's dependence

[97] L. J. Trinterud, "The Origins of Puritanism," *Church History*, XX (1951), No. 1, 37. Trinterud's excellent treatment focuses the genius of Puritanism in covenant theology.

[98] John Preston asserts that the covenant theology is the point of "greatest moment that a minister has to preach to his flock." (*New Covenant*, p. 351.)

upon God's grace and the relationship thereto of works. An examination of Wesley's use of the Puritan formulation indicates another important area of relationship between the two traditions.

By elaborating on a covenant theology, the Puritan divines attempted to explain further how man appropriates the grace of God offered to him in Christ and why he is required to perform certain duties and works which are not meritorious in God's sight. Perry Miller understands the Puritans to have viewed the covenant as an "extension" of the implications of orthodox Calvinism, which essentially preserves the sovereignty of God by retaining his unmerited initiative in salvation and which, at the same time, provides a rationale for man's obligation in terms of faith and moral duty.[99] As W. Adams Brown expresses it:

By the covenant God not only bound Himself to a certain definite line of conduct, so far as man was concerned, and in so far restricted the freedom of His own choice, but He made known in detail to His creature the nature and conditions of His gracious purpose and so removed the uncertainty to which he would otherwise have been exposed.[100]

The concept received elaborate treatment in Puritan literature, one of the most significant expositions being John Preston's work, *The New Covenant, or the Saint's Portion*.[101] This work serves as the principal source for comparison, for we can be sure that Wesley was familiar with this representative exposition of the Puritan formulation.

A principal feature of the covenant theology is its reiteration of the Reformation emphasis on man's salvation through divine grace rather than works. Hence, the Puritans distinguished two covenants—a covenant of works and a covenant of grace. In Preston's words:

The Covenant of Workes runs in these terms, *Doe this, and thou shalt live,* and I will bee thy *God*. This is the covenant that was made with *Adam* [in paradise.] AND THE COVENANT THAT IS EXPRESSED BY MOSES IN THE MORALL LAW, *doe this, and live*. The SECOND IS THE Cove-

[99] Perry Miller, *The New England Mind: The Seventeenth Century* (New York: The Macmillan Company, 1939), pp. 367 ff.

[100] Brown, "Covenant Theology," *Encyclopedia of Religion and Ethics,* ed. James Hastings (13 vols.; Edinburgh: T. & T. Clark, 1912), IV, 217.

[101] See Perry Miller, *The New England Mind: The Seventeenth Century,* p. 374, for an evaluation of its significance.

nant of Grace, AND THAT **runnes in these terms, Thou Shalt believe,** THOU SHALT [and] **take my Son** FOR THY *Lord,* AND THY SAVIOUR, and THOU SHALT LIKEWISE RECEIVE [accept of] **the gift of righteousness,** WHICH WAS WROUGHT BY HIM, FOR AN ABSOLUTION FOR THY SINNES, FOR A RECONCILIATION WITH ME, AND THEREFORE THOU SHALT GROW UP IN LOVE and OBEDIENCE TOWARD MEE, THEN **I will be thy** *God* AND THOU SHALT BEE MY PEOPLE.[102]

Preston points out that the covenant of works was made in paradise before the fall and required perfect obedience on the part of Adam—"Doe this, and live." This covenant was broken by Adam, representing all men, and as a consequence all men have thereafter been hindered by sin from fulfilling the requirements of perfect obedience. Nevertheless, God in his gracious mercy and on his own initiative alone establishes a new covenant with man, whereby man, in order to obtain its blessings, is required only to believe in Christ; through his death and resurrection Christ has gained reconciliation between man and God and is now counted for man's own righteousness—believe, and live. To believe is to have faith, and this faith is the only condition of the new covenant.[103]

Wesley's fullest endorsement of the covenant theology is found in an early sermon, "The Righteousness of Faith" (1742). Here Wesley adopts without hesitation the distinction between the two covenants and uses this formula as a major support of his conviction that man is saved not by obedience or works but solely by grace through faith in Christ.[104]

Preston, following Paul, pushes the covenant of grace back into the Old Testament, pointing out that Abraham and even Adam had their

---

[102] *New Covenant,* pp. 317-18 [*CL,* VI, 31]. Preston gives a good summary of the doctrine also in *The Breast Plate of Faith and Love,* Part I, pp. 18-21 [*CL,* V, 329-31].

[103] *New Covenant,* p. 359 [*CL,* VI, 40].

[104] *Sermons,* I, 132-39; cf. Harald Lindström, *Wesley and Sanctification,* pp. 89-90. Wesley's summary of the role of the two covenants clearly states his own, as well as the Puritan, understanding: "The covenant of works, in order to man's *continuance* in the favour of God, in His knowledge and love, in holiness and happiness, required of perfect man a *perfect* and uninterrupted *obedience* to every point of the law of God. Whereas, the covenant of grace, in order to man's *recovery* of the favour and life of God, requires only *faith,* living faith in Him who, through God, justifies him that obeyed not." (*Sermons,* I, 138; cf. II, 65; *Works,* VIII, 289.) Sugden may be correct when he says that the covenant of works is a "theological fiction" (*Sermons,* I, 131n.), nevertheless, it performed an important function in the thinking of Wesley and his Puritan mentors. For an incisive treatment of Wesley's use of the covenants, see John Deschner, *Wesley's Christology* (Dallas: Southern Methodist University Press, 1960), pp. 112-13.

significant relationships to God through a covenant of grace. Their relation to God was actually based on faith instead of works. Preston specifically notes the covenant of grace being "preached" by God in the Old Testament only to Adam and Abraham.[105] Wesley follows another Puritan exposition, as initiated by William Ames (d. 1633) and expanded by men such as Isaac Ambrose (d. 1663),[106] in maintaining a progressively fuller and clearer revelation of this covenant from Adam through Abraham, Moses, David, and the prophets.[107] These early covenants, while being real covenants of grace since they depended upon faith, were but types of the final covenant revealed in Christ.[108]

In all the covenants of grace the righteousness which God accepts as the fulfillment of the requirement of obedience is that of Christ—never that of man. Christ's righteousness is not only obedience to the commandments but obedience even unto death, making propitiation for man's sin. In the Old Testament the grace given in covenant is a type or shadow of what is fulfilled in the New; both are dependent upon Christ's righteousness in his obedience unto death. Christ agrees to fulfill the obedience required and man is able to have this righteousness counted for his own through faith in Christ.

Christ is the Mediator of the *Covenant*, it is he that declares the *Covenant* and, SECONDLY, it is he that BY THE INTERVENTION OF A CERTAINE COMPACT, OF CERTAINE ARTICLES OF AGREEMENT, hath reconciled the disagreeing parties, he hath gone between them, as it were, and hath undertaken for both sides; he hath undertaken on *God's* part, these and these things shall be done, ALL HIS PROMISES ARE YEA, AND AMEN, IN HIM: and AGAIN, he hath undertaken on our part to give satisfaction by his death, and likewise to make us obedient to his Father.[109]

---

[105] *New Covenant*, pp. 351-53.

[106] William Ames, *The Marrow of Sacred Divinity* (London: Edward Griffin, 1642), pp. 170-75; Isaac Ambrose, *Looking Unto Jesus, CL*, VIII, 116 ff.; see W. Adams Brown, "Covenant Theology," *Encyclopedia of Religion and Ethics*, IV, 218.

[107] *Sermons*, I, 136.

[108] *New Covenant*, p. 326 [CL, VI, 34]; *Sermons*, I, 136.

[109] *New Covenant*, p. 330 [CL, VI, 36].

Wesley's own formulation retains this christocentric orientation.[110]

For both Wesley and Preston the sole condition of the covenant of grace is belief, faith in Christ's death and resurrection, faith in the grace given through the covenant.[111] By the act of faith Abraham joined in covenant with God, and this act made the covenant valid for Abraham.[112] Through an act of faith, therefore, the covenant is sealed and its benefits appropriated by each believer.[113]

The Puritans insisted that even the ability to believe—to perform this act of faith—was the gift of the Spirit; only through this enabling gift can man appropriate for himself the covenant and its blessings.[114] Such was the logical outcome of their doctrine of original sin. In this Wesley concurs, for he also understands faith to be "the gift of God"; "No man is able to work it in himself." [115] Man must be enabled by God even to respond to grace.

[110] "Indeed, strictly speaking, the covenant of *grace* doth not require us to *do* anything at all, as absolutely and indispensably necessary in order to our justification; but only to *believe* in Him who, for the sake of His Son, and the propitiation which he hath made, 'justifieth the ungodly that worketh not,' and imputes his faith to him for righteousness." (*Sermons*, I, 137.) See Colin Williams, *John Wesley's Theology Today*, pp. 84-87, for a discussion of Christ as mediator in Wesley and the use of covenant of works and of grace therein. See John Deschner, *Wesley's Christology*, pp. 156, 162, on the christocentric nature of the covenants in Wesley.

[111] There was a divergence of opinion among the Puritans as to the conditionality of the covenant. Some, best represented in the seventeenth century by John Saltmarsh (d. 1647) and Tobias Crisp (d. 1643), argued that the covenant of grace was between God and Christ and therefore was not dependent upon man but simply applied to the elect. To counter the antinomian tendencies of this concept, Baxter, Daniel Williams, John Flavel, and others insisted upon conditionality. To accomplish this, one of the explanations offered, particularly by Daniel Williams, was a covenant of redemption made between God and Christ in heaven by which Christ agrees to save man, and to this is added the covenant of grace between God and the elect made through Christ. The former was without condition on man's part but the latter retains the condition of faith. (W. Adams Brown, "Covenant Theology," *Encyclopedia of Religion and Ethics*, IV, 218; David Shipley, "Wesley and Some Calvinistic Controversies," *Drew Gateway*, XXV (1955), 205-9). The rudiments of this covenant of redemption are seen in Preston's statement quoted above referring to a "certaine compact, of certaine articles of agreement" but here this covenant is largely seen as a metaphysical framework for the whole doctrine of covenant. Wesley rejects the covenant of redemption because he finds no scriptural base for it, but, more important, in his own day this covenant was interpreted as the covenant of election, whereby God and Christ agreed to save the elect—naturally, Wesley had no use for this, and consequently retained only the concept of a covenant of grace and a covenant of works. (*Works*, X, 238-42; 422-23.) He continually insists upon the conditionality of the covenant of grace. (*Works*, X, 238, 309; *Letters*, III, 379.)

[112] *New Covenant*, pp. 357-71; *Sermons*, I, 137.

[113] *Sermons*, I, 138; see Perry Miller, *New England Mind: The Seventeenth Century*, p. 378.

[114] W. Adams Brown, "Covenant Theology," *Encyclopedia of Religion and Ethics*, IV, 218.

[115] *Works*, VIII, 5.

Out of this total dependence on God's grace arose the Calvinistic doctrine of predestination, which restricts the enabling gift of grace to those persons "elected" by God. Rejecting this interpretation as unduly limiting God's grace to a select few, Wesley introduced his doctrine of prevenient grace to explain how the "enabling" came about. According to this doctrine *all* men (estranged from God by their original sin and totally unable of their own volition to reestablish their relationship to him) are *enabled* by God's gift of "preventing grace" to accept or reject saving or convicting grace.[116] Such an "enabling" grace *restores* to each man a measure of "free will" or, more correctly, a measure of responsibility for his own salvation, since the universality of prevenient grace gives every man the possibility of accepting or rejecting God's saving grace when offered.[117] In appropriating saving grace there is some "concurrence on man's part." [118] Synergism is qualifiedly admitted here but still within a Reformation context.[119] This is an attempt to take seriously the Protestant doctrine of original sin with its insistence upon total dependence on the mercy of God and to avoid the pitfalls of a Pelagian "inherent" free will and, at the same time, truly to restore a measure of responsibility to man. Man's responsibility thus restored by prevenient grace carries with it as a corollary the ability to distinguish right and wrong, good and evil. Part of the gift of prevenient grace is, then, man's conscience.[120] Through prevenient grace, man becomes a responsible moral agent.

[116] *Works*, VI, 512; "Free Grace," in *Works*, VII, 373-74; cf. *The Doctrine of Original Sin,* in *Works*, IX, 196 ff.

[117] *Works*, VIII, 285.

[118] *Ibid.*, X, 229-30.

[119] Colin Williams (*John Wesley's Theology Today*, p. 72) points out that Wesley's synergism can only be correctly understood when it is noted that this does not allow, as in a Pelagian concept, an upward movement of man's natural will nor a required moral level or standard to be achieved. Man cooperates in his salvation only in the sense of accepting or rejecting saving grace, and even this ability—or responsibility—is given by God's free gift of prevenient grace. David Shipley ("Methodist Arminianism in the Theology of John Fletcher," p. 417) and Robert Chiles ("Methodist Apostasy: From Free Grace to Free Will," *Religion in Life*, XXVII, 440-41) are not willing to call this cooperative element by the title "synergism" since even this is dependent on grace. Chiles suggests that Wesley moves "beyond these traditional distinctions to make a unique contribution to Christian thought!" It may be that Wesley's concept is unique and that this is only a qualified synergism, but in the sense that it does imply cooperation on man's part, divinely bestowed, the term may be used legitimately. See Lycurgus Starkey, *The Work of the Holy Spirit*, pp. 116 ff.

[120] *Works*, VII, 187-88; VI, 512.

Wesley's doctrine, however, is not without its own problems. To distinguish between two aspects of God's grace and to provide an explanation of how man appropriates the second instance of grace (saving grace) still does not explain his appropriation of the first instance of grace (prevenient grace). Wesley has provided only a partial explanation. Perhaps this is as much as is possible if, as in the Reformed tradition, man's total dependence on God is to be affirmed unequivocally and Pelagianism avoided, but it still leaves the question partially open. Other queries can also be raised about the doctrine. If some men appear to be more able to respond to saving grace than others, and conscience appears to be "strong" in some men but "weak" in others, has God endowed men equally with prevenient grace? If not, the question of election has only been pushed back one step through saving grace to prevenient grace, for God appears at least to favor, or if one prefers "elect," some men over others. The charges of unwarranted favoritism in God's election of some men over others, so often leveled against predestinarianism, might also be valid here.

Nevertheless, even if he were forced to admit the mysteries of such discrepancies evident between men in the state of prevenient grace, Wesley, unable to conceive that any man was totally void of conscience and contact with God, would probably answer this latter argument by pointing out that all men, no matter how low their degree of conscience or receptivity to God, are nevertheless "elected" by God to respond in moral action and to saving grace. Although some may be more richly endowed through prevenient grace, none are without it—"in all and for all." All are elected to receive prevenient grace and the opportunity for saving grace even if in varying degrees; by the same token, all are made responsible no matter to what degree. Wesley's construction may leave one with unexplained discrepancies which appear to indicate "degrees" of election; yet at least it avoids the predestinarian discrepancy whereby grace is offered to some while it is withheld from others. In addition, it does provide an explanation for each man's being a responsible moral agent.[121]

[121] Although Wesley rejects the limitation of election inherent in predestination, he affirms election in the sense of "a divine appointment of some particular men, to do some particular work in the world." (*Works*, X, 210). That he felt himself and his movement so appointed is without

Wesley's doctrine of prevenient grace was not without precedent in the Puritan ranks. Richard Baxter clearly could not accept an interpretation of God's grace which restricts it to the elect and he insisted on the universality of what he termed "common grace." [122] According to David Shipley, "Baxter's description of common grace is a striking precursor of what is found in Wesley's conception of an efficacious prevenient grace." [123] Baxter, like Wesley, insisted on the universality of a "common grace" which enables man to respond to God's offer of saving grace, thereby making man responsible. "He that made us without us, will not save us without us." [124] Here is another area of affinity between Wesley and the "Arminian wing" of Puritanism represented by Baxter.

It was noted above that a major function of the Puritan covenant theology was to provide a rationale for a believer's performance of obligations and duties. To enter into covenant means to take all the obligations, as Preston expresses it, "though there were nothing but Faith, yet that believing, brings with it, and works sanctification, and holiness of life." "Let any Man believe as Abraham did, and of necessity it will produce good works." [125] When one has believed and been reconciled to God, then the Spirit "writes the Law in his inward parts, that is it that breedes in him a holy disposition, that enables him in some measure to keepe the Law; it prints in him all those graces that give him strength to observe the commandments that God hath given him." [126]

Obedience to the commandments, which was required in the covenant of works and unattainable for sinful man, now issues out of faith. The standard of the commandments given in the old law now becomes

---

question. His famous comment about himself as a "brand plucked out of the burning" (from a fire in the Epworth rectory) to fulfill some special mission is only one example among many. (*Journal,* IV, 90; *Letters,* V, 15.) He was convinced that Methodism had been raised up to "reform the nation, particularly the Church, and to spread spiritual holiness over the land." (*Works,* VIII, 299.) Although Wesley denies, in response to one of his critics, that he felt such a "designation to extraordinary work," his constant affirmations contradict this denial. (*Works,* XIII, 409; *Sermons,* II, 344.)

[122] "Preface to the Readers," *Richard Baxter's Confession of His Faith,* p. vi.

[123] "Wesley and Some Calvinistic Controversies," *The Drew Gateway,* XXV (1955), 208.

[124] Baxter, *Aphorisms on Justification* (London: Printed for Francis Tyton, 1644), p. 95.

[125] *New Covenant,* p. 362 [*CL,* VI, 40]; see W. Adams Brown, "Covenant Theology," *Encyclopedia of Religion and Ethics,* IV, 217.

[126] *New Covenant,* p. 345.

again the standard of the new covenant, not on the basis of man's ability to obey but as a natural consequence of his faith.[127] The standard is still applicable to the believer's life; he is morally responsible for his act as a part of (or issue of) his faith. Wesley, though not needing this explanation to restore man to moral responsibility, saw in this covenantal insistence upon the necessity of works issuing from faith an antidote to antinomianism, and thus insisted that one was bound to obey the commandments, "under the covenant of grace, though not in order to his justification." [128]

The Puritan restoration of moral responsibility to the believer through the avenue of the covenant is open to the criticism that such a covenant is still restricted to the elect; although it provides a defense against antinomianism among these elect, it fails to extend its insight into the nature of the relation of faith and works to those outside the community of elected believers. Wesley's doctrine of universal prevenient grace offered him the possibility of circumventing this problem; therefore, he is able to accept and use the insights and distinctions of the covenant theology both to affirm man's dependence upon God's grace *and* to insist upon the necessity for moral responsibility and the holy life.

Along with the covenant theology elaborated in Puritan circles went its practical manifestations in outward form through church, national, and personal covenants. For the community of believers and the nation the covenants established concrete evidence of commitment to particular standards, and in the Congregational wing of the Puritan tradition it took the place of creeds and confessions. For the individual the psychological value of having expressed in outward form and statement an inward agreement is obvious. Equally valuable is the establishment of an express relationship which serves as a constant reminder of the covenant obligation solemnly entered into with God.

Wesley's perception of both the limits and the value of such cove-

[127] "In order that men should not presume upon the 'Absolute Promises' of the Covenant to give over trying, the federal God, . . . perfected the adroit device of incorporating the Covenant of Works into the Covenant of Grace, not as the condition of salvation but as the rule of righteousness. . . . 'For the Morall Law, the Law of the ten Commandments, we are dead also to the covenant of that Law, though not to the command of it.' " (Perry Miller, *The New England Mind: The Seventeenth Century*, p. 384.)

[128] *Letters*, III, 378; cf. *Works*, VIII, 289; *Sermons*, I, 138.

nants is clearly expressed in his comment on II Chronicles 15:12 in *Explanatory Notes upon the Old Testament*: "The matter of this covenant was nothing but what they were before obliged to. And tho' no promise could lay any higher obligation upon them, than they were already under, yet it would help increase their sense of the obligation, and to arm them against temptations. And by joining all together in this, they strengthened the hands of each other." [129]

To aid his own societies he provided them with a covenant service. Interestingly, the earliest use of such a service by Wesley in his societies coincides with the period during which he was laboring on the abridgments for *A Christian Library*, wherein he includes Joseph and Richard Alleine's formulations of a covenant and directions for its use.[130] Wesley's service is patterned on these forms.

Frederick Hunter correctly points out that Wesley had chosen out of the Puritan tradition a covenant form which was primarily a covenant between the believer and his God and not a church covenant. Richard Alleine's form was no doubt intended to be used corporately but still was an individual covenant, and so remained in Methodist use.[131] Leslie Church presents evidence to show that, in addition to the corporate covenant service, which had become by the late 1760's a traditional service of renewal by which the Methodists began the year, some of the early Methodists also prepared and signed personal covenants expressing their relationship to God.[132] Such was the original intent of the Alleine covenants.

There is little question that Wesley's advocacy of the covenant service among his followers came primarily out of the practical values he saw in its use, but Hunter proposes some interesting suppositions rela-

[129] *Explanatory Notes upon the Old Testament* (3 vols.; Bristol: Printed by William Pine, 1765), II, 1372.

[130] The first mention of "renewing in every point our covenant that the Lord should be our God" is in January, 1748 (*Journal*, III, 328), when Wesley was preparing materials for the *Library*. Covenanting is not mentioned again until 1755, after Wesley had published both of the Alleine formulas, and it is by this time in the form of a service. After this, the covenant is frequently mentioned and urged upon the societies. He records in the *Journal*, almost each time the covenant is mentioned, how it brought special blessing to the congregation and to him personally. (*Journal*, V, 98; VI, 222; VII, 133.)

[131] Frederick Hunter, "The Origin of Wesley's Covenant Service," *LQHR*, 164 (1939), 81.

[132] Leslie Church, *More About the Early Methodist People* (London: Epworth Press, 1949), pp. 274-77.

tive to the possibility of the carry-over of the covenant emphasis from Wesley's Puritan ancestors. Wesley, in 1755, urges one of the societies to practice "another means of increasing serious religion, which had been frequently practiced by our forefathers . . . namely, the joining in a covenant." [133] Hunter takes the reference to "our forefathers" to be a recognition on Wesley's part of his own Puritan ancestors using the covenant.

To support such a supposition Hunter suggests: (1) that John Westley, paternal grandfather of John Wesley, may have proposed to Joseph Alleine the use of the personal covenant in corporate worship; (2) that Samuel Annesley "probably" derived the idea of a covenant service from Richard Alleine and used it in his church at Little St. Helens after his ejection in 1662; and (3) that John Wesley was possibly familiar with the use of the covenant by John White, another grandfather, in forming New England colonists into a church.[134] In all these, Hunter is dependent upon probabilities and therefore the suggestion must be weighed accordingly, but he is on surer ground in suggesting a real awareness and dependence upon the covenant relationship in the Wesley household when he points out that Susanna Wesley urged her sons, Samuel and John, to remember the covenant they personally made with God. Apparently Susanna urged upon her children an appreciation for the covenant theology and the personal covenant, which she no doubt drew from her Puritan forefathers.[135] Wesley's adoption of the covenant service may, then, have been the result not only of its practical and religious value but also of his own appreciation of the covenant fostered by family background. In any case, in the use of both the covenant form of dedication and the theological formulation upon which it was grounded, Wesley displays a close affinity to Puritan precepts and practices.

[133] *Journal*, IV, 126.
[134] "The Origin of Wesley's Covenant Service," *LQHR*, 164 (1939), 85-86.
[135] Frank Baker ("The Beginnings of the Methodist Covenant Service," p. 215) supports this assumption that much of the emphasis on the covenant came to Wesley through his mother.

IV

THEOLOGICAL FOUNDATIONS: SANCTIFICATION, SIN IN BELIEVERS, FINAL JUSTIFICATION

1. Sanctification

We have seen that both the witness of the Spirit and the cementing of faith through covenant theology issue in a new life for the believer. Therefore, not surprisingly, a dominant emphasis upon the doctrine of sanctification is present in the works of both Wesley and the Puritans. For each, the encounter with God established through faith could mean little if it did not also mean constant transforming companionship and guidance in the vicissitudes of daily life.[1] This continuous experience of

---

[1] One of Wesley's favorite distinctions between justification and sanctification is to call justification the "relative" change in man and sanctification the "real" change. (*Sermons,* II, 446.) Richard Baxter provides a strikingly similar distinction when, in discussing salvation, he comments, "He [God] *never maketh a relative change, where he doth not also make a real change.*" (*Aphorisms on Justification,* p. 95, italics mine.)

renewal provides the reality which issues in the doctrine of sanctification.

The important truth of sanctification was never lost even in those branches of Protestantism most insistent on the priority and domination of justification by faith. To be sure, Luther essentially incorporated sanctification within justification without distinguishing between them, but the Calvinistic tradition retained the distinction without losing a valid stress upon either.[2] The English Reformation in all its branches had as one of its major elements the emphasis upon the sanctified, the holy, life. Both the Puritans and Wesley, in stressing this doctrine, were within the mainstream of their joint heritage.

In each tradition an emphasis upon the reality and necessity of sanctification manifests itself in the production of instructive writings relative to the Christian life. A brief survey of the Puritan writings used by Wesley in *A Christian Library* should be sufficient to indicate the major role given to instruction, with its theological basis, sanctification.[3] From the detailed instruction and regulation of daily life, or in Wesley's terms, the "supposed greater purity of their manners," [4] the sobriquet "Puritan" or "Precisian" drew its sting. As Horton Davies suggests, the name was "justified only as a description of the concern of the radical party that the Church of England should be reformed according to the 'pure' Word of God." [5] Nevertheless, their concern with purity in liturgical forms and church government carried over into their instructions in daily living, so that in the eyes of their contemporaries they were far too pure and precise in all areas. It is, of course, this insistence upon the practical application of divinity which strikes the responsive chord in Wesley.[6]

The parallels in the traditions lie not only in elaborate Christian instruction but in the essential features of the doctrine. With the Puritan

---

[2] For discussion of the relation of Wesley's doctrine to that of the Reformation leaders see Harald Lindström, *Wesley and Sanctification*, pp. 91-92.

[3] See Appendix I.

[4] Wesley, *A Concise History of England* (4 vols.; London: Printed by R. Hawes, 1776), III, 124.

[5] Horton Davies, *The Worship of the English Puritans* (London: Dacre Press, 1948), p. 2.

[6] Lycurgus Starkey, *The Work of the Holy Spirit*, p. 137, comments, "The closest parallels to be drawn between Wesley and seventeenth-century Puritanism are in this area of sanctification and inherent righteousness."

and the Reformed traditions, Wesley insists that sanctification, no matter how necessary, is nevertheless dependent upon faith—to give it any other base is to reinstitute salvation through an order of merit.

Faith is the condition, and the only condition, of sanctification, exactly as it is of justification. It is the *condition*: none is sanctified but he that believes; without faith no man is sanctified. And it is the *only condition*: this alone is sufficient for sanctification. Every one that believes is sanctified, whatever else he has or has not. In other words, no man is sanctified till he believes: every man, when he believes, is sanctified.[7]

John Owen declares in a similar passage, "Faith is the instrumental cause of our sanctification; so that, where it is not, no holiness can be wrought in us. . . . It is from faith in God through Jesus Christ, acting itself in obedience unto the gospel, that we purify or cleanse our soul, which is our sanctification." [8] Robert Bolton's *The Saints' Selfe-Enriching Examination* affirms, "Saving faith is the root and fountain of sanctification." [9]

The true importance of Wesley's affirmation that sanctification is solely dependent upon faith becomes evident with the application of Colin Williams' insight concerning perfection to the whole doctrine of sanctification. Williams, as well as Shipley, questions the widely held view of Cell that Wesley has in fact established "a necessary synthesis of the Protestant ethic of grace with the Catholic ethic of holiness." [10] If it were true, Williams maintains, that Wesley accepted a Catholic doctrine of holiness, he must accept its essential elements: the ability of man, with the help of grace, to rise up in a "ladder of merit" and to reach the goal or level of perfection. In the case of general sanctification man is enabled and required to reach a certain moral level before he may be saved (in order to assure the possibility of this, the concept of purga-

---

[7] *Sermons*, II, 453.

[8] *Concerning the Holy Spirit*, in Owen, *Works*, II, 488.

[9] *The Saints' Selfe-Enriching Examination* (London: Printed by Anne Griffin for Rapha Harford, 1634), p. 132 [*CL*, V, 219]; cited hereafter as *On Self-Examination*.

[10] George Cell, *The Rediscovery of John Wesley*, p. 361. Others who generally support such a concept include John L. Peters, *Christian Perfection and American Methodism* (Nashville: Abingdon Press, 1956), p. 21; W. E. Sangster, "Wesley and Sanctification," *LQHR*, 171 (1946), 219; Paul Sanders, "What God Hath Joined Together," *Religion in Life*, XXIX (1960), 493.

tory is needed).[11] Obviously, to accept these components is to accept the corollary doctrine of grace, which makes it essentially a helpmate to man's natural ability. Wesley rejected these concepts, insisting that no merit is required or possible for man, that salvation is a free gift of God without consideration of a standard or level of holiness. In doing this he not only affirmed a Protestant doctrine of grace but also a Protestant doctrine of sanctification in which faith is still the crucial element.[12]

Harald Lindström, in his excellent study, *Wesley and Sanctification*, contends that the gradual process of sanctification was far more integral to Wesley's concept of salvation than is frequently assumed. Too often, according to Lindström, investigation of Wesley's concept of salvation and the Christian life has been concentrated on the new birth and complete sanctification (Christian perfection) as "two isolated phenomena unconnected organically with his doctrine of salvation as a whole." [13] Since both of these events in Wesley's thought may be instantaneous, the gradual process of general sanctification is often minimized. Yet Wesley's emphasis upon the gradual process is obvious, for, though "entire sanctification" is a possibility and goal for all believers, by far the greater number of Christian believers will always be involved in the process.[14] The normal pattern of sanctification is constant spiritual and moral improvement of the Christian life, admitting many degrees within it. Through each state one needs to "grow in grace" and "daily to advance in the knowledge and love of God his Saviour." [15] That Wesley

[11] Colin Williams, *John Wesley's Theology Today*, pp. 174-75; see also David Shipley, "Methodist Arminianism in the Theology of John Fletcher," p. 267.

[12] "Wesley's view is one of sanctification by faith alone. In other words, Wesley puts his doctrine within the Protestant framework of justification by faith, not within the Roman framework of justification by faith and works. He put it within the order of personal relationship to Christ, not within the order of a legal relationship to a moral standard." (Colin Williams, *John Wesley's Theology Today*, p. 175.)

[13] *Wesley and Sanctification*, pp. 105, 123. "How much soever any man has attained, or in how high a degree soever he is perfect, he hath still need to 'grow in grace,' and daily to advance in the knowledge and love of God his Saviour." (*Sermons*, II, 156.)

[14] Lindström is correct when he notes that, although Wesley, in discussing salvation, concentrates upon the doctrines of justification and sanctification, it is "undoubtedly sanctification that received major attention." (*Wesley and Sanctification*, p. 15.)

[15] *Sermons*, II, 156. One of Wesley's favorite images is the designation of the various stages as that of child or newborn babe, a young man, and finally, a father or mature adult, in the faith.

himself was aware of the importance of the gradual process and of his own task in cultivating it is evident in his comment to his brother Charles, in 1766: "Go on, in your *own way,* what God has peculiarly called you to. Press the *instantaneous* blessing: then I shall have more time for my peculiar calling, enforcing the *gradual* work." [16]

The gradual nature of the process of sanctification within the Puritan tradition is shown by the title of one of Owen's chapters: "Sanctification, a Progressive Work." [17] Through persuasive and constant work within the lives of believers the Holy Spirit is gradually "renewing in them the image of God," so that progressively, by degrees, one becomes more holy.[18]

This common insistence upon the gradual nature should not be allowed to obscure the real distinction between Wesley and the Puritan tradition, in that Wesley incorporated into the gradual process the possibility of present, instantaneous, entire sanctification or perfection.[19] For the Puritans the process is never consummated within this life, and entire sanctification comes only at or after death.[20] Wesley's insistence

[16] *Letters,* V, 16; John Peters, *Christian Perfection and American Methodism,* pp. 65-66, asserts that the gradual process is very important even within the state of perfection. The instantaneous beginning only starts a gradual maturing which is of great consequence.

[17] *Concerning the Holy Spirit,* in Owen, *Works,* II, 453; cf. *Sermons,* II, 447 and 454, where Wesley also indicates that sanctification is to grow in the "image of God"; cf. *Explanatory Notes,* p. 900 (II Pet. 3:18); *Letters,* V, 81.

[18] *Concerning the Holy Spirit,* p. 453.

[19] *Sermons,* II, 459; *Works,* XI, 380, 442. Although Wesley at times clearly distinguishes between sanctification and perfection or entire sanctification (*Works,* IX, 388), there is some tendency to coalesce these "stages." Sanctification as both an instantaneous and a gradual process is identified with perfection as early as the 1744 conference and as late as 1770 (*Letters,* V, 215). Instead of perfection being the ultimate capstone of a gradual process of sanctification, it can be an instantaneous gift. As a result, Wesley can speak of sanctification as both "an instantaneous and a gradual work." (*Letters,* V, 215; *Sermons,* II, 240.) "Whoever would advance the gradual change in believers should strongly insist on the instantaneous." (*Works,* VIII, 329; cf. VIII, 293-94.) This conflating of the two is only possible because Wesley's perfection "admits of a thousand degrees." (*Letters,* V, 215.) As Lindström indicates, both aspects of instantaneous and gradual must be held together (*Wesley and Sanctification,* p. 122). Sanctification must be taken to include both the gradual process present in the life of all believers *and* Wesley's doctrine of Christian perfection, or entire sanctification, which is a possibility for all and not necessarily the culmination of the gradual process. Including both these meanings, it stands in the salvation process between justification and final salvation. John Peters (*Christian Perfection and American Methodism,* pp. 63-64) provides a helpful summary of the various meanings and usages of such words as perfection, sanctification, and entire sanctification in Wesley's various works.

[20] *Concerning the Holy Spirit,* in Owen, *Works,* II, 477.

111

upon the possibility of such an instantaneous completion of sanctification, goes beyond the Puritan understanding but, even so, never loses sight of the gradual element of "growth in grace."

This gradual process provides the context for the whole body of instructions concerning the Christian life. Even though such teachings, for Wesley, may apply to the "entirely sanctified," they are principally intended for the instruction of the believer who, far from living a perfect life, is struggling to understand the meaning of Christian behavior among the diverting interests of daily affairs. One cannot understand the magnetic appeal that Wesley had for the common man of his day and the Puritans had in their own day, without recognizing the role played by Christian instruction. As Wesley says, his peculiar work is to "enforce the gradual work."

Sanctification has always been considered by Christian theologians to be part of the work of the Holy Spirit (Rom. 15:16, I Cor. 6:11, II Tim. 2:13). The agency of the Holy Spirit in the believer's sanctification is most fully amplified by Wesley in his early sermons, "The Circumcision of the Heart" (1733), "On Grieving the Holy Spirit" (1733), and "On the Holy Spirit" (1736).[21] These early sermons express complete dependence upon the Spirit for the sanctifying purification of life.

We are convinced, that we are not sufficient of ourselves to help ourselves; that, without the Spirit of God, we can do nothing but add sin to sin; that it is He alone who worketh in us by His almighty power, either to will or do that which is good; it being as impossible for us even to think a good thought, without the supernatural assistance of His Spirit, as to create ourselves.[22]

The emphasis found here is never lost and is expressed throughout his ministry.[23] Tying the work of the Spirit to that of Christ, Wesley can exclaim, "As all *merit* is in the Son of God . . . so all *power* is in the Spirit of God; . . . all true faith and the whole work of salvation, every good thought, word, and work, is altogether by the operation of the

---

[21] Of these sermons, only "The Circumcision of the Heart" is included among the standard sermons and therefore "endorsed" throughout his life as a doctrinal standard.

[22] *Sermons,* I, 268.

[23] *Sermons,* I, 166; II, 94; *Letters,* V, 7; II, 71; *Works,* VIII, 352; IX, 378.

Spirit of God." [24] The same emphasis is, of course, a cornerstone of the Puritan presentation, typified by Owen's insistence that "he [the Spirit] is the immediate author of every good or gracious acting in us." [25]

In this formulation of sanctification as a work of the Spirit, neither Wesley nor the Puritans diverge from traditional orthodox statements. If there is any distinction, it is in the emphasis placed upon the Spirit's role in the process of sanctification. Wesley may have been able to give a wider scope to man's own part in this process; nevertheless, the Puritans did not allow emphasis on the Spirit to negate man's responsibility in the process. Owen insists that, while the Spirit is the effective cause, it is "our own work also in a way of duty." [26] The antinomian tendencies of a radical dependence upon the Spirit are always rejected.

As we have seen, the culmination of the sanctification process for the Puritans was in the complete moral and spiritual perfection of the believer at the moment of death. However, some of their number expounded a doctrine of perfection of "intent," "sincerity of heart," which may be fruitfully compared with Wesley's own doctrine.

Gordon Wakefield in his work, *Puritan Devotion,* points out that William Dell had taught a doctrine of perfection and that persons such as Richard Greenham gave full credit to the scriptural inferences of perfection without affirming "absolute unspottedness in this life." John Preston's *The New Covenant,* however, is the fullest treatment of the doctrine, according to Wakefield.[27] Wesley's abridgment of this work provides a readily available text for comparison. Preston's major characterization of perfection is perfection of the heart; that is, a heart dedicated singularly and solely to God.

[24] *A Farther Appeal to Men of Reason and Religion,* in *Works,* VIII, 49.

[25] *Concerning the Holy Spirit,* in Owen, *Works,* II, 459; *The Westminster Confession,* p. 12; Isaac Ambrose, *The Practice of Sanctification,* in *The Works of Isaac Ambrose* (London: Printed by H. Fisher, n.d.), p. 78 [*CL,* VIII, 6].

[26] *Concerning the Holy Spirit,* in Owen, *Works,* II, 475. Wesley's sentiment toward Owen is expressed in a letter to John Newton wherein, commenting on how others fail to stress "zeal and care for practical holiness" when teaching imputed righteousness, he says, "They do not enforce it, as Dr. Owen does, with whom (though I do not like some of his opinions) I should never have disputed had he been alive now." (*Letters,* V, 5.)

[27] Wakefield, *Puritan Devotion,* pp. 137-39; Samuel Shaw's *Communion with God* (Glasgow: Printed for William Collins, 1829), p. 303 [*CL,* XIV, 320] includes statements which suggest a belief in perfection, though no extended comment amplifies the doctrine. Wesley claims that even Bunyan actually allows in his *Holy War* a real sense of perfection although he does not acknowledge it as such. (*Works,* VI, 423.)

SO NOW **he is a perfect man with God, that** FIRST **hath a whole heart; that is, such a heart whereof every part, and facultie is sanctified; there is no part of it, but it is seasoned with grace, there is no wheele in all the soule, but it is turned the right way,** ACCORDING TO THAT, I THESS. 5. HE IS SANCTIFIED THROUGHOUT, IN BODY, SOULE, AND SPIRIT, I SAY, WHEN A MAN SHALL FINDE EVERYTHING WITHIN HIM READIE TO PRAYSE THE LORD, AND TO LOOKE TOWARD THE LORD, ALL THAT IS WITHIN HIM. **There is not anything within him, of which he can say, the bent of it is another way.**[28]

Wesley's statements are a close parallel to this: perfection is "purity of intention, dedicating all the life to God. It is the giving God all our heart; it is one desire and design ruling all our tempers. It is the devoting, not a part, but all our soul, body, and substance to God." [29]

Wesley published what he termed his first "sentiments of Christian Perfection" in a work entitled *The Character of a Methodist.* Comparison of this tract with Preston's formulation reveals that Wesley used exactly the same characteristics for perfection and in the same order as Preston had used for the "sincere heart." For both, this is to have "purity of heart," a heart which casts out all sin; to have a "single eye," a heart that looks upon one thing; to have integrity of heart, every part and interest dedicated to God; and finally, to follow all the commandments and ordinances of God without fail in any of them.[30] Wesley's tract was written, according to him, in 1739 and his abridgment of Preston was probably made a few years later (1746-47), so no direct dependence can be demonstrated, but it is noteworthy that the same "characteristics," along with the same scriptural support and in the same order, are found in Preston's treatment of the subject.

The similariy of interpretation is found also in the presentation of perfection as a higher level or stage to be sought and expected in the Chris-

[28] *New Covenant,* p. 229 [*CL*, VI, 27-28].
[29] *Works,* XI, 444. "Here is the sum of the perfect law, the circumcision of the heart. Let the spirit return to God that gave it, with the whole train of its affection—Other sacrifices from us he would not, but the living sacrifice of the heart hath he chosen. . . . Be no design, no desire admitted there, but what has Him for its ultimate object." (*Ibid.,* XI, 368; cf. 371-72.)
[30] *New Covenant,* p. 220 *et passim* [*CL*, VI, 26-28]; *Works,* XI, 372-73. For Wesley's expanded treatment of these explanations see his third sermon, "Upon Our Lord's Sermon on the Mount" (*Sermons,* I, 356 ff.), and his eighth sermon of that series for comments on "singleness of eye." (*Sermons,* I, 471 ff.)

tian life. Preston's insistence that a believer's "constant and ordinary work" is "every day to make his heart perfect" corresponds to Wesley's admonition to his followers to "go on to perfection." [31] This should not be misinterpreted as meaning that either man understood perfection as a state attained by man's efforts; rather they both insisted that perfection was a gift of God's grace.[32]

A major distinction between Wesley and Preston lies in what each was willing to say about sin. Preston, recognizing that man's human infirmities inevitably cause him to sin, asserts that whatever perfection is available to the believer is only the perfection of intention, of dedication, of sincerity; it is perfect direction toward the goal of life, God. Commenting on Phil. 3:12-14, he says:

> The meaning is this; this is my course, saith the apostle: I have not yet attained to perfection; but this I do, I aim at the utmost, even at "the prize of the high calling of God in Jesus Christ": I aim even at the top of perfection, and *I follow hard to it:* and, saith he, not only I, but "as many as are perfect, let them be thus minded"; where, by the *perfect,* he means, you see not one that hath already a perfect heart, but one that is sound hearted.[33]

Preston's perfection of the "sound heart" is an imperfect perfection that presses on toward the goal of real perfection obtained when the taint of sin is taken from man at death; therefore, he never speaks of perfection as being completed in the present. Perfection of the sound heart is the ultimate ideal to be sought in this life and is to be expected of all believers when they are most attuned to God.

Wesley, on the other hand, attempts to circumvent the problem of sin in the perfected man by distinguishing between two types of sin:

[31] *New Covenant*, p. 259 [CL, VI, 29]; *Letters*, V, 6; VI, 103, 137.

[32] *New Covenant*, p. 395. It should be remembered in any discussion of Wesley's doctrine of perfection that the doctrine in its fullest form guards, on the one hand, against a concept of perfection which tends toward dismissing the necessity of good works because of one's "perfected" state. On the other hand, it credits all perfection to the work of Christ so that the "perfected" are always in need of the "merits of Christ" and must always be in a constant communion with him. The severance of communion with Christ is a constant threat to perfection. Perfection is no merit for man but provides all the more reason to praise God for his grace given in Christ. Perfection, like justification, is gained through faith, not merit.

[33] *New Covenant*, p. 258 [CL, VI, 28].

To explain myself a little farther on this head: (1) Not only sin, properly so called, (that is, a voluntary transgression of a known law,) but sin, improperly so called, (that is, an involuntary transgression of a divine law, known or unknown,) needs the atoning blood. (2) I believe there is no such perfection in this life as excludes these involuntary transgressions which I apprehend to be naturally consequent on the ignorance and mistakes inseparable from mortality. (3) Therefore *sinless perfection* is a phrase I never use, lest I should seem to contradict myself. (4) I believe, a person filled with the love of God is still liable to these involuntary transgressions. (5) Such transgressions you may call sins, if you please: I do not, for the reasons above-mentioned.[34]

This definition gave him, like Preston, a "perfection that is imperfect." [35] By refusing to call sins those acts which are involuntary and those present because of man's "corruptible nature," he could and did maintain that "perfection" is presently available within this life. In this interpretation he attempted to eliminate the confusion caused by presentations such as Preston's which, although talking about one "whose heart is perfect with God," [36] actually push perfection into the future.

However, it may be questioned whether Wesley has really moved beyond what Preston was attempting to formulate in his presentation of the doctrine. Without affirming complete moral perfection, Preston attempts to recognize a perfection of personal commitment which produces love and service and goes beyond occasional moral failures. That he must call these failures sins, and Wesley did not consider himself obligated to do so, is not of major consequence. Both are concerned with an overarching perfection of the whole person which is the motivating force of the personality and which discounts occasional failures. Neither could accept a "perfection of degrees" which would not demand continual increase.[37] Thus, although Wesley's perfection was a present

---

[34] *Works*, XI, 396. It would be difficult to reconcile this concept of "involuntary transgression" with Wesley's own earlier criticism of a perfection which means only that a man does not willfully or habitually sin. (*Sermons*, II, 159.) Surely voluntary and involuntary transgression is what is meant by willingly and unwillingly sinning. For comment on the dangers of this definition of sin and Wesley's inconsistencies at this point see R. Newton Flew, *The Idea of Perfection in Christian Theology* (London: Oxford University Press, 1934), p. 327; Colin Williams, *John Wesley's Theology Today*, pp. 179-80).

[35] Williams, *John Wesley's Theology Today*, p. 168.

[36] *New Covenant*, p. 259 [CL, VI, 29].

[37] *Ibid.*, p. 215; *Sermons*, II, 156.

possibility, it still must improve or increase in love, just as Preston demanded a constant increase in love. Preston's concept of perfection, on the other hand, certainly allowed some sense of "present perfection" in his concentration on purity of intention or dedication present now in a believer. Both authors sought a very similar, if not identical, end product —a pure, perfect, or sound heart in the believer.

The following passage from Preston exemplifies how close their concepts were with respect to the essence of the perfected heart. As can be seen, Wesley cut the passage extensively but retained the core of the message. The passage vividly illustrates how Preston conceived what Wesley termed man's "corruptible infirmities" and their place in the life of the perfected man.

Now what is it to be pure? THAT IS PURE WHICH IS FULL OF ITSELF, AND HATH NO OTHER HETEROGENEALL THING MINGLED WITH IT; SO, that heart is *pure*, WHICH HATH NO SINNE IN IT, which is holy, WHICH HATH A RENEWED QUALITIE OF GRACE, WHICH HATH AN INWARD REGENERATE MAN, THAT [which] will mingle with no sin, THAT IS FULL OF ITSELFE, AND ADMITS NOT THE MIXTURE OF ANY SINNE. MY BELOVED, I MUST BE WARILY UNDERSTOOD HERE, I SAY, IT ADMITS NOT THE MIXTURE OF ANY SIN. It is true, sin may cleave, and adhere to a man, as drosse doth to the silver, BUT IT MINGLES NOT WITH THE REGENERATE PART, NOR THAT CONSTITUTION OF A MAN'S HEART, IT IS NOT WEAVED INTO THE TEXTURE OF HIS HEART; IT IS NO INGREDIENT INTO THE VERY FRAME, AND FABRICKE OF IT, but though sinne be here, yet the heart still casts it out of itselfe, it resists it, and rejects it, and purifieth and cleanseth itselfe from it, THIS PROPERLY IS A PURE HEART.[38]

John Peters suggests that the idea of love's expelling sin from the heart, so aptly stated here by Preston, is the most appropriate formulation used by Wesley to express the essence of his doctrine. In Wesley's words, "It is love excluding sin; love filling the heart, taking up the whole capacity of the soul." "For as long as love takes up the whole heart, what room is there for sin therein?" [39]

[38] *New Covenant*, p. 219 [CL, VI, 26-27]; *cf.* Alleine, *Vindiciae Pietatis*, p. 87.
[39] John Peters, *Christian Perfection and American Methodism*, pp. 58-59; *Sermons*, II, 448, 457.

Wesley's doctrine of perfection had many sources,[40] and it would be unrealistic to claim any real dependence upon Preston, but certainly there is a realistic affinity between the doctrine of perfection taught by the two men. The very least that can be said is that the doctrine was present in the Puritan tradition and Wesley was not only familiar with its formulation there but thought it significant enough to include one statement of it among his abridgments.

2. Sin and Repentance in Believers

While, in Wesley's understanding, perfection was the privilege of a few, the normal experience was sanctification through a gradual elimination of sin accompanied by growth in grace. Such growth can only take place when the believer is conscious of his own sin and in repentance is anxious, through grace, to overcome his sin.

Esteem for the Puritan emphasis on the reality of sin in believers and the necessity of repentance was in a large measure the result of Wesley's own conflict in the early 1740's with the Moravians in England. They taught that once a man was converted he was entirely sanctified, sin was no longer a threat to him, good works were not necessary, and the means of grace were irrelevant to salvation. Wesley's reaction to this form of antinomianism was to separate himself from the movement and to attempt to counteract such teaching by showing the reality of sin in believers and the necessity for their continued repentance. The conflict was similar to that which had occurred the century before when some of the more "radical" branches of the Puritan tradition had taught antinomian doctrines which were rejected and condemned by the majority of the Puritan divines. Those who in their writings fought antinomianism are commended by Wesley in this passage, which, though quoted before, is instructive for the present discussion.

They are continually tearing up the very roots of Antinomianism, by shewing at large, from the oracles of God, the absolute necessity, as of that legal repentance which is previous to faith, so of that evangelical repentance

---

[40] For his own description of these sources, see the early pages of *A Plain Account of Christian Perfection*, in *Works*, XI, 366-70. R. Newton Flew in his comprehensive work, *The Idea of Perfection in Christian Theology*, traces these sources through various traditions to the early church.

which follows it, and which is essential to that holiness, without which we cannot see the Lord.[41]

The expressions "legal repentance" and "evangelical repentance" (or "gospel repentance") used here were technical theological terms of the Puritan era. Robert Bolton defines legal repentance as that which is "a necessary preparative to the infusion of faith." [42] It is termed legal because it is the repentance to which one is driven when he becomes conscious of his abject sinfulness through the preaching of the law.

Evangelical repentance, according to John Owen, consists of "**godly sorrow for sin, WITH ITS RELINQUISHMENT, [and leaving of it] proceeding from faith, love, and abhorrency of sin, ON ACCOUNT OF FATHER, SON, AND SPIRIT, BOTH LAW, AND LOVE.**" [43] It is necessary for the continuation of a constant fellowship between the believer and God. Insistence upon the necessity of such evangelical or gospel repentance presupposes the reality of sin in the lives of believers.

Several of the titles of treatises included in *A Christian Library* suggest the general outlines of the Puritan treatment of this particular subject: *Of the Mortification of Sin in Believers: The Necessity, Nature and Means of It* and *The Nature, Power, Deceit, and Prevalency of the Remainders of Indwelling Sin in Believers* by John Owen; *A Rebuke to Backsliders: And a Spur for Loiterers* by Richard Alleine; and *A Gospel-Glass: Representing the Miscarriages of English Professors, or, A Call from Heaven, to Sinners and Saints, by Repentance and Reformation, to Prepare to Meet God* by Lewis Stuckley. This latter work states that "the great design of this publication is, to reduce *professors* to a more awful, humble, serious repentance towards God." [44]

---

[41] *CL*, IV, 107.

[42] Bolton, *On Self-Examination*, p. 59 [*CL*, V, 201]. Wesley does not use these technical terms in his own exposition but comments on this type of repentance as that "which is a conviction of our utter sinfulness, and guiltiness, and helplessness; and which precedes our receiving that kingdom of God, which our Lord observes, is 'within us.'" (*Sermons*, II, 380.)

[43] Owen, *On Communion*, p. 241 [*CL*, XI, 63].

[44] Lewis Stuckley, *A Gospel-Glass: Representing the Miscarriages of English Professors or A Call from Heaven, to Sinners and Saints, by Repentance And Reformation, to Prepare to Meet God* (London: R. Edwards, 1809), p. x [*CL*, XIX, 232]. Italics mine. Cited hereafter as *A Gospel-Glass*.

The nature of the sin which is found in believers is clearly stated by Wesley:

There does still *remain*, even in them that are justified, a *mind* which is in some measure *carnal;* . . . an *heart bent to back sliding*, still ever ready to "depart from the living God"; a propensity to pride, self-will, anger, revenge, love of the world, yea, and all evil: a root of bitterness, which, if the restraint were taken off for a moment, would instantly spring up; yea, such a depth of corruption, as, without clear light from God, we cannot possibly conceive.[45]

"Inward" sin is principally noted here, for Wesley assumes that the true believer will cast off outward sin, though he recognizes that the believer is nevertheless capable of relapsing into both inward and outward sin. The carnal mind, the genesis of man's sinful nature, is not eradicated from man upon justification but continues to produce sins which require continual recognition and repentance in order that one may "grow in grace."

Both Owen and Wesley base their concept of the "enmity" between natural man and God on Gal. 5:7, "the flesh lusteth against the spirit." This sin, for Owen, is not, as in Wesley, primarily inward but encompasses the whole spectrum. "**Nor are these lusts of the flesh only whereby men act their sensuality in riot, drunkenness, uncleanness, and the like; but they comprehend all the actings OF THE LOVE of sin whatever, in all the faculties and affections of the soul.**" [46] Owen's description of sin found in the believer is quite elaborate, showing how it "wars" against the grace present in the believer, setting itself in opposition to the general purpose of the soul; how it deceives the soul by drawing its attention away to worldly things; and how any success it has in this work causes it to grow and the grace found in man to diminish proportionately. The major consideration, nevertheless, is that the believer is constantly torn by the conflict of the flesh and the spirit, necessitating conscious acknowledgment of the reality of sin.[47]

[45] *Sermons*, II, 385; cf. 367 ff.
[46] *The Nature, Power, Deceit, and Prevalency of the Remainders of Indwelling Sin in Believers*, in Owen, *Works*, XIII, 45 [CL, X, 137].
[47] For extensive catalogs of sin in believers see *The Nature, Power, Deceit, and Prevalency of the Remainders of Indwelling Sin in Believers*, p. 45 [CL, X, 137], and Lewis Stuckley, *A Gospel-Glass*, pp. 4 ff. [CL, XIX, 239 ff.].

120

Sin in believers necessitates true repentance (evangelical repentance) for this sin: "a conviction of all this sin *remaining* in *their hearts* is the repentance which belongs to them that are justified," or "one kind of self-knowledge, the knowing ourselves sinners, yea, guilty, helpless sinners, even though we know we are children of God." [48] As this quote shows, Wesley, out of his struggle with the antinomians, seems to be so concerned with the recognition of the reality of this sin in believers that in his definition of repentance the stress falls on "conviction" or "self-knowledge" with no attention given to what Owen calls "a Godly sorrow for sin." Wesley evidently assumes that recognition and conviction will bring contrition, which in turn will allow God, through grace, to establish holiness. For Owen and the Puritans, repentance explicitly includes contrition, or in Robert Bolton's words, "to bewaile our sins from the bottome of our hearts," which naturally entails recognition.[49] Wesley's presentation no doubt better served his immediate purposes, but the Puritan emphasis on contrition rather than conviction is a truer definition of this repentance.

Bolton and Owen also regard the true believer as one who is more conscious of his sin than even the man who, convinced of his sin, is ready through repentance to enter into faith. Bolton affirms that once a person becomes a believer his eyes search further for his sins. "Comfort of remission must serve as a precious *Eye-salve,* both to cleare their sight, that they may see more, and with more detestation; and to enlarge their Sluices, as it were, to poure out repentant teares more plentifully." [50] Wesley's exposition of repentance as conviction of sins, which range from unprofitable conversation to sins of omission, is equally a stress upon the believer's increased awareness of his sin.

Several of the treatises which Wesley abridges give extended directions for the eradication of sin in believers. Among these directions for mortification, as outlined by Owen, are the recognition of the sin; conviction of one's guilt relative to this sin; repentance for the sin through consideration of the sin, particularly accompanied by meditation; and finally,

[48] *Sermons,* II, 385, 380.
[49] Bolton, *On Self-Examination,* p. 129 [*CL,* V, 218].
[50] Bolton, *Instructions for a Right Comforting of Afflicted Consciences* (London: Printed by Felix Kyngston for Thomas Weaver, 1631), p. 289 [*CL,* VI, 61].

121

through faith, dependence upon Christ's ability and willingness to relieve one from this sin.[51] Wesley's concentration in his sermons on the reality of sin in believers and the necessity of repentance did not lead him to specific directions, but his appreciation for these instructions prompted him to abridge them for his own followers.

Another similarity between the presentations of Wesley and the Puritans is the insistence that the regenerate are dependent in this repentance upon the work of grace through the Spirit, just as they were in their first repentance. As Wesley indicates, believers, for all of their newness and escape from their old lives, "are no more able now *of themselves* to think one good thought, to form one good desire, to speak one good word, or to do one good work, than before they were justified. . . . They can, it is certain, do all these things; but it is not by their own strength. . . . It is the *mere* gift of God: nor is it given all at once, as if they had a stock laid up for many years; but from moment to moment." [52] Owen, following his general pattern, clearly marks out this evangelical repentance with its resultant mortification of sin as the work of the Holy Spirit. The Spirit convinces, reveals Christ as the relief for this sin, and is the "author and finisher of our sanctification; gives new supplies in influences of grace for holiness AND SANCTIFICATION." [53]

Clearly a real affinity exists between Wesley and the Puritan tradition in their doctrines of sin and repentance in believing Christians. The affinity is indicated not only by Wesley's appreciation for the Puritan teaching and by the similarities between their respective teachings but also by his specific commendation and use of the Puritans in his own struggles against antinomianism.

3. Final Justification

The culmination of the "order of salvation" occurs, for Wesley, in what he calls "final justification." It has been shown that Wesley's doctrine of justification retained its Reformation character through its

---

[51] *The Mortification of Indwelling Sin in Believers*, in Owen, *Works*, VII, 425 ff. [*CL*, X, 116 ff.]; cf. Stuckley, *A Gospel-Glass*, pp. 367-83 [*CL*, XIX, 433-43]; Richard Alleine, *A Rebuke to Backsliders: And a Spur to Loiterers*, *CL*, XVIII, 306 ff.

[52] *Sermons*, II, 389.

[53] *The Mortification of Sin in Believers*, p. 429 [*CL*, X, 118]; cf. Alleine, *A Rebuke to Backsliders: And a Spur to Loiterers*, *CL*, XVIII, 321.

insistence upon faith; however, it differed from the Calvinistic formulations of his own day which contained antinomian tendencies by giving positive value and importance to a believer's obedience and works in the final salvation event. His attraction to Baxter's and Goodwin's statements on justification was precisely at this point, for they had interpreted obedience and works as necessary to final justification.

As Lindström has indicated in his summary of Wesley's development of the concept,[54] immediately after 1738 Wesley tends to deprecate any concept of a second or "final justification" which takes notice of obedience or good works as a condition. However, a justification which refers to "our acquittal at the last day" is noted early,[55] and in the antinomian controversies of 1740 and 1770-74 Wesley not only accepts such a concept, interpreted in his own way, but uses it as a chief weapon against his opponents. Even as early as 1744 he speaks of the justification that was spoken of by St. Paul and St. James as being two different justifications—one indicating justification by faith alone and the other justification at the point of judgment, which is made on the basis of "those works which spring from it [faith]." [56] In *A Farther Appeal to Men of Reason and Religion* (1745) he asserts:

With regard to the *condition* of salvation, it may be remembered that I allow, not only faith, but likewise holiness or universal obedience, to be the *ordinary condition* [italics mine] of final salvation; and that when I say, Faith alone is the condition of present salvation, what I would assert is this: (1) That without faith no man can be saved from his sins; can be either inwardly or outwardly holy. And (2) That at what time soever faith is given, holiness commences in the soul. From that instant "the love of God" (which is the source of holiness) "is shed abroad in the heart." [57]

It is clear from this passage that Wesley shared the Puritan insistence that by its very nature faith must produce works. "Works do not give life to faith, but *faith begets works,* and then is perfected by them." [58] Faith is present "together with" works in all cases.

[54] *Wesley and Sanctification,* pp. 205 ff.
[55] *Works,* VIII, 46.
[56] *Ibid.,* p. 277; cf. *Letters,* IV, 178-79.
[57] *Works,* VIII, 68-69.
[58] *Explanatory Notes,* pp. 862-63. (James 2:22); italics mine.

In the *Minutes* of the 1770 conference the stress upon works had become so strong in opposition to antinomianism that Wesley, though claiming salvation is not by "merit of works, but by works as a condition," could still wonder if it was not splitting a hair to question whether we are not saved "for the sake of our works." [59]

As an answer to the violent opposition which arose over these *Minutes* of 1770, the conference of the following year issued this statement:

Whereas the Doctrinal points in the Minutes of a Conference, held in London, August the 7th 1770, have been understood to favour Justification by Works: Now the Revd. John Wesley and others assembled in Conference, do declare, That we had no such meaning; and that we abhor the Doctrine of Justification by Works, as a most perilous and abominable Doctrine. And as the said Minutes are not sufficiently guarded in the way they are expressed, we hereby solemnly declare in the sight of God, that we have no trust or confidence but in the alone merits of our Lord and Saviour Jesus Christ, for Justification or Salvation, either in Life, Death, or the day of Judgment. And although no one is a real Christian believer (and consequently cannot be saved) who doth not good works, where there is time and opportunity, yet our Works have no part in meriting or purchasing our justification from first to last, either in whole or in part.[60]

Here Wesley clearly returns the doctrine to its Reformation base but just as clearly retains the stress upon the necessity of works. The phrase "where there is time and opportunity" indicates, however, the secondary, though necessary, role of works. Commenting on the final judgment in Matt. 12:37, Wesley says, "Your words as well as actions shall be produced in evidence for or against you, to *prove whether you was a true believer or not.*" [61] As John Deschner succinctly states it: "These works do not lay hold of eternal life; it is rather that the lack of them may cause God to withhold his grace." [62]

Lindström suggests that Wesley's distinction between "merit" and

[59] *Works*, VIII, 337-38; *Letters*, V, 264.

[60] *Journal*, V, 427. Wesley's insistence upon man's dependence on Christ's merit is best seen in his sermon "The Lord our Righteousness" (*Sermons*, II, 420-41).

[61] *Explanatory Notes*, p. 65 (Matthew 12:37), italics mine.

[62] *Wesley's Christology*, p. 179.

"condition" is made more precise by John Fletcher, Wesley's major ally in the struggle with the extreme Calvinists, when he defines final justification as one in which the believer is "justified by the evidence of works." [63] Here, as in Wesley's comment, it is not upon the merit but upon the witness of the works that final justification rests.

Wesley's early distinction between two justifications crystallizes into a concept of justification which insists, first, upon a present justification totally dependent upon faith in the righteousness and merit of Christ, and, second, upon a final justification incorporating the obedience, holiness, and good works which spring from that faith. Both are ultimately based on faith. As Deschner points out, it is through the avenue of final justification that Wesley brings to bear the concept of judgment. Whereas in present justification forgiveness and reconciliation are dominant, in final justification judgment is taken into full account.[64] In both justifications the central element is still Christ and his atoning work, for all works, no matter how they "evidence" a man's faith, are ultimately dependent on the grace of God offered to man in Christ. Held in tension, the two justifications recognize God's judgment as well as his mercy in Christ *and* man's wretchedness as well as his obedience gained through grace.

Is it possible to relate this insistence upon a twofold justification to the theories of justification present in Puritanism? David Shipley is convinced that "every element in Wesley's answer . . . to theoretical antinomianism, even to the precise detail of the concept of a double justification, had been set forth in the seventeenth century," that is, in English Presbyterianism.[65] Shipley locates the concept of double justification in the works of Richard Baxter and John Flavel (d. 1691).

[63] *Wesley and Sanctification*, p. 212. "Although from first to last, the merits of my life and death *purchase* or *deserve* thy justification; yet in the day of judgment thou shall be justified by thy works; that is, thy justification, which is purchased by my merits, will entirely turn upon the evidence of thy works, according to the time and opportunity thou hast to do them." (John Fletcher, *Checks to Antinomianism*, I, 107.)

[64] *Wesley's Christology*, pp. 178-79.

[65] "Wesley and Some Calvinistic Controversies," *The Drew Gateway*, XXV, 205. It should be noted that some forms of a double justification concept are found in Anglican circles. (See Deschner, *Wesley's Christology*, p. 188.) Wesley refers to such a distinction in Bishop George Bull's "Harmonica Apostolica." (*Letters*, V, 264.)

Baxter's *Aphorisms of Justification* contains a distinction of two elements in justification. Baxter, in his vivid phraseology, comments, "Justification is either 1. in Title or Sence of the Law, 2. or in Sentence of Judgment. The first may be called Constitutive; the second Declarative; the first Virtual, the second Actual." [66] By "Title of Law" he understands "justification as done in this life" which is "a gracious Act of God, by the promise or grant of the New Covenant, acquitting the offender from the Accusation and Condemnation of the Old Covenant, upon consideration of the Satisfaction made by Christ and accepted by the sinner." [67] Justification by "sentence of Judgment" is, however, a "future thing, not yet done" which is "a gracious Act of God by Christ, according to the Gospel, by sentence at his publique Bar, acquitting the sinner from the Accusation and Condemnation of the Law, . . . upon consideration of the satisfaction made by Christ, accepted by the sinner, and pleaded for him." [68] This justification at judgment, although a justification by faith, is nevertheless dependent upon the performance of the human conditions of the new covenant; therefore, "the Justification which we have in Christ's own Justification is but as to the particular offenders, and none can lay claim to it, till he have performed the conditions; nor shall any be personally justified till then." Consequently, "men that are but thus conditionally pardoned and justified, may be unpardoned and unjustified again for their non-performance of the conditions." [69] Justification is then "not a momentaneous Act; begun and ended immediately upon our Believing: but a continued Act; which though it be in its kind complete from the first, yet it is still doing, till the finall Justification at the Judgment day." [70]

The conditions of the covenant are not simply faith but the "necessary, immediate, inseparable products of Faith"—sincere obedience and

[66] *Aphorisms of Justification*, p. 183.
[67] *Ibid.*, p. 185.
[68] *Ibid.*, pp. 184, 188-89.
[69] *Ibid.*, p. 196.
[70] *Ibid.*, pp. 233, 194. Baxter outlines some ten "steps toward our final and full Justification," calling the sixth ("The change of our Relation upon our actual Faith") and the tenth ("Our final Justification at the Great Judgment") those which are "directly and properly the Justification by Faith." (*Ibid.*, p. 195.)

126

works of love.[71] Therefore, "Faith only doth not justify in opposition to the works of the Gospel; but those works do also justify as the secondary remote parts of the condition of the covenant." [72] Baxter's metaphor illuminates what he (and Wesley) is striving to convey. "Actual Obedience (as part of the Condition) doth . . . goe before our justification as continued and confirmed. For though our Marriage Contract with Christ doth give us the first possession, yet it is the Marriage faithfulness and duties, which must continue that possession." [73]

In Wesley's abridgment of the *Aphorisms*, "Justification in Title of Law" becomes simply "justification," and justification "by sentence of Judgment" becomes "final justification." Clearly, Wesley could closely identify his own concept of final justification with Baxter's justification at judgment. Baxter uses the phrase "finall justification" and Wesley is certainly not misrepresenting him by substituting it here.[74] Shipley may be correct when he claims that "Wesley's phrase 'final justification' is taken from Baxter" but there is little evidence to support his statement except that the phrase is found in the work of both men and that Wesley used Baxter's treatise.[75]

The attraction of Baxter's treatise for Wesley is obvious since they essentially agreed that (1) justification is not a "once for all" event but has two loci—present and final justification; (2) final justification, or the culmination of the justification process, comes at the judgment event; (3) in this final justification a believer's obedience and good works will

[71] *Ibid.*, p. 241; cf. pp. 235-36. Baxter's publication of the *Aphorisms* drew stinging attacks upon him which he attempted to answer in his work *Richard Baxter's Confession of Faith;* at least he hoped to clear up misunderstanding through this work. Here the distinctions between the justifications are reiterated, and obedience exemplified in works as a condition of final justification is ably defended. (See particularly pp. 47-55.)

[72] *Ibid.*, pp. 289-90. "To conclude: It is most clear in the Scripture, and beyond dispute, that our Actual, most proper, compleat Justification, at the great Judgment, will be according to our Works, and to what we have done in flesh, whether Good or Evil: which can be no otherwise than as it was the Condition of that Justification."

[73] *Ibid.*, p. 333. Richard Alleine's insistence upon faith *and* works as necessary for salvation is very close to this exposition, though Alleine does not propose a second justification. (*Vindiciae Pietatis*, pp. 90 ff.)

[74] *Aphorisms of Justification*, pp. 195, 233.

[75] Shipley, "Wesley and Some Calvinistic Controversies," p. 208. This statement of Shipley's is curiously incongruous with his concluding remarks that he has made no attempt "to prove that Wesley was in any way dependent upon or influenced directly by the English Presbyterians." (*Ibid.*, p. 210.)

count as a "secondary" condition, and consequently, man's moral responsibilities are integrally related to justification itself; (4) faith is nevertheless the ultimate foundation of both justification events; and (5) it is upon "the consideration of the satisfaction made by Christ" that both justifications depend. It is also significant that Wesley's own use of the term "final justification" really comes into prominence after the publication date of the abridgment (1745), although, as we have seen, the basic concept was present before this time. It would no doubt be going beyond the bounds of the evidence to claim that Wesley was directly dependent upon Baxter for his own concept—it is more likely that it was molded out of the necessities of his role in the antinomian controversy—but he certainly found here congenial and familiar concepts which he widely used.

It was noted above that Shipley finds the meaning of a continuing and final justification also in the thought of John Flavel,[76] but is it possible to find it in other Puritans? Fletcher thought so and devoted a generous section of his work *Checks to Antinomianism* to expounding the concept from the Puritan divines.[77] One would not expect to find here the esteemed John Owen, but indeed the following passage reveals how Fletcher used Owen in defense of his own position:

Suppose a person freely Justified by the Grace of God through Faith in the Blood of Christ, without respect unto any Works, Obedience, or Righteousness of his own: we do freely grant: (1) that God doth *indispensably require personal obedience of him,* which may be called his Evangelical Righteousness; (2) that God doth *approve* of, and accept in Christ this Righteousness so performed; (3) that hereby that Faith whereby we are justified is *evidenced,* proved, manifested, in the sight of God and men; . . . (5) that upon it, we shall be *declared Righteous* at the last day, and without it none shall be. And if any shall think meet from hence to conclude unto an *Evangelical Justification,* or call God's acceptance of our Righteousness by that name, I shall by no means contend with them. And wherever this inquiry is made, not how a sinner *guilty of death* and obnoxious unto the Curse, shall be pardoned, acquitted and justified, which is by the Righteousness of Christ alone imputed unto him; but how a man that professeth *Evangelical faith,* or Faith in Christ,

---

[76] *Ibid.,* pp. 209-10.
[77] *Checks to Antinomianism,* I, 276-93.

shall be tried, judged, and whereon as such he shall be justified, we grant that it is and must be by his own personal obedience.[78]

Fletcher correctly recognizes here a concept very close to his own, particularly as it stresses works as the *evidence* of the faith and as it allows at least a qualified (evangelical) justification of the believer based on obedience. Owen, looking at the professing believer, can affirm this, yet his fear of justification by works will not allow him to affirm that works have a place in justification; therefore, in the last chapter of this treatise he specifically denies a second justification.[79] On one hand, one must reject Owen as a Puritan precursor of Fletcher's and Wesley's doctrine but, on the other, it can be maintained that in the passage quoted Owen expresses much of the underlying content of what Wesley and Fletcher were trying to formulate. This, of course, can only be said in clear recognition that the bulk of Owen's argument stands against a twofold justification and is best understood as interpreting the same justification from differing perspectives.[80]

It is interesting to note the curious similarity between one of the objectives of Wesley's final justification and the Puritan doctrine of the

[78] John Owen, *The Doctrine of Justification by Faith Through the Imputation of the Righteousness of Christ, Explained, Confirmed, and Vindicated* (London: Printed for R. Boulter, 1677), pp. 222-23. Cf. John Preston, *The Breast Plate of Faith and Love*, Part II, p. 101 [CL, V, 382].

[79] *The Doctrine of Justification by Faith Through the Imputation of the Righteousness of Christ, Explained, Confirmed, and Vindicated*, p. 572. Owen, like Wesley after him, in discussing the reconciliation of Paul's and James's statements on works, points out that these two apostles, respectively, treat faith in two different senses. Paul interprets faith as "the means of our justification," while James interprets it as a description of a "dead" faith. He also allows that they treat justification in different senses—Paul in terms of an "absolute justification before God," James as the evidence or manifestation of this justification as is shown in true "professors" of the faith. Wesley makes this two justifications; Owen prefers to call it one. (*Ibid.*, pp. 557-82; cf. *Letters*, IV, 178-79; *Explanatory Notes*, p. 863 [James 2:24].)

[80] Isaac Ambrose in his work, *Practice of Sanctification*, recognizing that justification is not simply one event, distinguishes between initial, progressive, and perfective justification. Here Ambrose attempts to guard against the dangers inherent in a justification which has already taken place and cannot therefore be counted as operative in terms of our present sin. His progressive justification is then an attempt to apply the merits of Christ to forgiveness of daily sins. In the final day, one is finally perfectly justified. Such a present application corresponds to Wesley's insistence upon a "moment by moment" relationship to God, but does not attempt to take into account man's responsibility in terms of obedience. Ambrose was at least aware of the problems of a "once for all" justification and attempted to deal with them constructively. (*Works*, pp. 76-78 [CL, VIII, 3-5].)

"perseverance of the saints," which Wesley rejected on the basis of its incorporation of a Calvinistic concept of election. One aspect of final justification is its sustaining role in the life of the believer. The hope and promise of final justification, incorporating moral responsibility dependent on God's sustaining grace, is a bulwark against a believer's "falling away" from the faith. Viewed as a sustaining agency, the doctrine has the same objective as the doctrine of perseverance. Chapter XVII of the *Westminster Confession* assumes the continuing sustaining love of God as the basis of that perseverance which does not allow the elect to fall away from faith. The authors of this statement of the doctrine were, however, aware of its dangers and call specific attention to the moral responsibility of these elect and the possibility of their damaging sinfulness even within the framework of perseverance. Wesley would no doubt reject any suggestion of correlation between his concept of final justification and the doctrine of perseverance. He strenuously rejected all implications that man *could not* "fall from grace," which was a major and inherent tenet of the doctrine; therefore, he rejected the whole concept. Nevertheless, whether he would have recognized it or not, one aspect of *both* final justification *and* perseverance is to sustain the faithful by providing an assurance of grace and a bulwark against falling away from one's "first faith."

What may be said in evaluation of Wesley's concept of final justification? One must agree with John Deschner that Wesley's "doctrine of justification . . . must not be read as a considered, balanced piece of doctrinal instruction" but is probably best understood as "a journal of his theological pilgrimage." [81] Interpreted in this way, the questions which one may raise relative to the doctrine may be more congenially dealt with.

Deschner, speaking from the christological perspective, raises the question of whether insofar as Wesley fails to give full value to Christ's "imputed active obedience" he has not actually, in the doctrine of justification, strayed farther from Calvin than he thinks. [82] Deschner is

[81] *Wesley's Christology*, p. 180.

[82] "I think on Justification just as I have done any time these seven-and-twenty years, and just as Mr. Calvin does. In this respect I do not differ from him an hair's-breadth." (*Journal*, V, 116.)

convinced that Wesley in doing this fails to see the full significance of the active obedience of Christ in his priestly office, particularly as "we participate in Christ's active as well as passive righteousness through the Holy Spirit, in the Church." [83] In this Deschner may be correct, and if Wesley had recognized a more legitimate role for this active obedience, he might have avoided "breaking justification in two"; with Owen he would have avoided distinguishing between two justifications and only affirmed that one must be clear what person—sinner or professor of the faith—he is talking about when he speaks of justification. In other words, he could have claimed that he speaks of the same justification but viewed from differing perspectives. Wesley, of course, then would be Owen or Calvin and not Wesley, and we must evaluate him as he is and not as he might have been.[84] Actually, in the context of the antinomian controversy Wesley and Fletcher saw no alternative to subordinating Christ's active obedience, for, as they saw it, to do otherwise would be to vitiate any real "active obedience" or moral responsibility on man's part. Here their Arminian synergism plays an active role in determining their formulation just as it does in Baxter and Goodwin.[85]

The real question to be asked, however, is whether a doctrine of final justification does not, on the one hand, threaten the positive and continuing value of the initial justification, making it less than truly complete; and, on the other hand, does not a final justification which ultimately depends upon faith threaten the real necessity of works? Obviously, we can defend Wesley here by affirming with Deschner that this is not a balanced piece of doctrinal instruction and therefore has its problems and inconsistencies. We may also answer that, if the two

[83] *Wesley's Christology*, p. 183.

[84] One should not assume that Deschner fails to recognize this. He points out that for all its problems Wesley's doctrine of justification still lays particular stress on Christ's priestly work and, indeed, "Wesley is not Calvin here: Wesley is much more interesting simply as Wesley, even in his doctrine of justification."

[85] John Goodwin's work, *Imputatio Fidei, or a Treatise on Justification* (London: Printed by P. O. and G. D., 1642) is an extended examination of Christ's imputed righteousness in which he rejects the imputation of Christ's active obedience "performed to ye moral law." In this work he distinguishes between a constitutive and a declarative or pronunciative justification (pp. 111-12) which reminds one of Baxter's formulation. Goodwin intimates that the declarative justification, as an actual justification, must include the sense of Matt. 12:37 and James 2—that is, works are considered in the declarative justification. Nevertheless, there is little made of this distinction by Goodwin and it plays no major role in his argument.

justifications as presented by Wesley are held in dynamic tension, we gain both a Reformation doctrine of faith and a genuinely fruitful attempt to affirm that man has moral responsibility, whereas one without the other lacks an important truth.[86]

[86] Shipley quotes Fletcher to show this tension, "So work with that earnestness, constancy and unweariness in well doing, as if thy works alone were able to justify and save thee; and so absolutely depend and rely upon the merits of Christ for justification and salvation, as if thou never hadst performed one act of obedience in all thy life. . . . It is a difficult thing to give each of these its true due in our practice." (*The Works of John Fletcher,* II, 397.) Shipley can then comment that this is an "eminent example of the Wesleyan logical dialectic which holds in unresolved tension the antitheses which have no synthesis." ("Methodist Arminianism in the Theology of John Fletcher," pp. 267-68; cf. Wesley, *Works,* VII, 204-5.)

SUMMARY OF PART II
THEOLOGICAL FOUNDATIONS OF THE CHRISTIAN LIFE

Investigation of the theological bases of practical divinity has revealed some close affinities between Wesley's own theological position and that of representative theologians of the Puritan tradition.

First, as a practical and/or theological concern it is the common interest of Wesley and the Puritans in the "experimental" nature of religion which determines their major theological affinities. From this concern arises the emphasis upon the personal relationship between the believer and God epitomized in the insistence upon the possibility of a real "assurance" of salvation. Here also is the ground for the emphasis upon the disciplined, obedient life of faith worked out in sanctification and culminating in final salvation.

Second, Wesley's defense and use of Puritan expressions of the Protestant doctrine of original sin indicate his recognition of a theological affinity in this doctrine.

133

Third, Wesley is in concord with a primary tenet of the Puritan tradition in his insistence on "justification by faith" as the basis of Christian life. His implied identification of his own interpretation of that doctrine with that of the Arminian Puritans, Baxter and Goodwin, through publication of their works and through his high recommendation of them, marks a strong agreement with, if not dependence upon, a Puritan explication of this doctrine.

Fourth, if one is allowed to concentrate one's attention upon the joint affirmation by Wesley and the Puritans of the reality of the experience of assurance, without dismissing the real divergences and differences, it is possible to say that at this point the two traditions are most closely allied. Wesley's identification of his doctrine with that of the early Puritans shows his own recognition of this affinity. Identification does not necessarily entail dependence; yet identification does indicate a valid and real relationship. The motivating spirit and general understanding of the Christian life found in both movements may be identified with this reality of personal contact with God. Here they are at one.

Fifth, Wesley's use of covenant theology, although not identifying him with any particular Puritan divine unless the abridgment of Preston is considered to be such, certainly identifies him with an emphasis of the whole tradition. The use of a covenant in his own societies indicates the significance of this concept. His exposure to covenant theology in his family makes clear the Puritan ancestry of this important formulation; therefore, there can be little question of real dependence upon the Puritan tradition.

Sixth, although the Puritans and Wesley were not alone in their insistence upon an elaborate doctrine of sanctification, it still serves as a distinguishing mark of both traditions. Wesley's emphatic retention of faith as the basis of that sanctification draws him close to the Puritan interpretation and relates him to the specifically Protestant rather than "Catholic" understanding.

Seventh, Wesley's special appreciation for the Puritan formulation of the doctrine of sin in believers with its corollary, repentance in believers, and the similarities of his own presentation to that of the Puritans indicate concurrence between the two traditions at this point.

134

Eighth, Wesley had at least one Puritan precursor of his elaborated doctrine of "final justification" in the work of Richard Baxter. The strong affinity here is without question, in view of Wesley's use of Baxter's *Aphorisms*. The doctrine itself was essentially an attempt to formulate fruitfully the truth which the vast majority of the Puritan divines insisted upon, i.e., that the obedience and works of the true believer are necessary requirements of his life and will be considered in his final judgment.

This examination of the "order of salvation" which lies behind and is, at the same time, an actual part of the teachings concerning the Christian life reveals, then, these areas of close affinity and at least the possibility of real dependence.

Part III: THE CHRISTIAN LIFE

V

THE BEGINNINGS, SIGNIFICANCE, AND CHARACTER
OF THE CHRISTIAN LIFE

The Evangelical Revival of the eighteenth century, in its description of daily living, struck a responsive chord in the mind and heart of the common man, who in his more serious moments questioned his mode of living and saw in the Christian ideal hope for a better life, both here and hereafter. Much of the same appeal and a similar response had been the experience of the Puritan movement of the century before.

As a result, John Wesley's Methodism, like Puritanism, became known for its insistence upon a true, pure, consistent, and dynamically active life of love modeled after the life of Christ. Whether or not such a distinction was sought by either movement, it became the hallmark of both.

For this insistence both movements have been either praised or criticized, according to the prejudices of the commentator.[1]

Due to this special interest in the Christian life, the number and range of Puritan and Methodist materials available for comparison and analysis is phenomenal. An investigation of affinities, therefore, is confronted with the problem of selection. A full survey in this area would require a complete catalog and systematic analysis of teachings which touch practically every imaginable life situation. In order to limit the investigation and to examine relatively concrete instances of correspondence between the two traditions, representative teachings have been selected from three sources: (1) those in which Wesley related his own teachings to those of the Puritans through recommendation and use of their works or through inclusion of these teachings in *A Christian Library*; (2) those in which both movements display a peculiar interest or emphasis; (3) those in which Wesley, through his action or practice, relates himself to Puritan precepts or practice.

In order to keep before us Wesley's appreciation of the Puritan teachings relative to the Christian life, it is well to review once again his evaluation of that "peculiar excellency" of the Puritan divines: "[They] instruct us . . . how to use the faith which God has given, and to go from strength to strength. They lead us by the hand in the paths of righteousness, and shew us how, in the various circumstances of life, we may most surely and swiftly grow in grace, and in the knowledge of our Lord Jesus Christ." [2] As this passage indicates, the dominant interest for Wesley in all teachings relative to Christian living is that they ultimately lead one to a closer conformity to Christ. They must provide the climate for "growth in grace."

Instruction in Christian living, while describing the true Christian life, awakened interest in such a life. In addition it brought many nominal Christians to a conscious recognition that they not only failed

[1] A late eighteenth-century commentator identifies the two movements on the basis of the exactitude of their application of religion: "They who go now under the name of Methodists, were in the days of our forefathers called *Precisians,* terms of their own devising, importing that the bearers of them had carefully squared out their religion by line and level." (Quoted by T. E. Owen, *Methodism Unmasked: or the Progress of Puritanism* [London: Printed for J. Hatchard, 1802], p. ix.)
[2] *CL,* IV, 107-8.

to apply their faith to their lives but often failed to recognize the necessity for such application. The latter result was of particular significance to the Puritans and Wesley since most Englishmen considered themselves Christians by virtue of their baptism and membership in the national church—whether or not they practiced their religion. Instruction and challenge to accept conversion used in this way offered a real tool for work among the people, for it was equally applicable to those within and without the church.

One of Wesley's major attempts to provide instruction took place in his latter years. In January, 1782, Wesley and his able assistant, Thomas Coke, established a society for the distribution of reading materials among the poor at practically no cost to the reader. Wesley's object is seen in his comment upon the establishment of the society: "I cannot but earnestly recommend this to all those who desire to see true, scriptural Christianity spread throughout these nations. Men wholly unawakened will not take the pains to read the Bible. They have no relish for it. But a small tract may engage their attention for half-an-hour; and may, by the blessing of God, prepare them for going forward." [3] The plan was to subsidize the publication of various tracts containing "true, scriptural Christianity" and to distribute these almost free to the poor and to those "unconverted" or uninterested souls whom one might have opportunity to contact. [4]

Thirty tracts appeared in 1782 under the auspices of this society, on which were printed, according to Green, the words, "This book is not to be sold, but given away." [5] Wesley seemed quite pleased with the success of this new project. He comments later in that same year to Thomas Davenport:

Our little Society for dispersing religious books among the poor has now spread them through all England. Two of the books which they disperse are

[3] [H. R. O.], "Tract Societies," *The Wesleyan Methodist Magazine,* LXX (1847), 270.
[4] " 'A Plan of the Society, instituted in January, 1782, to Distribute Religious Tracts among the Poor.' 1. Every member must subscribe half-a-guinea, a guinea, or more, annually. 2. A proportionable quantity of tracts shall be delivered yearly to each subscriber, according to his subscription, and as nearly as possible at prime cost, and carriage paid. 3. Every subscriber shall have a right to chuse his own tracts, if he please: otherwise he will receive a proportionable variety of the whole" (*ibid.*).
[5] *Bibliography,* p. 217.

141

Alleyne's Alarm and *Baxter's Call to the Unconverted*. Any person that sub-scribes half a guinea or a guinea yearly will have four times as many books sent down as he could otherwise purchase with that sum. It seems this is one of the most excellent charities that we can be concerned in.[6]

Of the tracts which were distributed in this manner, twenty-one of the thirty tracts were Wesley's own sermons and tracts, all of which had previously been published in some form. These ranged from his sermon "The Almost Christian" to various "words" such as his "Word to a Drunkard." The other tracts included two contemporary sermons by Fletcher and Oliver; three tracts by Wesley's mentor, William Law, including his work, *A Serious Call to a Holy Life*; and four of Puritan vintage. Alleine's and Baxter's works are joined by Wesley's abridgment of *John Janeway's Life* and Janeway's *Token for Children*, which Wesley had published as early as 1749. In publishing these works Wesley was not only providing instruction but was printing his evangelism. The distinction of almost all these tracts is that they were designed to provide a witness to the Christian life for those who were not converted to that way of life. Even Janeway's *Token for Children* is an account of the conversion and holy lives of several children.

1. The Beginnings of the Christian Life

Neither Wesley nor the Puritans were original in the use of instruction, but the success of both their movements witnesses to the fact that they were masters in the art of its application. Our present concern is Wesley's use of some of the Puritan literature designed to bring a person, be he an avowed sinner or nominal Christian, to the beginnings of Christian life—to conversion.

As indicated above, Wesley found two Puritan works of special value: Joseph Alleine's *An Alarm to Unconverted Sinners* and Richard Baxter's *A Call to the Unconverted*.[7] Alleine's work, published in 1672, was widely acclaimed and cherished. Edmund Calamy indicates that twenty thousand copies of the tract were sold in this first edition and fifty

[6] *Letters*, VII, 155.

[7] These works are used as representative Puritan treatments of this topic although several other treatises included in Wesley's *Library* quite adequately deal with this subject: Robert Bolton's *On Self-Examination*; Hugh Binning's *Fellowship with God*; Richard Alleine's *Vindiciae Pietatis*; Isaac Ambrose' *The Doctrine of Regeneration*; and Lewis Stuckley's *A Gospel-Glass*.

thousand more three years later under the title *The Sure Guide to Heaven.*[8] Whether these figures are accurate or not, the work was, without question, extremely popular well into the nineteenth century. Wesley not only included this work in *A Christian Library,* but he also used it as a source of his covenant service. In addition, he seems to have made use of the work in instructing the societies, particularly in their preparation for covenanting, for his *Journal* entry of April 13, 1757, records: "On *Good-Friday,* in the evening, at the meeting of the society, God was eminently present with us. I read over and enlarged upon Joseph Alleine's *Directions for a Thorough Conversion to God,* and desired all who were able would meet me on Monday that we might 'perform our vows to the Lord.' "[9] He also recommends the version included in the *Library,* along with Richard Alleine's *Vindiciae Pietatis,* to Samuel Furly for a good example of instruction in Christian piety.[10] These references testify that the work was one of those which Wesley regularly used as instructive material for his own people. As we have seen, a quarter of a century later the tract again comes into prominence among the Methodists when it is one of those published by Wesley through his tract society.

The work by Baxter is the only one of the thirty which seems specifically to have been abridged by Wesley for his series of tracts, although the abridgment of Alleine is a new one and not a reprint of that included in the *Library.* Baxter's work, *A Call to the Unconverted,* was first printed in 1657, and, like Alleine's *Alarm,* enjoyed renown as one of the most significant Puritan writings. In fact, Baxter himself in late life comments that this work had enjoyed "unexpected success, beyond all the rest that I have written, except *The Saints' Rest.*"[11]

[8] Edmund Calamy, *The Nonconformist's Memorial,* II, 319.

[9] *Journal,* IV, 200. This reference to "Directions for a Thorough Conversion to God" is a reference to one of the chapters in Alleine's tract.

[10] *Letters,* III, 207.

[11] He continues, "In a little more than a year there were twenty thousand printed by my own consent, and about ten thousand since, besides many thousands by stolen impressions, which poor men stole for lucre's sake. Through God's mercy, I have information of almost whole households converted by this small book, which I set so light by: and as if all this in England, Scotland, and Ireland, were not mercy enough to me God (since I was silenced) hath sent it over in his message to many beyond the seas; for when Mr. Elliot had printed all the Bible in the Indian language, he next translated this my *Call to the Unconverted,* as he wrote to us

The similarity of these two treatises is obvious even from their titles. They were both originally addressed to the congregations which these men served and were, no doubt, sermons before being printed. The printed tracts, while designed for a wider audience, retain the sermonic intimacy. Baxter makes clear how he hopes his treatise will be used: "The use this Part is published for, is 1. For Masters and Parents to read often in their Families, if they have servants or children as yet unconverted. 2. For all such unconverted persons to read and consider themselves. 3. For the richer sort, that have any pitty on such miserable souls, to give to the unsanctified that need them: (if they have not fitter at hand to use and give.)" [12]

That the tract is primarily designed to challenge those not yet in the community of the faithful is clear; yet the whole text of the treatise cries out to the lackadaisical Christian to recognize his true state. It is the latter who most concern Alleine, for in his words, "The numbers of unconverted Souls among you call for my most earnest Compassions and hasty Diligence to pluck them out of burning." [13]

In order to establish clearly to whom they are addressing themselves, both Baxter and Alleine incorporate descriptions of the unconverted. Obviously, those who live in open sin, i.e., the drunkards, the thieves, the openly covetous, etc., are unconverted; yet many who assume that they are converted testify through their lives to the falsity of their assumption. Such a person is one who, though not living in outward evil, is inclined to self, making the "principal business of his life to prosper in the world." [14] Religion which is used to one's own ends is no religion

here. And yet God would make some further use of it, for Mr. Stoop, the pastor of the French Church in London, being driven hence by the displeasure of superiors, was pleased to translate it into French; I hope it will not be unprofitable there; nor in Germany, where it is printed in Dutch." (Richard Baxter, *A Call to the Unconverted* [Paris, Ky.: Printed by John Lyle, 1815], p. iv.)

[12] Baxter, *A Call to the Unconverted* (London: Printed by R. W. for N. Simmons, 1669), introduction; cited hereafter as *Call*. [Wesley's Abridgment: 2nd ed.; Dublin: Printed by R. Napper, 1795.]

[13] Joseph Alleine, *An Alarm to Unconverted Sinners* (London: Printed by Nevil Simmons, 1672), p. 1; cited hereafter as *Alarm*. [Wesley's Abridgment: 2nd ed.; Dublin: Printed by R. Napper, 1794.]

[14] *Call*, pp. 31-35 [W.A., pp. 14-16]. W.A. in the bracketed references indicates Wesley's abridgment of the treatise.

at all.[15] The formality of religious practice should not deceive one:

Friends and Brethren, *be not deceived, God is not mocked*, Gal. vi. 7. Whether it be your Baptism, or whatever else you pretend, I tell you, from the Living God, that, if any of you be prayerless Persons, or unclean, or malicious, or covetous, or riotous, or a Scoffer, or a Lover of evil Company, (PROV. XIII. 20) in a word, if you are not holy, strict, and self-denying Christians, (HEB. XII. 4 MATT. XVI. 24) you cannot be saved, EXCEPT YOU BE TRANSFORMED BY A FARTHER WORK UPON YOU, AND RENEWED AGAIN BY REPENTENCE.[16]

In Alleine's doctrinal description of the unconverted, the Puritan definition is quite clear: "Regeneration and remission are never separated: the unsanctified are unquestionably unjustified, and unpardoned." [17]

Having established the nature of the unconverted, our authors then define conversion. Alleine succinctly defines it as "the thorow change both of the heart, and life." [18] **"He saith it must be a total change, and you must be holy, and new creatures, AND BORN AGAIN; and you think that it is enough to patch up the old man, without becoming new."** [19] The converted man will have a new direction to his life—his mind, his will, his affections, fears, joy, love, sorrows, every aspect of his life is now turned in a new direction. He desires "nothing in all the world so much as that Christ may be magnified in him." [20]

Using the fear of eternal damnation and the promise of new life, as well as contrasting God's judgment with his mercy and compassion, both Alleine and Baxter appeal to the emotion and the reason of their congregations and readers. Baxter is sure that "God taketh Pleasure in Men's Conversion and Salvation, but not in their Death or Damnation: he had rather they would Return and Live, than go on and die." [21] Therefore, God promises, commands, admonishes, and reasons with man in order

---

[15] "When they have so much as will save them, (as they suppose,) they will look no farther, and so shew themselves short of true Grace, which will ever put men upon aspiring to further perfection." (*Alarm*, p. 97 [W.A., p. 70].)

[16] *Alarm*, p. 12 [W.A., p. 29].

[17] *Alarm*, p. 122 [W.A., p. 82]; cf. Isaac Ambrose, *The Practice of Sanctification*, in Ambrose, *Works*, p. 79 [*CL*, VIII, 7].

[18] *Alarm*, p. 19 [W.A., p. 32].

[19] *Call*, p. 135 [W.A., p. 46].

[20] *Alarm*, p. 30 [W.A., p. 37].

[21] *Call*, p. 69 [W.A., p. 28].

to convince him to accept conversion. Alleine, although concentrating more on the miseries and danger of the man who refuses to accept conversion ("Turn or burn"),[22] also stresses the joy of God over one who accepts conversion.

Baxter contributes a helpful section answering typical objections of the common man to the gospel message, such as: all men are sinners; therefore, why should I endeavor to live a holy life; "we will have a store of company" in hell; "professors are not any better than other men"; we are not gross sinners; "you would make men mad under the pretense of converting them"; you make "too much ado" about religion, etc.[23] Although Wesley omitted some of these from his abridgment, he included the most important and very likely recommended these to his societies as answers to those who would ridicule them.

Probably the most important sections of both these treatises for Wesley, outside of their attempt to convince the unconverted of their condition, were the ones containing directions for those who would seek the blessedness of the Christian life through conversion. Baxter's directions, with which one may assume Alleine was familiar, were written a decade before Alleine's and are incorporated almost in their entirety in this later work with some additions and revisions in the order of presentation. Beginning with a caution to recognize the nature and necessity of conversion, Baxter's directions laid out a plan which, through serious meditation, prayer, and study of the Word, will bring one to renounce all sin. A person is then able to deliver himself, through Christ, to God and give himself "unreservedly, absolutely, and universally" to him. This should be done without delay and should be accompanied by the rejection of evil company who would no doubt endanger the keeping of such firm resolutions.[24] Alleine's presentation provides greatly expanded comment upon each direction and his additions are principally in the recognition of one's state and in pointing out that the laws of holiness are accepted willingly by one who experiences conversion. His most important addition is, of course, the form of covenant by which one ob-

[22] *Alarm*, p. 81 [W.A., p. 63]; Baxter uses the same phrase, *Call*, p. 186 [W.A., p. 58].
[23] *Call*, pp. 144-54 [W.A., pp. 49-51].
[24] *Call*, pp. 224-37 [W.A., pp. 67-72].

jectively binds oneself to God after his conversion.[25] Wesley's abridgments of the respective treatises retain the entire set of directions with the usual abbreviation of hortatory material and of what he evidently considered to be unnecessary expansion of particular points.

The attraction of these treatises for Wesley lay in (1) their clear and precise appeal to all, churched and unchurched, to recognize the absolute necessity of a changed and holy life, (2) their description of both the converted and the unconverted, and (3) their method of direction by which a person offers himself to God in order that the Holy Spirit, acting with his spirit, might be able to effect the change. They were ideally suited for the purpose of preparing a person for the Christian message and then presenting it to him in such a way that he might begin the Christian life.

Wesley's own presentation of the gospel to the uncommitted, or the falsely committed, is distinguished from these treatises in the emphasis placed upon the various elements. For instance, in his writings there is little of the description of the fiery torments of hell spelled out so vividly by Alleine[26] and more emphasis upon the promises of the blessedness of salvation, particularly as they relate to this life.[27] Furthermore, Wesley is perhaps somewhat more successful in holding in balance the emphasis upon inward holiness with that upon outward manifestations.[28]

All these authors, including Wesley, were faced with the dilemma of how one is to insist upon inward holiness as the real criterion of Christian conversion, while in reality one can only judge the outward actions of another and must infer from these the inward condition. As a result, although stress may be placed on the necessity of a change in the heart, the criterion by which one is to distinguish the unconverted

[25] *Alarm*, pp. 136-77 [W.A., pp. 89-107]. His advice given to the one who would join in the covenant indicates how he thought it should be used: "This Covenant I advise you to make, not only in Heart, but in Word; not only in Word, but in Writing; and that you would, with all possible Reverence, spread the Writing before the Lord, as if you would present it to him as your act and deed; and, when you have done this, set your hand to it, keep it as a Memorial of the Solemn Transactions that have passed between God and you, that you may have recourse to it in Doubts, and Temptations." (*Ibid.*, p. 170 [W.A., p. 104].)

[26] See Alleine's section titled "The Furnace of Eternal Vengeance is heated ready for thee," *Alarm*, p. 128 [W.A., p. 83].

[27] *Sermons*, I, 300.

[28] *Ibid.*, pp. 304-7; p. 390.

man from the converted is by how he acts. If one is to judge a congregation and evaluate most of its members as unconverted, as both Baxter
and Alleine continually do, one makes this judgment upon the basis of
outward manifestations. Therefore, the description of the unconverted
and the admonitions found in Baxter and Alleine appear to stress outward manifestations, even though this may not have been their intention.
Wesley is far from escaping the same charge but seems to have made a
more conscious effort to guard against the dangers inherent in this situation.[29] Finally, and perhaps this is simply a matter of the changes in
preaching styles over the century that had intervened between his time
and that of the Puritans, Wesley does not use the long and involved discourses found in Baxter and Alleine which plead with the people to accept the faith.[30] Wesley admonishes and advises one to examine himself
and accept the gospel but not with the same verboseness or pleading
fervor found in these Puritan authors.

2. The Significance and Character
of the Christian Life

Direction and Destiny

The most famous and succinct Puritan statement of man's purpose is
found in the Westminster *Shorter Catechism*: "Man's chief end is to
glorify God and enjoy him forever." Such glorification and enjoyment
of God is not, however, only a future heavenly event. It is presently
exemplified in how one lives—in a Christian life. Both the present direction of a believer's life and his ultimate destiny are bound up in the
glorification of God.

Such glorification springs from faith. Neither the Puritans nor Wesley
were interested in instruction in Christian living simply on moral
grounds. This would have been merely seeking a better or more congenial life for man in the world. The Christian life is rather, as we have

[29] Wesley's sermon on the dangers of judging others shows his concern that one be careful
in this area. *Ibid.*, pp. 517-31.
[30] For discussion of the changes in preaching styles and interests in the period, see Charles
Smyth, *The Art of Preaching* (London: SPCK, 1953); E. C. Dargan, *The History of Preaching*
(2 vols.; London: Hodder and Stoughton, 1905), II; F. R. Webber, *A History of Preaching in
Britain and America* (3 vols.; Milwaukee: Northwest Publishing House, 1952), I.

seen repeatedly in this study, the product of true faith in Jesus Christ. Such faith establishes a genuine and living relationship between God and a believer. This relationship, of its very nature, issues forth in an active life of obedience and love—love directed both to God and the neighbor and consequently away from self. Seen from this perspective, the purpose and aim of the Christian life is to carry into one's daily life the intimate personal relationship which exists between God and the believer, and thereby to glorify him.

There is, however, another perspective from which the direction and destiny of Christian life may be viewed. A Christian life is also the way one must live in order to enjoy the promised salvation both now and in the future life. Although faith, in Puritan thought as well as Wesley's, is the sole condition of the covenant which leads to salvation, the Christian life of love and good works is a secondary part of this very condition. This should not be interpreted to mean the reinstitution of salvation by works, since the sanctified Christian life is still dependent upon faith and God's grace both for its inception and its continuation. Nevertheless, the direction and destiny of Christian life presented in this manner shifts the emphasis to that salvation which such a life will bring to the believer. The purpose of a Christian life may, then, be viewed from two different, though complementary, perspectives: (1) it is a life which, in free response to God's mercy and love, is lived for his glorification and (2) it is a life which a person lives in order to sustain his own salvation.

Although the Puritan treatises Wesley incorporates in *A Christian Library* include both perspectives, the latter predominates. With proper reservations against understanding it as a new salvation by works, Bolton's presentation of the direction and destiny of a Christian life of obedience and love is quite clear.

There is no greater encouragement, or stronger motive to STIRRE [excite] a man to an eager and earnest pursuite of the meanes, than to propose unto him an end wherein at length his heart may repose; as in a concurrence of all comforts and contentments. To which, there is no possibility of attainment, but by purenesse of heart, holinesse of life, constancie in course of sanctification, which onely leade unto the face, and presence of God; where, and with whom alone is the highest per-

fection of blisse, a river of infinite pleasures, the well of life, and end-
less rest of all created desires.[31]

Thomas Manton's formulation is in the same vein:

The gospel is not a naked, unconditionate offer of pardon and eternal
life in favour of sinners, but upon most convenient terms, for the
glory of God, and the good of men, and enforced by the strongest obligations upon them TO RECEIVE HUMBLY AND THANKFULLY THESE
BENEFITS. The promises are attended with commands to repent, believe,
and persevere in the uniform practice of obedience. . . . His [Christ's]
end was to enable and induce us to return to God, as our rightful Lord
and proper felicity, from whom we rebelliously and miserably fell by
our disobedience, in seeking for happiness out of him. Accordingly the
gospel is called "the law of faith" as it commands those duties upon
the motives of eternal hopes and fears.[32]

Richard Baxter holds together both understandings of the direction
and destiny of Christian life; yet, as this passage from *The Saints' Everlasting Rest* indicates, the emphasis falls on the necessity of such a life
for salvation.

I call a Christian's happiness the end of his course, thereby meaning, as
Paul, (2 Tim. iv. 8,) the whole scope of his life. For salvation may, and
must be, our end, so not only the end of our faith, though that principally, but of all our actions; for as whatsover we do, must be done
to the glory of God, WHETHER EATING, DRINKING, ETC., so must they all
be done to our salvation. THAT WE MAY BELIEVE FOR SALVATION, SOME WILL
GRANT, WHO YET DENY THAT WE MAY DO, OR OBEY FOR IT.[33]

Such a presentation provided the ground of charges that the Puritans had
reinstituted legalism. Baxter, speaking against the charge that "to make
salvation the end of duty, is to be a legalist," defends this presentation of

[31] Robert Bolton, *A Discourse About the State of True Happiness* (London: Printed by
Felix Kyngston for Thomas Weaver, 1631), p. 1 [*CL*, IV, 243]; cited hereafter as *True Happiness*.
[32] Thomas Manton, *Twenty Sermons*, in *The Works of Thomas Manton* (22 vols.; London:
James Nisbet and Co., 1871), II, 175-76 [*CL*, VII, 166].
[33] *The Saints' Everlasting Rest*, in Baxter, *Works*, XXII, 36 [*CL*, XXII, 11-12].

the aim of Christian life by insisting that duty is a necessary element in man's participation in the salvation process.[34]

Even though Baxter admits that the text of his discourse (Heb. 4:9)[35] may refer to the rest (salvation) that one enjoys in this life as well as the "rest of eternal glory," [36] he insists that one must consider the future rest toward which his life is moving to be "the very first stone in the foundation of religion." For the Puritans Christian life is most advantageously presented as that crowning glory—eternal salvation—be it defined as true happiness, everlasting rest, or "seeing God." [37]

Wesley shared with the Puritans both interpretations as to the direction and destiny of the Christian life. His comment on I Corinthians clearly states the understanding of Christian life as glorification of God.

Devote and employ all ye have, and all ye are, entirely unreservedly and forever, to His glory.

In all things whatsoever, whether of a religious or civil nature, in all the common, as well as sacred, actions of life, keep the glory of God in view, and steadily pursue in all this one end of your being, the planting or advancing the vital knowledge and love of God, first in your own soul, then in all mankind.[38]

Wesley, like the Puritans, however, tends to express the purpose of Christian life in terms of its obligation and necessity to salvation.[39] A

---

[34] "It is not a note of a legalist neither; it hath been the ground of a multitude of late mistakes in divinity, to think that 'Do this and live,' is only the language of the covenant of works. It is true, in some sense it is; but in other, not: The law of works only saith, 'Do this,' that is, perfectly fulfil the whole law, 'and live,' that is, for so doing: but the law of grace saith, 'Do this and live' too; that is, believe in Christ, seek him, obey him sincerely, as thy Lord and King; forsake all, suffer all things, and overcome; and by so doing, or in so doing, AS THE CONDITIONS WHICH THE GOSPEL PROPOUNDS FOR SALVATION, you shall live. . . . In a word, you must both use and trust duty in subordination to Christ, but neither use them nor trust them in co-ordination with him." (*Ibid.*, pp. 32-33 [*CL*, XXII, 9-10].)

[35] "There remaineth, therefore, a rest for the people of God."

[36] *The Saints' Everlasting Rest*, in Baxter, *Works*, XXII, 20.

[37] Bolton, in the passage above, incorporates the concept of the "vision of God" which was a common expression of the nature of salvation for both the Puritans and Wesley. For a detailed study of the development and importance of this classical medieval view of Augustine and Aquinas, see K. E. Kirk's *The Vision of God* (London: Longman, Green, and Co., 1931).

[38] *Explanatory Notes*, pp. 602-3 (I Cor. 6:20); p. 617 (I Cor. 10:31).

[39] *Sermons*, II, 454, 458-59.

Christian life of love and good works is a secondary, "remote" condition of salvation; therefore, such a life is to be lived in order to sustain salvation.

"Without holiness no man shall see the Lord," shall see the face of God in glory. . . . No, it cannot be done; none shall live with God, but he that now lives to God; none shall enjoy the glory of God in heaven, but he that bears the image of God on earth; none that is not saved from sin here can be saved from hell hereafter; none can see the kingdom of God above, unless the kingdom of God be in him below.[40]

Wesley makes a conscious effort to hold the present and future salvation together. "It is not something at a distance: it is a present thing; a blessing which, through the free mercy of God, ye are now in possession of." Salvation may, then, be extended "to the entire work of God, from the first dawning of grace in the soul, till it is consummated in glory." [41] This concept of salvation as including both present and future life allows a full recognition of the aim of Christian life to be a present and future fulfillment of faith. Nevertheless, Christian living, in its present manifestations, is directed toward the ultimate relationship of a believer to God revealed in Christ, and Wesley's presentation never loses this understanding.

Wesley's inclusion of the Puritan formulations, properly edited, indicates his approval of their presentations, and these passages from his own works show that he is in essential agreement with their understanding of the direction and destiny of Christian life. Neither the perspective of present and future reward nor that of the glorification of God excludes the other. They are simply different facets of one object, the Christian life—the central concern for Wesley and the Puritans. Wesley vividly expresses this concern in his description of the rise of the Methodist movement:

In 1729, two young men, reading the Bible, saw they could not be saved without holiness, followed after it, and incited others so to do. In 1739 they

[40] *Works*, X, 364.
[41] *Sermons*, II, 445; cf. *Explanatory Notes*, p. 22 (Matt. 3:2).

saw holiness comes by faith. They saw likewise, that men are justified before they are sanctified; *but still holiness was their point.* God then thrust them out, utterly against their will, to raise a holy people.[42]

Holiness as Its Design

Whatever the direction and destiny of the Christian life, its character is holiness (as expressed in Wesley's statement) or godliness—conformity to the love of God expressed in Jesus Christ throughout every aspect of a man's personal and social life. Puritan works found in the *Library* ably substantiate such a characterization.

For the Puritans and Wesley true religion is threatened by a life unproductive of love and good works. On the one hand, the threat is intellectual acceptance of and acquiescence in the truths of the Christian gospel which fail to relate these truths to one's daily actions; as one writer says, "Religion is a *truth 'according to godliness,'* not according to *speculation* only, and *notion.* Wheresoever these fundamental truths are embraced, there is godliness with them; a man cannot embrace religion in truth, but he must be godly." [43] On the other hand, the threat comes from the hypocrite who carries on the outward forms of true religion, living an upright moral life graced with performance of outward religious duties, but who does this not from an inward motivation of true relationship to God but for his own selfish ends.[44] To these may be added the antinomian danger of interpreting faith as freeing one from the obligations of good works and moral law. Any of these misinterpretations of true Christian life threaten the vitality of present religion as well as its ultimate object.

O study to get the image and impress of Christ upon you within. Begin with your hearts, else you build without foundation. Labour to get a saving change

---

[42] *Works,* VIII, 300 (italics mine). Joseph Alleine states the same sentiment: "He [the Christian] pitches upon God his blessedness, and upon Christ as the principal, and holiness as the subordinate means, to bring him to God." (*Alarm,* p. 30 [W.A., p. 37].)

[43] Richard Sibbes, *A Fountain Opened,* in Sibbes, *Works,* V, 461 [*CL,* VI, 56]; cf. Isaac Ambrose, *Looking Unto Jesus,* in Ambrose, *Works,* pp. 144-46 [*CL,* VIII, 102-4].

[44] Robert Bolton indicates that there is a "Formall Hypocrit" who deceives even himself since in times of trial or suffering he quite honestly pledges to live a true Christian life but fails to carry this out when the spiritual affliction has passed. (Bolton, *Instructions for a Right Comforting of Afflicted Consciences* [London: Printed by F. Kyngston for T. Weaver, 1631], p. 290 [*CL,* V, 62]; Bolton, *True Happiness,* pp. 67 ff. [*CL,* IV, 278 ff.].)

within, or all external performances will be to no purpose. And then study to show forth the power of godliness in your life. Let piety be your first and great business. . . .

But piety without charity is but half of Christianity, or rather impious hypocracy. We may not divide the tables. See therefore that you do justly, and love mercy; and let Equity and Charity run like an even thread throughout all your dealings.[45]

Alleine here makes clear the necessity of carefully examining both the inward and the outward manifestations of religion. These inward and outward aspects of the Christian life, distinguished but not separated, constitute the foci of the Puritan treatment of the Christian life. To promulgate specific instructions is to expand on one or the other of these aspects of life.[46] Wesley's approach is essentially the same with a constant insistence upon the joint nature of the two aspects.[47]

What, then, is the character of these elements? Part of it has, of course, been indicated. Alleine's call for a believer to seek "to get the image and impress of Christ upon you within" gives some definition of the inward holiness (and is much the same as Wesley's formulation).[48] In Sibbes's phrase, it is "the inward bent of the soul."[49] The love of God permeating all the interests, affections, and "tempers" of the person is regarded as inward holiness. For Wesley such inward holiness constitutes the immediate fruits of new birth when God's love begins to expel "the love of the world, the love of pleasure, of ease, of honour, of money, together with pride, anger, self-will, and every other evil temper; in a word,

---

[45] Joseph Alleine, "A Counsel for Personal and Family Godliness," in *Christian Letters* (London: Printed by J. Darby for N. Simons, 1672), pp. 113-14 [*CL*, XIV, 173-74] "If thou have respect onely to the Commandments of the first table, and outward performance of religious services; but neglect duties of the second, AND CONSCIONABLE CARRIAGE TO THY BRETHREN; Thou art but a Pharisie, and formall Professor: If thou dealest justly with thy neighbor, and yet bee a stranger to the mystery of godliness, CANST NOT PRAY, SANCTIFIE THE LORDS DAY, SUBMIT TO A SINCERE AND SEARCHING MINISTRIE, ETC. WHICH THE FIRST TABLE ENJOYNES; Thou art but a meere civill man." (Bolton, *Walking with God*, p. 22 [*CL*, IV, 334].)

[46] Hugh Binning, *Fellowship with God*, in *The Works of Hugh Binning* (London: A. Fullarton and Co., 1851), p. 307 [*CL*, XVII, 54]; Thomas Manton, *Twenty Sermons*, in Manton, *Works*, II, 238 [*CL*, VII, 234]. Samuel Shaw, *Immanuel: or a Discovery of True Religion* (Glasgow: Printed by R. Urio, 1749), p. 68 [*CL*, XIV, 296-97].

[47] *Sermons*, I, 378, 449.

[48] *Ibid.*, II, 446.

[49] Richard Sibbes, *A Fountain Opened*, in Sibbes, *Works*, V, 460 [*CL*, VI, 55].

changing the earthly, sensual, devilish mind, into 'the mind which was in Christ Jesus.' " [50]

Outward holiness consists of all that a person does and is in relationship to the world but particularly to his fellowman. Here is included all religious, political, occupational, and social relationships which make up life. Outward holiness is to act in all these situations out of love and in obedience to God's commands. Bishop Hall ably sums up both the inward and outward holiness in his comment on good works, which, though not all inclusive, is indicative of the directions of a holy life.

The fruits of faith are good works: whether inward, within the roof of the heart, as love, awe, sorrow, pity, zeal, joy, and the rest; or outwards towards God, or our brethren: obedience and service, to the one; to the other, relief and beneficence. These he bears, in his time: sometimes, all; but, always, some.[51]

The outward works noted here correspond roughly to Wesley's own distinction between "works of piety" and "works of mercy." [52]

The character of a Christian life, while most appropriately defined in terms of inward and outward holiness, derives from the relationship one has with God. Wesley's attraction to the works of Samuel Shaw is not far to be sought, for Shaw's treatise on *Communion with God* is an elaborate treatment of the communion and fellowship with God which stand behind all true religion.

RIGHT [real] fellowship with God is a communion of hearts and natures, of will and affections, of interests and end: to have one heart and will, the same interest and ends with God, is to be truly godly; a God-like man is the only godly man: a Christ-like nature brought into the soul

---

[50] *Sermons*, II, 446. Cf. Robert Bolton, *Walking with God*, pp. 58-59 [CL, IV, 342-43].

[51] Joseph Hall, "Letter to My Lady Mary Denny," in Hall, *Works*, VII, 234 [CL, IV, 195].

[52] "Works of piety; such as public prayer, family prayer, and praying in our closet; receiving the supper of the Lord; searching the Scriptures, by hearing, reading, meditating; and using such a measure of fasting or abstinence as our bodily health allows. . . . Works of mercy; whether they relate to the bodies or souls of men; such as feeding the hungry, clothing the naked, entertaining the stranger, visiting those that are in prison, or sick, or variously afflicted; such as the endeavouring to instruct the ignorant, to awaken the stupid sinner, to quicken the lukewarm, to confirm the wavering, to comfort the feeble-minded, to succour the tempted, or contribute in any manner to the saving of souls from death." (*Sermons*, II, 455-56.) Robert Bolton uses the phrase "works of mercy," distinguishing as Wesley does between "spiritual" and "corporal" works of mercy. (Bolton, *Walking with God*, p. 256 [CL, IV, 390-91].)

DOTH ONLY [does alone] denominate a man a LIVING [true] **Christian. It is not speaking together, but loving and living together, that brings God and the soul into one.**[53]

Wesley's own descriptions of Christian perfection—the believer in whom true holiness has become a reality—are based upon such a communion and conformity of man to God.

Shaw's description of how and why a Christian acts as he does serves as an informative summary of the character of the Christian life.

As to the outward acts of service which the true Christian DOTH performs, he is freely carried out towards them, without any constraint OR FORCE. If he keep himself from the evils of the place, and age, and company wherein he lives AND CONVERSES, it is not by restraint, which is upon him merely from without him, but by a principle of holy temperance planted in his soul: it is the seed of God abiding in him that preserves him from commission of sin, I JOHN III. 9. He is not kept back from sin as a horse by a bridle, but by an inward AND SPIRITUAL change made in his nature. On the other hand, if he employ himself in any external acts of moral or instituted duty, he does it freely, not as of necessity, or by constraint. If you speak of acts of charity, the godly man gives from a principle of love to God, and kindness to his brother; AND SO cheerfully, not grudgingly, or of necessity, 2 COR. IX. 7. . . . If you speak of righteousness or temperance, he is not over-ruled by power, or compelled by laws, but INDEED ACTED [actuated] by the power of that law which is WRITTEN AND engraved upon his mind. If you speak of acts of worship, whether moral or instituted, in all these he is also free, as to any constraint. Prayer is not his task, or a piece of penance, but it is the nature cry of a new born soul; . . . he prays, because he wants, and loves, and believes.[54]

---

[53] Shaw, *Communion with God*, p. 211 [*CL*, XIV, 303].

[54] Shaw, *Immanuel: or a Discovery of True Religion*. p. 75 [*CL*, XIV, 231-32]. It should be remembered in establishing holiness as the character of the Christian life Wesley and the Puritans were only carrying on an ancient tradition reaching back to the earliest Christian eras, as R. Newton Flew ably shows in his work *The Idea of Perfection in Christian Theology*. L. J. Trinterud maintains that the emphasis on piety was an English religious trait, principally Augustinian in character and present even in medieval English Church life. ("The Origins of Puritanism," *Church History*, XX [1951], 40.)

Conscience as Its Director

In order for a believer to be sustained in the holiness of an authentic Christian life he must have guidance and direction. In the discussion of the covenant theology it was noted that for both Wesley and the Puritans the law as defined in Scripture is incorporated under the gospel as the standard for Christian living. The law present in Christianity includes not only the Ten Commandments but also the commandments of Jesus, as well as the example of his own life. Although no longer required as the condition of justification or sanctification, it is now, along with love, the standard defining the good works which are a natural consequence of faith.[55]

How was such a standard to be made applicable to the life of the individual believer? It could not be adequately applied by some external authority such as the minister, a friend, or the congregation, for, though they might judge the outward manifestations, they could never truly judge the inward motivation. Hence, the conscience of the individual Christian must become the means by which one evaluates his own conformity to the standard.

Because of this significant role of the conscience in Christian life, much of the Puritan literature concerns itself with examinations of conscience and its operations in the life of the individual. An almost natural outgrowth of such a concern and interest was the endeavor to define how a true Christian conscience should interpret the various situations of life. Such efforts produced the vast Puritan casuistical literature. Although this casuistry was extensively elaborated in the latter half of the seventeenth century, it began with some of its most significant formulations in the works of William Perkins (*A Discourse of Conscience*, 1595; *The Whole Treatise of the Cases of Conscience*, 1606) and William Ames (*Conscience, with the Power and Cases Thereof*, 1639). The standard format for Puritan ethical application became the "cases of conscience," which served parishioners as a practical guide to a "tender" conscience. Richard Baxter and his contemporaries represent the full flower of the

---

[55] "Nor yet do we so establish the moral law (which it is to be feared too many do), as if the fulfilling it, the keeping all the commandments, were the condition of our justification: if it were so, surely 'in His sight should no man living be justified.' But all this being allowed, we still, in the Apostle's sense, 'establish the law,' the moral law." (*Sermons*, II, 73.)

Puritan endeavor to instruct the average church member in how to apply his conscience to the task of determining true Christian action.[56]

Even though Wesley does not follow the general form of the "cases of conscience" in his own writings, he carries out the intent of such work in much of his ethical writings, particularly his various instructions and "words" ("Of Riches," "On Dress," "A Word to a Freeholder," etc.). For purposes of this study, however, Wesley most closely relates himself to the Puritan exposition of the conscience in his sermon entitled "On Conscience," in which he depends directly upon a sermon of his grandfather, Samuel Annesley, "How May We be Universally and Exactly Conscientious?"

This sermon is the first in a volume entitled *The Morning Exercises at Cripplegate*. Annesley sponsored in 1661, after the pattern set for him by Thomas Case, a series of early morning lectures by prominent Puritan divines in his church at Cripplegate. Originally designed to provide additional opportunity for corporate prayer as well as to give instruction, particularly in "practical godliness," these lectureships were sporadically continued by Annesley and others through the next thirty years. Annesley edited and published four volumes containing lectures delivered in this fashion.[57] The lecture used by Wesley introduces the whole series and is intended by Annesley to define conscience in order that the following "select cases of conscience" may be better understood and applied.[58] Wesley abridged this lecture or sermon for *A Christian Library*.

In introducing his own sermon on the topic, Wesley comments that conscience is one of the most familiar expressions of men and yet grossly misunderstood. He points out that there have been numberless treatises written upon the subject (many only confusing the issue), yet "there is

[56] For a thorough exposition of Richard Baxter's casuistical endeavors, see James M. Phillips, "Between Conscience and Law: The Ethics of Richard Baxter" (Unpublished Ph.D. dissertation, Princeton University, 1959).

[57] In 1844, James Nichols edited a new edition of these volumes, adding two others originally edited by Thomas Case. Collating the various impressions or editions, since later editions published during the lifetime of the various authors were corrected and expanded, Nichols produced a "standard" text. He provides an informative introduction on the occasion and importance of these lectures in the Nonconforming community. It is this edition which is used in this study. (Samuel Annesley, *The Morning Exercises at Cripplegate, St. Giles in the Fields, and in Southwark*, ed. James Nichols [5th ed., 6 vols.; London: Printed for Thomas Tegg, 1844], I, vi; cited hereafter as *Morning Exercises*.)

[58] Annesley, "How May We be Universally and Exactly Conscientious?" *Morning Exercises*, I, 1.

158

still wanting a discourse upon the subject, short, as well as clear. This, by the assistance of God, I will endeavour to supply, by showing, First, the nature of conscience; and, Then, the several sorts of it; after which, I shall conclude with a few important directions." [59] His choice of Annesley's sermon as a guide among the multitude of those available[60] may be explained by the fact that it is essentially practical in its orientation.[61] Annesley tells us that he intends "to wave the determination of that school-dispute, whether it [conscience] be an act, or an habit, whether of the understanding, or will or both; whether it be a distinct faculty, or power, how far born with us, and far acquired. I willingly let pass all that doth not further the design I drive at, namely, an universal and exact conscientiousness." [62] No doubt such a sentiment struck a responsive note in Wesley, anxious as he was to jettison speculation wherever possible. He shares Annesley's wish to occupy oneself with definitions only insofar as they offer clarity and a basis of application.

Wesley begins his sermon by quoting Dr. Annesley's definition of conscience:

This word, which literally signifies, *knowing with another*, excellently sets forth the scriptural notion of it. So Job: (xvi. 19) "My witness is in heaven." And so the Apostle: (Rom. ix. 1) "I say the truth, my conscience also bearing me witness in the Holy Ghost." In both places it is as if he had said, "God witnesseth with my conscience." Conscience is placed in the middle, under God, and above man. It is a kind of silent reasoning of the mind, whereby those things which are judged to be right are approved of with pleasure; but those which are judged evil are disapproved of with uneasiness.[63]

[59] *Works*, VII, 186.

[60] Not only were the Puritans interested in the role of conscience but it was a common topic among theologians of the period. Wesley could easily have drawn from the Anglican works such as Bishop Sanderson's *Lectures on Conscience and Human Law* and Jeremy Taylor's *Rule of Conscience*, to mention only two. Wesley comments that the "best treatise on the subject which I remember to have seen is translated from the French of Mons. Placette," but he continues that this is much too long and therefore not likely to be very useful. (*Ibid.*)

[61] Wesley's sermon "On Conscience," was a late production, according to his *Journal* written in 1788 (VII, 359). Before this he seems to have recommended his grandfather's sermon as found in *A Christian Library* for instruction in the area. (*Letters*, V, 200.)

[62] Annesley, "How May We be Universally and Exactly Conscientious?" *Morning Exercises*, I, 3.

[63] *Works*, VII, 186-87. Wesley in this quotation is not completely accurate in transcribing Annesley's statement nor does he note that part of the statement is quoted by Annesley from Brockmand, but there are no significant changes or omissions.

In Annesley's sermon the above quotation is an expansion of the following brief definition of conscience: "Conscience is man's judgment of himself, of his estate and actions as they are subjected unto the judgment of God." [64] Wesley's own formulation states quite simply what the conscience is for the Christian: "It is that faculty of the soul which, by the assistance of the grace of God, sees at one and the same time, (1.) Our own tempers and lives,—the real nature and quality of our thoughts, words, and actions; (2.) The rule whereby we are to be directed; and, (3.) The agreement or disagreement therewith." [65]

Conscience used in the sense of discovering the Christian's conformity to God's law and judgment seems, however, to leave little place for "natural conscience," or the ability of all men to discern right and wrong. Both Annesley and Wesley allow such a natural conscience, but it is of secondary importance to them. Annesley defines this natural ability in the more traditional sense as "the relics of the image of God after the fall," and comments no further on it.[66] From Wesley's perspective, there is a more convenient explanation. Man's ability to distinguish good and evil is "a branch of that supernatural gift of God which we usually style preventing grace." "For though in one sense it may be termed natural, because it is found in all men; yet, properly speaking, it is not natural, but a supernatural gift of God, above all his natural endowments." [67] Wesley, using this explanation, can then insist not only that conscience is dependent upon God, since it is a gift, but also that

[64] Annesley, "How May We be Universally and Exactly Conscientious?" *Morning Exercises,* I, 3.
[65] *Works,* VII, 189.
[66] Annesley, "How May We be Universally and Exactly Conscientious?" *Morning Exercises,* I, 5.
[67] *Works,* VII, 187-88. As Lindström indicates, there are occasional instances in which Wesley expresses "the opinion that a certain residue of knowledge of the law was preserved after the Fall." Harald Lindström, *Wesley and Sanctification,* p. 47. (See *Sermons,* I, 400; II, 43.) Also in his sermon "The Heavenly Treasure in Earthern Vessels," Wesley comments on natural conscience in a passage discussing the remains of the image of God after the Fall and there mentions both the understanding of conscience as a "natural attribute" and as one "superadded by the grace of God," evidently willing to allow either as valid explanations. (*Works,* VII, 345.) It is possible to understand both these explanations as necessary and complementary if one is seen as the gift of creation and the other as part of the gift of sanctification. In any case, Wesley's normal formulation is that conscience is a part or branch of prevenient grace. (*Sermons,* II, 445.)

it is activated by the Holy Spirit. "In all the offices of the conscience, the 'unction of the Holy One' is indispensably needful." [68]

Wesley's understanding of prevenient grace as the first step in the process of salvation leads him in this sermon to conflate the two senses of conscience, that of natural man and that of the Christian.

This is properly the account of a good conscience; which may be in other terms expressed thus: a divine consciousness of walking in all things according to the written word of God. It seems, indeed, that there can be no conscience which has not a regard to God. If you say, "Yes, there certainly may be a consciousness of having done right or wrong, without any reference to him;" I answer, This I cannot grant: I doubt whether the very words, right and wrong, according to the Christian system, do not imply, in the very idea of them, agreement and disagreement to the will and word of God. If so, there is no such thing as conscience in a Christian if we leave God out of the question. [69]

Wesley here follows Augustine, who in a strikingly similar passage comments: "The virtues which it [the soul] seems to itself to possess, and by which it restrains the body and the vices that it may obtain and keep what it desires, are rather vices than virtues so long as there is no reference to God in the matter." [70]

If, then, conscience is restored to fallen man by prevenient grace, Wesley may be correct in declaring that there is no conscience "which has not a regard to God." Yet, this is certainly not the same *enlightened* conscience which guides one into "walking in all things according to the written word of God." A true Christian conscience defined, as both Wesley and Annesley insist, as one aware of "the rule [the law and commandments] by which we are to be directed" is far different from the ordinary unbeliever's conscience, which nevertheless is able to discern good and evil. [71]

[68] *Works*, VII, 190.
[69] *Ibid.*
[70] *The City of God*, in *Basic Writings of St. Augustine*, ed. Whitney J. Oates (2 vols.; New York: Random House, 1948), II, 504. Wesley in reflecting Augustine here joins the Puritans and other theologians. Baxter states it thus: "There is no virtue, truely so called, which is not theological as well as moral." (*The Saints' Everlasting Rest* in Baxter, *Works*, XXIII, 36.)
[71] Annesley's presentation does not contain the same confusion of two types of conscience. Along with his definition of natural conscience as a relic of the image of God, he defines a

It must be remembered that Wesley was defining the conscience for use within the Christian community; therefore, his insistence that all knowledge of good and evil must refer to God is quite adequate, framed as it is within a theological context. It is doubtful, however, if his answer would have been accepted by the fledgling empiricism of his own day, which would claim that the use of the terms "good" and "evil" have a legitimate application in situations which are not specifically religious and have no primary reference to ultimate ends.[72] In contrast, the theological understanding of good and evil, deriving its meaning essentially by reference to God, is, of course, concerned primarily with the ultimate end and religious significance of any particular action.

Wesley's insistence that the conscience cannot function without the activation of the Holy Spirit and his application of this statement even to natural conscience, since it is a "branch" of prevenient grace, finds no equivalent in Annesley. Annesley naturally assumes the activation of the Christian conscience by the Spirit but he does not stress this aspect. Neither is there any need for the Holy Spirit to be peculiarly operative in the conscience of the natural man, unless, of course, one wants to point out that creation itself assumes some operation of God in the life of every man. In any case, Wesley, probably because he is arguing a point, is much more insistent upon the role of the Spirit in activating and sustaining the conscience of all men.

Another aspect of these definitions is significant. Annesley's statement, apparently approved by Wesley, that conscience is somehow "in the middle, under God and above man," suggests that conscience is in some sense a separate entity external to man, judging him. This reflects

believer's conscience as one activated by "the light of Divine revelation" in "the standing rule of Scripture, and God's extraordinary discoveries of himself, whether by dreams, visions, or prophecies, or other spiritual communications." (Annesley, "How May We be Universally and Exactly Conscientious?" *Morning Exercises*, I, 5.)

[72] In fact, it is just such a sentiment expressed by "Professor Hutcheson, late of Glasgow" that Wesley is attempting to refute. This was, no doubt, Francis Hutcheson (1694-1746), moral philosopher at Glasgow, correspondent of David Hume, and effective lecturer "on the evidences of Christianity." Although Wesley dismisses him as an atheist since he would not allow that good action must always refer to its reward, he was well known in his own time as a defender of the Christian tradition, even though his theology was decidedly liberal for that day and he may be considered an originator of British utilitarianism, which, of course, in later hands slipped from its Christian moorings. (*DNB*, XXVIII, 333.)

a tendency to hypostatize conscience as the judge of man.[73] Conscience is somehow "over-against" man in this presentation. Wesley's own comment that conscience is not natural but "above all his natural endowments" might also reflect such tendencies, yet this concept should not be given too much weight; and allowance should be made for literary license in expression, since the burden of both Annesley's and Wesley's presentations leaves little doubt that conscience is a part or faculty of man's own nature, judging his own actions. It does, however, indicate the extremely important place that conscience held in the thinking of both the Puritans and Wesley.

Moving beyond the definition of conscience, Annesley treats the "kinds" of conscience and Wesley considers the "sorts of consciences," but there is no significant dependence in Wesley upon his grandfather's work in this section. Annesley's treatment is quite extensive, giving definition, cause, and cure for six types of conscience (sleepy, seared, erring, doubting, scrupulous, and trembling) which he did not consider to be sufficient and therefore closes with brief statements concerning the true conscience, that is, the "good honest" conscience and the "good quiet" conscience. Wesley's definition of a good conscience is essentially that given above in his definition of conscience itself, to which he adds a tender conscience, or one which is "exact in observing any deviation from the word of God" and corresponds roughly with Annesley's comments on a good conscience. He does not concern himself with the negative types used by Annesley, except to mention the hardened or seared conscience which may discern the correct action but dismisses, without self-condemnation, the failure to act in accordance with its insights, and the overly scrupulous conscience which fears when there is no reason to do so and consequently either condemns without cause or fails to act, fearing that the judgment might be wrong.[74]

Wesley returns to direct dependence on Annesley's sermon when he closes his own sermon by extensively quoting Annesley's "directions"

[73] For a discussion of such hypostatization in Baxter and other Puritan divines, see J. M. Phillips, "Between Conscience and Law: The Ethics of Richard Baxter," pp. 182-83.
[74] Annesley, "How May We be Universally and Exactly Conscientious?" *Morning Exercises,* I, 23-37; Wesley, *Works,* VII, 192-94.

for acquiring a good conscience, giving credit in a footnote to the fact that they are the work of his grandfather. Annesley gives ten directions and then in closing adds four more which are "generally sufficient, when others cannot be had"—these latter he considers to be actually the "spirit" or summary of the more elaborate set. Wesley condenses these fourteen to ten and then liberally abridges them, which, interestingly enough, he had not done in the *Library* edition of this sermon. Annesley conveniently summarizes the ten directions, allowing one an insight into the nature of the instruction:

For the *integrity* and *quiet* of your consciences, observe the rules proposed, as punctually as you would physicians' bills in a tedious sickness. (1.) Avoid sinning, as you would a train of gunpowder. (2.) Be as quick in your repentance, as in a pleurisy. (3.) Live under the apprehended presence of the jealous God. (4.) Examine your hearts, as princes sift out treason. (5.) Pray for suitable grace, as starving persons cry for food. (6.) Let every action be as an arrow shot at a mark. (7.) Think of God as a wise physician. (8.) Be as vile in your own esteem, as you are in the eyes of a captious enemy. (9.) Live upon Christ, as the child of the womb lives upon the mother. (10.) Love God (as near as possibly you can) as God loves you.[75]

Wesley omits four of these and includes those which Annesley added as expressing the spirit or essence of the directions: Consult duties, not events; what advice you would give to another, take yourselves; do nothing on which you cannot pray for a blessing; think and speak and do what you are persuaded Christ himself would do in your case, were he upon the earth.[76] The directions were, of course, good instruction for the Christian man in any case and might have been applied to many areas besides the conscience, but they typify the kind of practical instruction which is so much the concern of the Puritans and so attractive to Wesley.[77]

[75] Annesley, "How May We be Universally and Exactly Conscientious?" *Morning Exercises*, I, 34.

[76] Curnock calls Wesley's closing quotation from Annesley's sermon "a fine example of the Annesley-Wesley teaching on Holiness" thereby relating the Puritan-Wesleyan emphasis upon holiness. (*Journal*, VII, 359 n.)

[77] The almost compulsive use of "directions" throughout Puritan literature appears to have been an important element in his choice of their works. Directions for covenanting, for con-

In addition to the analysis of conscience found in the sermons of Annesley and Wesley, another Puritan use of conscience is noteworthy. Investigating and commenting upon all areas and situations of life, the Puritans were led to deal with those of their congregations who suffered an "afflicted conscience." Because of the importance of such a state, since it might threaten the whole tenor of a Christian life, the subject is a recurring theme in their writings and merits the attention of whole treatises. Representative works in the area are Robert Bolton's *Instructions for Rightly Comforting Afflicted Consciences;* Bishop Hall's *Heaven Upon Earth, or, Of True Peace of Mind;* and Thomas Goodwin's work, *A Child of Light Walking in Darkness; Or, a Treatise Shewing the Causes by Which, the Cases Wherein, and the Ends for Which God Leaves His Children to Distress of Conscience.*

Those suffering from an afflicted conscience are treated by the Puritans as two differing groups. First, there are those whose afflicted consciences are a sign of their readiness to receive the comforting message of the gospel. Such a state is usually the result of having had the accusations of the sinful state presented to one who is now ready for the peace of the gospel. In Bolton's terms, the responsibility of the minister in this case is "first, to wound by the *Law,* and then heal by the *Gospel.*" [78] It is primarily this type of afflicted conscience with which Bolton and Hall are concerned. Bolton's treatise might well serve as the manual for the Christian minister in dealing with one in a state of affliction, for it is not only full of advice about how to apply comfort but, just as important, how to avoid the errors of offering comfort to those who are not ready.

The second type of afflicted conscience is found in the believer who has experienced conversion and the life of faith but is now suffering doubt and temptation. Thomas Goodwin's treatise deals specifically with this condition, describing it in his comments on light as it is used in Eph. 5:13.

---

version, and now for gaining a true conscience have already played a significant role in this study. Other sets of directions are included in the *Library,* such as Bolton's *General Directions for a Comfortable Walking with God* and Whateley's *Directions for Married Persons.*

[78] Robert Bolton, *Instructions for a Right Comforting of Afflicted Consciences,* p. 131 [*CL*, V, 17]. Wesley's appreciation for the treatise is witnessed by his recommendation of it to answer the questions of one of his followers. (*Letters,* VII, 64.)

When therefore here he says he hath no *light*, the meaning is, he wants ALL PRESENT [the] sensible testimonies of God's favour to him; he sees nothing that may give SENSIBLE present witness of it to him; God's favour, and his own graces, and all the sensible tokens and evidence thereof, which are apprehended by spiritual sight, are become all as absent things, as if they were not, or never had been; that light which ordinarily discovers these as present he is clean deprived of.[79]

As the subtitle of Goodwin's work indicates, he assumes that there is always purpose in such afflictions; therefore, he emphasizes God's justice and purpose in these afflictions, God's mercy for one who keeps faith during such trials, the duty of offering comfort to such, and closes with the almost inevitable "directions for those who are deeply troubled." Bolton's treatise deals with this type of affliction of conscience, though concentrating on the first type. He also instructs one in the way to rectify the situation. Central in both sets of instructions is the admonition to seek by every means possible, to know why one is so afflicted, that is, examine by the use of the conscience itself the state of one's life which might have led him into this disturbed moment. Whether or not one is able to discover the problem this way, the solution to an afflicted conscience is true dependence upon the promises of the Scripture and a steady attendance upon these scriptures. Added to this is the use of prayer (Goodwin emphasizes seeking the prayers and help of others as well) and the ability to wait "in the constant use of all ordinances and means of comfort" [80] for the relief which will assuredly come to the one who seeks it.

Wesley's inclusion in the *Library* of these treatises, designed specifically for those facing such a situation, witnesses to his appreciation of their work and his use of it in his own instruction. His dependence upon Annesley's treatment of conscience, both for its definition of conscience

[79] Thomas Goodwin, *A Child of Light Walking in Darkness* (London: Printed by F. G. for R. Dawlman, 1659), p. 14 [*CL*, VI, 235]. Wesley's own description of this state is similar: "He [God] now 'hides His face and they are troubled'; they cannot see Him through the dark cloud. But they see temptation and sin, which they fondly supposed were gone never to return, arising again, following after them again, and holding them in on every side. It is not strange if their soul is now disquieted within them, and trouble and heaviness take hold upon them." (*Sermons*, I, 330.)

[80] Thomas Goodwin, *A Child of Light Walking in Darkness*, p. 312 [*CL*, VI, 300].

and its instructions relative to the attaining and nurturing of a good conscience, plus his particular commendation of the Puritan treatment of the disturbed conscience,[81] indicates another area of real affinity with the Puritan tradition. Although conscience may not play as large a role in the theology and teaching of Wesley as it did in that of the Puritans, it does have an extremely important function in Wesley's scheme and he is at least partially dependent upon the Puritan tradition for his own understanding and presentation of it.

---

[81] *CL,* IV, 107.

VI

THE SPHERES OF THE CHRISTIAN LIFE: THE INDIVIDUAL AND THE FAMILY

At the outset of this section the necessity for selecting materials from the mass available was mentioned. This necessity is particularly evident in an attempt to discuss specific teachings as they relate to the various areas of human life, since almost every conceivable human situation is dealt with, usually in detail, by the Puritans. This is compounded by the fact that any attempt to credit many of the specific ethical teachings of Wesley to the influence upon him of the Puritan tradition presents certain problems. Wesley's stringent application of extremely rigorous ethical norms to the lives of all believers and his ability to challenge large numbers of people to accept such an ideal no doubt offended the Latitudinarian theologians whose rationalistic moral teachings, though definitely widespread, were not equal to the Wesleyan

168

rigidity of demand.[1] However, in the previous century a substantially more rigorous ethical ideal and teaching had been a distinguishing feature of theologians of the Established Church. As a result, both Puritans and Anglicans of the seventeenth century concentrated on moral instruction within the Christian framework. Such instruction may have originated from somewhat different presuppositions—the Anglican on a more Arminian base, tending to emphasize the works of a good Christian as a primary necessity for salvation in view of man's own moral, though corrupt, abilities. Their understanding, therefore, tended toward legalism. The Puritans, on the other hand, as has been noted, with no less an emphasis on works, still rigidly subordinated these works to faith and grace. Nevertheless, though they may start from somewhat different bases, a substantial amount of strikingly similar, and in some cases almost identical, ethical instruction is found in both Puritan and Anglican writings of the period. To credit Wesley's teachings on a particular subject to either tradition by itself is in danger of misrepresentation. For example, Wesley's appreciation of the value of time stems from his study of William Law and Jeremy Taylor, although it is a major emphasis of the Puritans as well.[2] Examples do not need to be multiplied in order for one to appreciate the problem. Either, or both, traditions may be claimed as the mentor for many of the specific teachings.

Some explanation of the blending of the two streams in Wesley is suggested by his comment, quoted above, that while he and his brother Charles discovered justification by faith as the entrance to Christian life and holiness, nevertheless, that holiness which they had earlier been convinced was the way to salvation was still their goal.[3] Wesley, as a high-church Anglican, began with a legalistic framework of ethical teaching. Into this framework was forced the truth that "holiness comes by

---

[1] See Archbishop Tillotson's exposition of the "reasonableness" of laws and commands as quoted in Horton Davies' work, *Worship and Theology in England: 1690-1850*, p. 56.

[2] Wesley's sermon entitled "On Redeeming the Time" quotes extensively William Law's treatise, *Redeeming the Time from Sleep*; see *Works*, VII, 71 ff. The first rule of Jeremy Taylor's *Rules and Exercises for Holy Living* also deals with the subject. On the Puritan side, Sir Matthew Hale discusses the redemption of time in his *Contemplations, Moral and Divine* (London: Printed by William Godbid for William Shrowsbury, 1676), pp. 15 ff. [*CL*, XVII, 225 ff.] It is a concern for Herbert Palmer in his *Memorials of Godliness and Christianity in a Discourse of Making Religion Ones Business* (London: Printed for Samuel Crouch, 1681), pp. 14-18 [*CL*, XII, 10-11].

[3] See above, p. 152.

faith"; yet the end result, so far as its manifestation in Christian living was concerned, was the same—holiness. In other terms, Wesley's avid search for holiness is cut off the old tree of Anglican legalism and grafted upon a new tree—Reformation faith.[4] Now nourished by different roots, the fruit is still holiness. Though holiness now had a new root, none of its imperative nature was lost for Wesley, and what had always been a primary concern is reinforced.

To avoid the pitfalls inherent in an attempt to distinguish where Wesley may have gleaned a particular teaching, this study is limited: (1) to Puritan literature recommended and used by Wesley; (2) to selected areas within each sphere of the Christian life in which Wesley shares the Puritan interest and emphasis; and (3) to those areas where Wesley's practice reflects Puritan tradition.

With this caution in mind and working within these limitations, specific teachings are discussed as they relate to the various spheres of everyday life—those of the individual, the family, the church, and the world.[5] Obviously, while each sphere of life may be distinguished from the others, they are not to be separated, for each reflects and involves the others.

1. The Individual

I desire to have my Affections moulded by Religion, and towards it; my thoughts, and words, and deeds, to be all *exercises of Religion*, and my very *cessation* from *work commanded by Religion*, and *limited* and *circumstantiated* by Religion. My eating, drinking, sleeping, journeying, visiting, entertaining of friends, to be all *directed* by *Religion*: and that, above all, I may be *serious* and *busie* in the *acts* of *Religion*, about the Word, Prayer, Praises, Singing, Sacraments, not only that the duties in each kind be performed, but *religiously* performed, with life, and vigour, with Faith, Humility, and Charity.[6]

This description of the religious life by Herbert Palmer portrays the Puritan understanding of how an individual will reflect in his life his religious concerns. Religion will permeate all areas and aspects of life—

[4] This metaphor is drawn from John Deschner's provocative treatment of the interrelation of the Anglican and Reformed theologies in Wesley. (Deschner, *Wesley's Christology*, pp. 177, 185.)
[5] The "spheres" used here are those marking the fourfold division of Richard Baxter's work *A Christian Directory*, and are traditional divisions in casuistical writings.
[6] Herbert Palmer, *Memorials of Godliness and Christianity*, p. 2 [CL, XII, 5]; cf. Robert Bolton, *Walking with God*, p. 29 [CL, IV, 335].

none will be exempt from its direction. As a consequence, a primary consideration of that life is a thorough and honest knowledge of exactly who one really is. To obtain such knowledge, a truly religious man will make it one of his concerns to examine himself rigorously and consistently. Self-examination is, therefore, a prominent concern for the individual Puritan.

In view of its importance, it is treated in some fashion by most of the Puritan instruction which Wesley includes in *A Christian Library*, but Wesley seems to have particularly appreciated and commended an extensive commentary on the subject, Lewis Stuckley's work, *A Gospel-Glass*. This is one of the few works abridged in the *Library* which Wesley indicates he used in instructing the societies. Soon after the publication of the *Library* Wesley notes in his *Journal*, "I began reading that excellent book, 'The Gospel-Glass,' to the morning congregation: a method which I find more profitable for 'instruction in righteousness' than any other manner of preaching." [7] It is impossible to know how extensively Wesley practiced this type of instruction or how often this particular work was used. However, his continuing appreciation for the work is clear, for in January of 1791, only a few months before his death, he notes having one of the most active of his society members, Elizabeth Richie, read it again to him. [8]

As one may surmise from the title, Stuckley attempts in this treatise to place before the believer a mirror, in order that he might examine himself. This is a special mirror silvered with the gospel, so that one's reflection is actually the reflection of his conformity or deviation from the gospel standards of conduct. With this aid one's conscience can examine itself and commend or rebuke, whichever is appropriate. Stuckley's approach is principally negative in that it points to the major deviations, the sins of the believer, but throughout is the concern to be certain that one examines oneself carefully and honestly. On the necessity of such self-examination he comments:

[7] *Journal*, IV, 189. Wesley used Bolton's treatise, *Walking with God*, for the same purposes. (*Ibid.*, IV, 94.)

[8] *Journal*, VIII, 122. For comments on Wesley's reading habits and particularly his dependence upon someone to read aloud to him in his later years, see Frank Baker, "A Study of John Wesley's Readings," *LQHR*, 168 (1943), 140-45; 234-42.

There are few things more commanded US, than to try and examine our HABITS [hearts] and lives: EXAMINE YOURSELVES, ETC. PROVE YOURSELVES, ETC. We are apt to be strangers to ourselves, to cheat ourselves with vain PRESUMPTUOUS hopes, to rest in notions; therefore *Examine yourselves*, take an experimental knowledge of yourselves: we are apt to prove others, and centure them; therefore, *Prove* YOUR OWNSELVES [yourselves]; begin at home, try your state, try your actions, bring the metal to the touchstone, see whether it be sound or counterfeit; try your faith, whether it be temporary or saving; prove your repentance, whether it be thorough or superficial; examine your love, whether it be sincere or hypocritical; and your obedience, whether it be universal or partial.[9]

This passage makes it clear that self-examination is, for the Puritan, a constant, never-ending task.[10] For Stuckley the first responsibility of self-examination is to turn inward to our hearts, trying them to see if they are truly set on Christ. Such inward examination is to be followed by examination of outward action. Every action should be examined, but at least once each day a believer should stop to examine himself thoroughly, principally by the Scriptures.[11] The account of a Puritan layman's day given for Sir Matthew Hale begins the day with resolve to set a "watch over my own infirmities and passions" and to close the day by casting "up the accounts of the day."[12]

Robert Bolton's *A Treatise on Self-Examination* approaches the subject in terms of the special use of self-examination as a preparation for receiving the Lord's Supper. In this sense it becomes

an holy worke of the soul, whereby it casteth its eye, AND REFLECTETH upon itselfe, and so looks through itselfe, makes an exact survey and search into every corner, and takes a true SCANTLING AND estimate of its spiritual state.

FIRST, in this GODLY exercise OF EXAMINATION, a man by the touchstone

---

[9] *A Gospel-Glass*, pp. 158-59 [CL, XIX, 330].
[10] *Ibid.*, pp. 162-63 [CL, XIX, 332-33]; cf. Bolton, *Walking with God*, p. 150 [CL, IV, 372].
[11] *A Gospel-Glass*, p. 161 [CL, XIX, 332].
[12] Gilbert Burnett, *The Life and Death of Sir Matthew Hale* (London: Printed for W. Shrowsbury, 1682), pp. 11-12 [CL, XVII, 109-10]. Cf. Herbert Palmer, *Memorials of Godliness and Christianity*, p. 32 [CL, XII, 8].

of God's Word, . . . doth try whether his conversion be sound and saving, OR COPPER AND COUNTERFEIT; . . . [and whether he have] First, Knowledge; Secondly, Faith; Thirdly, Repentance; Fourthly, New Obedience; Fifthly, Love. . . .

He must also revise these SAVING GIFTS AND CHRISTIAN graces, and consider how they wax or waine, fade or flourish, languish, or are in life, that so he may proportionably prepare and apply spiritual preservatives or restoratives.[13]

In essence, the treatise is an exposition of how a person is to test and examine his knowledge of his relationship with God but particularly how he is to determine the true state of his faith. It exemplifies how self-examination, a daily responsibility, may also be used for the special occasions of Christian renewal.[14] Sibbes reminds one that such an examination is not simply a moral one, for it is aided through the work of the Holy Spirit, which enlightens the Christian's conscience, helping it distinguish right and wrong, to discern how well one conforms to the gospel pattern.[15]

Wesley's own concern for self-examination was deep-seated, the aftermath of his early endeavors to seek salvation through personal discipline, as is indicated in *A Scheme of Self-Examination: Used by the First Methodists in Oxford*. Here are presented questions which will bring before a person every action and thought, religious and secular, personal and social.[16] A constant admonition to both preacher and layman was to "watch" and "try" oneself.[17] Self-examination is especially useful and important in determining the cause of "spiritual darkness"—those

---

[13] Bolton, *On Self-Examination*, pp. 17-19 [CL, V, 188].

[14] Bolton's use of self-examination is not limited to this special case. Self-examination is again evident as he warns of the particular danger inherent in the normal Christian life: "Let me advise AND FOREWARNE with as great earnestness AND HEARTINESSE as I can possibly, all Gods Children, that . . . they would watch over themselves VERY EXTRAORDINARILY, AND with singular care AND HEEDFULNESSE, in the use and enjoyment of things lawfull IN THEIR OWN NATURE. . . . For more, saith a worthy Divine, perish WITH PROPOSTEROUS FOLLOWING OF LAWFULL THINGS [by lawfull things], then by unlawfull courses." (*Walking with God*, p. 206 [CL, IV, 378].)

[15] Richard Sibbes, *Bowels Opened, or A Discovery of the Neere and Deere Love, Union, and Communion betwixt Christ and the Church*, in Sibbes, *Works*, II, 47 [CL, VI, 160]; cited hereafter as *Christ and the Church*.

[16] *Works*, XI, 521-23.

[17] *Ibid.*, VIII, 315, 323.

times of afflicted conscience and also those times when the fortunes of the work seem to be adverse.[18]

Even though there is little question that, as a personal concern, Wesley's interest in self-examination was grounded in his early legalism, it is clear that he recognized an affinity between his own training and the teachings of the Puritans in this area. For the instruction of his people in this matter he turned, at least in part, to that tradition which had made self-examination such a primary ingredient in the life of the common man. It is most likely that much of Wesley's concern with self-examination stemmed from his home training where Susanna, reflecting her Puritan heritage, must have laid such a concern upon the hearts of her children.

Methods of self-examination might vary, but in the Puritan tradition one of the principal supports of this task was the keeping of a daily diary. The diary provided not only the record of daily events but the chance to evaluate those events. Here it was that one recorded the results of "casting his accounts." William Haller maintains that the diary served as the Puritan confessional and thereby played a singularly important role in their spiritual lives.[19] Theirs was an age of renewed popular interest in biography and history, so that some of their interest in diaries may be thus explained; but the keeping of the diary was far more than a literary interest, for it served as the daily record of their relationship to God as they could best be aware of it.

Wesley's own careful use of a diary throughout his long life serves the same purpose for him and is the basis of the later published *Journal*. Adam Clarke, one of Wesley's preachers and a leading Methodist theologian of the early nineteenth century, ties Wesley's habit of keeping a diary to the example set for him by his Puritan grandfather, John Westley, who seems to have recorded "not only the most remarkable events of God's providence in his behalf, but more especially the operations of the Divine Spirit upon his heart." [20] Curnock points out that

---

[18] *Sermons*, II, 256-57; *Letters*, VIII, 241. As might be expected, such use is made of self-examination in Puritan treatises also. See Thomas Goodwin, *A Child of Light Walking in Darkness*, pp. 263-64 [*CL*, VI, 288].

[19] William Haller, *The Rise of Puritanism*, p. 98.

[20] Adam Clarke, *Memoirs of the Wesley Family*, p. 23; cf. J. Whitehead, *The Life of John Wesley, A.M.*, I, 2.

this statement is not contradictory to Wesley's own introduction to his *Journal,* which states, "It was in pursuance of an advice given by Bishop Taylor, in his 'Rules for Holy Living and Dying,' that . . . I began to take a more exact account than I had done before, of the manner wherein I spent my time," for it only indicates that he now kept a "more exact account." [21] Curnock may be correct,[22] but it must be admitted that Clarke's supposition is largely a matter of conjecture and must be weighed accordingly, especially in view of Wesley's acknowledgment of Taylor's influence at this point. Nevertheless, the suggestion is attractive; and the fact that there is evidence to indicate that the Puritan tradition of diary keeping was a part of the family heritage may at least allow one to consider this Puritan practice as one factor which encouraged Wesley's own use of a diary.

Self-examination leads naturally to the necessity of self-denial or the denial of the selfish interests and motivations which lie at the base of the sins discovered through the process of examination. For Wesley self-denial was a natural and necessary element in a Christian's life. Consequently, in his sermon on the subject he criticizes, on the one hand, the Predestinarians, Antinomians, and Ranters of his own day, who either discount it altogether as a reinstitution of "salvation by works" or fail to appreciate its significance. On the other hand, he is not satisfied with the general treatises on the subject, especially those of the mystics, because they "deal in generals only" without coming to the particulars which affect common men, or they detail the "particulars" such as imprisonment, tortures, the giving up of lands, etc., which are not likely to be the lot of the common man.[23] His own exposition of the topic is to lie somewhere between these two extremes.

If the Predestinarians of his own day were not willing to stress the necessity of self-denial, they had at that point strayed from their Puritan heritage, for it is a recurring theme in Puritan literature. Wesley must have found in these writings a position somewhat similar to his own, for

[21] *Journal,* I, 42-44; *Works,* I, 3.
[22] Curnock also suggests that the first notebook in which John Wesley kept a diary was one that had belonged to his grandfather Westley. It was given to John by his father Samuel, with the advice "that he should imitate the example of his grandfather whose name he bore." (*Journal,* I, 45.)
[23] *Sermons,* II, 283, 285.

the Puritan divines insisted upon the necessity of self-denial and at the same time pointed out what this meant in the common life. The topic is treated in many of the Puritan works Wesley includes in the *Library* but receives special attention in Isaac Ambrose's tract, *The Practice of Sanctification,* in which he defines self-denial as

a total, thorough, utter abnegation of a man's own ends, counsels, affections, and a whole prostration of himself, and of all that is his under Christ Jesus. And thus we have the meaning of Christ, *If any man will come after me, let him deny himself;* i.e. let him lay aside his own wisdom as an empty lamp, his own will as an evil commander, his own imaginations as a false rule, his own affections as corrupt counsellors, and his own ends as base and unworthy marks to be aimed at. . . . In the regenerate man, all the supernatural gifts and graces, all the moral endowments and abilities, all the natural powers and faculties of the soul, with all the members of the body, and all the labours of the life . . . must do obeisance, and be made subject unto Jesus Christ.[24]

This characterization of self-denial as the turning of man from his own will, goals, purposes, and inclinations to those of God corresponds to Wesley's definition of self-denial as "the denying or refusing to follow our own will, from a conviction that the will of God is the only rule of action to us." [25] Wesley is even closer to Richard Alleine, who points out that one cannot serve both Christ and self at the same time: "If you will not deny yourselves, you deny your Lord; and if you can deny yourselves in anything, you will deny Christ in nothing." [26] Wesley concentrates on the aspect of will, but there is never any question that he means to include all affections, goals, abilities, etc.—all of man is to be completely consecrated to God.

Ambrose details self-denial in its various aspects by indicating that we must be willing to deny (1) our sinful selves or our corruptions and concupiscence (Wesley's corrupt nature of man); (2) our external relations or those natural human relations even of family that may stand between man and God; (3) our special gifts or endowments, such as learning, wisdom, power, etc., which might interfere with singular

---

[24] *The Practice of Sanctification,* in Ambrose, *Works,* p. 87 [*CL,* VIII, 20]; cf. Joseph Alleine, *Divers Practical Cases of Conscience Satisfactorily Resolved* (London: Printed for Nevil Simmons, 1672), p. 24 [*CL,* XIV, 191].

[25] *Sermons,* II, 286.

[26] Alleine, *Vindiciae Pietatis,* p. 315 [*CL,* XVIII, 186-87].

service of God; (4) our worldly profits and pleasures when these tend to sin instead of God; (5) our honor, praise, and good name among men when they are "snares or baits unto sin"; (6) our very life if this is required; and finally, (7) any spiritual pride or any credit for the graces of God which may be present in us.[27] Ambrose is careful to indicate that what is to be denied may be in itself good and useful, but must be cast from one when it tends to interfere with one's following after God. When they are used or sought for what they do for the self, they are sinful and must be denied. Wesley, while not listing the aspects which must be denied, manages to comment on most of those given by Ambrose. As indicated in his criticism of the previous treatments of the subject, he is more concerned with the giving up of pride, self-will, seeking after place and wealth—things which tend toward the world— than he is those things which he doubts the common man will be called upon to abandon, such as family or life itself. Therefore, he might well criticize Ambrose and other Puritans for inclusion of these; yet many of the Puritans had been called upon to make the kind of self-denying sacrifices which these things indicate and as a consequence these aspects were much closer and more real to them than they were to the average Methodist. In any case, the "particulars" of self-denial are evident throughout the Puritan treatises, and Wesley must have agreed with Stuckley's designation of what is to be denied as "all your sinful lusts, . . . all your worldly advantages, . . . all self, self-will, self-righteousness, self-sufficiency, self-confidence, and self-seekings."[28] Self-denial served as the touchstone of true Christian life, and the Puritans, as well as Wesley, were convinced that without self-denial one could hardly expect to lead a Christian life.[29]

---

[27] *The Practice of Sanctification*, in Ambrose, *Works*, pp. 87-107 [*CL*, VIII, 20-47]. Bolton distinguishes approximately the same areas: "Be content to denie thy selfe, thy worldly wisdome, NATURALL WIT, CARNALL REASON, ACCEPTATION WITH THE WORLD, excellencie of learning, FAVOUR OF GREAT ONES, CREDIT AND applause, with the most; thy passions, profits, pleasures, preferments, neerest friends, ease, libertie, life, everything, anything." (Bolton, *Walking with God*, p. 52 [*CL*, IV, 340].) Cf. Thomas Goodwin, *The Tryall of A Christian's Growth* (London: Printed for R. Dawlman, 1643), pp. 14 ff.

[28] Stuckley, *A Gospel-Glass*, pp. 31-32 [*CL*, XIX, 255].

[29] "No Walking with God, no sweete communion, and sound peace at his Mercy-Seate, except for his sake, AND KEEPING A GOOD CONSCIENCE, thou be content to denie thy selfe." (Bolton, *Walking with God*, p. 52 [*CL*, IV, 339-40]; cf. p. 313 [*CL*, IV, 12]; Ambrose, *The Practice of Sanctification*, p. 87 [*CL*, VIII, 20].)

Wesley's commendation of the Puritans' ability to teach one how to "grow in grace" or to go from strength to strength[30] is reflected in his selection of their works, for here again is a theme recurrent through most of these writings. Arising from their conviction of the necessity of sanctification, such an emphasis is only natural, for they were convinced that a person does not stand still in his faith but that it must always increase. Discussed in many of the treatises, it is the topic of Thomas Goodwin's work, *The Tryall of a Christian's Growth.*[31] Convinced that "there is therefore as great a necessity to grow as to be born again or else we cannot enter into heaven," Goodwin, in typical Puritan style, gives instruction or tests by which one may ascertain the nature of such growth. True growth in grace is the growth of those bases of all Christian life, such as love, faith, and humility.[32] Growth in these will produce growth in gifts, opportunities, and fruits, which, considered by themselves, do not necessarily indicate true growth. All fruits, gifts, etc., grow more spiritual, with the result that renewal and increase come to graces which may already be present in substance. Credit must, of course, be given to God for the increase, it is his work and not ours, even though he "doth proportion his influence to our endeavours," and it may be said that, in this limited sense, we are "fellow-workers." [33] Goodwin is joined by other Puritan divines in insisting on the necessity of growth in grace. Bolton sees it as a test of conversion and "an inseparable companion of spiritual life." [34] Sibbes picturesquely comments, "He [God] doth not only give them a stock of grace at the beginning, but also helps them to trade. . . . He not only plants graces, but also waters and cherishes them." [35] The list need not be extended to show that growth in grace is a constant theme in these works used by Wesley and, as he indicated, for which he felt a strong attraction.

Wesley's affinities with the Puritan teachings on self-examination, self-

[30] *CL*, IV, 108.

[31] *The Tryall of a Christian's Growth* [*CL*, VII, 49 ff.].

[32] *Ibid.*, p. 70 [*CL*, VII, 56].

[33] *Ibid.*, p. 167 [*CL*, VII, 86].

[34] Bolton, *On Self-Examination*, p. 287 [*CL*, V, 244]; cf. *Walking with God*, pp. 312, 339-40 [*CL*, IV, 400, 416]; Stuckley, *A Gospel-Glass*, p. 378 [*CL*, XIX, 441].

[35] Richard Sibbes, *Christ and the Church*, p. 13 [*CL*, VI, 139]. Cf. Preston, *New Covenant*, pp. 258-60 [*CL*, VI, 28-29].

denial, and growth in grace serve to indicate only representative areas of mutual concern and interest relative to instruction in the religious life of the individual Christian. He offers at least one specific recommendation of Puritan patterns in the furthering of personal religion. In the 1763 Minutes and the two editions which followed, Wesley, questioning his preachers about their own personal religious practice, asks them if they follow the "instituted" means of grace such as prayer, reading the Scriptures, and "meditating: at set times? How? By Bishop Hall's, or Mr. Baxter's rule? How long?" [36] It is possible that he is suggesting here the use of Bishop Hall's *Meditations and Vows,* which was available to Wesley's followers in *A Christian Library.* The reference to Baxter's rule may indicate several treatises since meditation is essentially the subject of *The Saints' Everlasting Rest,* also available in the *Library,* as well as part of the instruction in *Gildas Salvianus, The Reformed Pastor,* which, as we shall see, is recommended to his preachers by Wesley in other connections. In any case, Wesley clearly depends upon Puritan mentors to provide instruction in this important area. The Methodist "Rule of Meditation" prescribed in official conference session is Puritan in origin. This is particularly interesting in light of his background in an Anglican tradition that was strongly oriented toward meditation. Perhaps the practical nature of the instruction written principally for the common man would, in Wesley's view, make it more acceptable and appealing to his own flock as well as his ministers. [37]

Other areas of affinity between Wesley and the Puritans in terms of particular teachings and their application to the various circumstances of life are no doubt discernible, [38] but these may serve to indicate the rela-

[36] Minutes (1763) in *Minutes of the Methodist Conferences, 1744-1798* (London: John Mason, 1862), p. 550; cited hereafter as *MMC.*

[37] A curious note in Wesley's letter dated June, 1764, to Miss Margaret Lewen concerning reading and *meditating* on the Scriptures indicates Wesley's recommendation of Matthew Henry's commentary, as well as Wesley's evaluation of it in comparison to his own *Explanatory Notes.* For supplementary reading to this study of Scripture he comments: "If you would save yourself the trouble of thinking, add Mr. Henry's 'Comment': If you would only be assisted in thinking, add the 'Explanatory Notes.'" (*Letters,* IV, 247.)

[38] The vast expanse of Wesley's practical ethical teachings, ranging in sermons and tracts over such diverse areas as, among many others, marriage, vocation, dress, time, conversation, recreation, and, of course, money, provides a fertile field for comparison of his teachings with the Puritans' teaching in the same areas, but such would unduly extend the scope of this study. The similarities are obvious and no doubt account for Wesley's contemporaries' comparing him

179

tionship between the two traditions as they provide guidance for their followers in terms of their personal religious life.

2. The Family

A major factor in the success of the Puritan movement in ministering to its people was its insistence upon the necessity of family religion. Recognizing the incalculable importance of the intimate relationships of the home, the Puritan divines made instruction in family religion and training a primary ingredient in their teachings. This same insistence upon the family is found in Wesley. Even though Wesley's band meetings and class meetings supplemented and served as an intimate fellowship of individual Christians, he recognized the importance of family training and continually insisted upon regulation and instruction in this area. That such instruction was effective is demonstrated by Leslie Church's study which reveals that "the first Methodists were distinguished for many things, but nothing more became them than their 'sense of family.' " [39]

The Puritan works included in the *Library* reveal numerous commentaries upon the proper conduct of family religion, as well as instruction relative to the proper relationship between, and responsibility of, each member of the family. Such instruction is not lacking in the Anglican materials selected by Wesley for the *Library*, but they treat the subject in a much more cursory fashion, and the Puritan commentaries far outnumber these.[40]

Convinced that the household is in essence the model on which all other social relations are built, the Puritan divines insisted that the authority of the master of the house carried privileges and responsibilities similar to those of a civil governor. Instruction in family religion and responsibility begins, therefore, with the insistence that the governors of the household, the father as well as his helpmate, realize the gravity of their positions. John Kitchin states the responsibility thus:

---

with the Puritans. Professor Davies cogently suggests that "in effect, Wesley's ethical sermons provided for the spiritual illiterates what another Arminian, Baxter, had given the Puritan élite in his *Christian Directory*." (*Worship and Theology in England, 1690-1850*, p. 156.)

[39] Leslie Church, *The Early Methodist People* (London: Epworth Press, 1948), p. 222.

[40] See Wesley's abridgment of Jeremy Taylor's work, *The Rules and Exercises of Holy Living*, CL, IX, 186-88, and Anthony Horneck's work, *The Happy Ascetic*, CL, XVI, 367-73.

That father that does not correct his child when he goes amiss, is justly corrected for his faults; and it is the pattern of God's judicial proceedings. As He visits the iniquities of the fathers upon the children who *imitate* them; so He visits the iniquities of the children upon the fathers, who *countenance* and indulge them. . . . Thus must family governors be accountable to God for every lamb in the fold, for every child in the family, for every servant in the house. . . . "Husband, father, master, wife, give account of thy husbandship and give account of thy fathership, give account of thy mastership, give account of thy wifeship." [41]

Richard Alleine's comment puts the case in even stronger terms: "Now, where there is a charge of Souls, there must be an account given of Souls. . . . If any in the house perish through thy neglect, thy life shall go for his life, thy Soul for his Soul." [42] The religious care of the child is, then, part of the express command of God—a duty which cannot be overlooked.

Although Wesley shares this understanding of the role of the parent and the responsibilities thereof before God,[43] he is also appreciative of the Puritan insistence that it is principally through family religion and education that God will raise up a new generation to carry on his church and a well-ordered society. William Whateley points out that only through the progeny of fruitful and legitimate marriage can there be a "flourishing estate of every church and commonwealth." [44] Richard Baxter, concerned with the necessity of proper education, states, "The very welfare of Church and State lieth mainly on this duty of well educating children; and without this, all other means are like to be far less successful." [45] Family worship and religion, the very cornerstone of a good education and proper training of the child, is then more than merely a personal affair but has much larger implications. Wesley sees it also as the way in which the revival of religion in his own time would be

[41] John Kitchin, "How Must We Reprove, That We May Not Partake of Other Men's Sins," in *Morning Exercises*, I, 135 [*CL*, XXI, 434]; cited hereafter as "How Must We Reprove." Cf. Stuckley, *A Gospel-Glass*, p. 222 [*CL*, XIX, 370].

[42] Alleine, *Vindiciae Pietatis*, p. 353 [*CL*, XVIII, 209]; cf. *The Saints' Everlasting Rest*, in Baxter, *Works*, XXIII, 146 [*CL*, XXII, 216].

[43] Wesley, *On Family Religion*, in *Works*, VII, 79.

[44] William Whateley, *A Bride-Bush; or a Direction for Married Persons*, p. 17 [*CL*, XII, 263]; cited hereafter as *Directions for Married Persons*.

[45] *The Saints' Everlasting Rest*, in Baxter, *Works*, XXIII, 150 [*CL*, XXII, 218].

carried forward—otherwise, it would "in a short time die away." [46]

The family itself, therefore, in view of the importance of the religious training therein, serves as a church. "Why hath God given the name of Churches to Christian families, but because of those holy services which are to be done publikely in the family? Whereby they are all sanctified, and become even houses of God to dwell in." [47] "He that makes his House a *little church*, shall find, that God will make it a *Little Sanctuary*." [48]

Wesley's insistence that the Methodists must maintain constant attention to the duties of family religion not only is expressed in his sermons on this subject ("On Family Religion," "On the Education of Children," "On Obedience to Parents") but also is a recurring theme in his instructions to his ministers: "Do all you can herein, if not all you would. Inquire in each house, Have you family-prayer? Do you read the scripture in your family? Have you a fixed time for private prayer? Examine each as to his growth in grace, and discharge of relative duties." [49]

For a pattern of Christian family worship Wesley turned to the Puritan Philip Henry. Henry's "Method of Family Prayer" is part of the "particular" instructions which the Methodist preachers were to give in the families under their care. [50] Printed as a part of *The Life of Mr. Philip Henry*, it had been abridged for the *Library* by Wesley. [51] He does not appear to have published it separately; therefore, it may be assumed that he expected them to use the *Library* edition, for he consistently urged it upon his people as a pattern for their own families.

---

[46] *Works*, VII, 77; VIII, 316.

[47] Whateley, *Directions for Married Persons*, p. 91 [CL, XII, 295]. "It will never be said to your glory, *the church in your house*: but may it not be said, there is a nest of snakes, a cage of devils in your house?" (Stuckley, *A Gospel-Glass*, p. 241 [CL, XIX, 383].)

[48] Matthew Henry, *An Account of the Life and Death of Mr. Philip Henry* (3rd ed.; London: Printed for J. Lawrence, J. Nicholson, etc., 1712), p. 59 [CL, XXVIII, 291]; cited hereafter as *Philip Henry*. Cf. Kitchin, "How Must We Reprove," *Morning Exercises*, I, 135 [CL, XXI, 434].

[49] Minutes (1763), MMC, p. 456. The first sentence of this quotation is almost a paraphrase of Baxter's admonition on this same subject: "O Sirs, if you cannot do what you would do for them, do what you can." (*The Saints' Everlasting Rest*, in Baxter, *Works*, XXIII, 165 [CL, XXII, 228-29]. Cf. *Works*, VIII, 302 ff.)

[50] *Works*, VIII, 315.

[51] Wesley identifies this "Method" with that printed in *Philip Henry* in the Minutes of 1766: "Read publicly that part of Mr. Philip Henry's life, enforcing it as a pattern." MMC, p. 53.

Philip Henry's method of family worship is a classical account of the Puritan pattern for the religious training of the family. As such it serves as a representative treatment of the subject. Beginning with the insistence that one must follow the practice of private worship, or "Closet-worship," as the first step in religious cultivation, Henry then urged his parishioners always to join together as husband and wife in prayer. "This Sanctifies the Relation, and fetcheth in a Blessing upon it, makes the Comforts of it the more sweet, and the Cares and Crosses of it the more easie, and is an excellent Means of preserving and encreasing Love in the Relation." [52] Together with these practices and central in the family life as a whole were the daily worship periods.[53] These were normally the morning and evening prayers held early in the morning before the cares of the day crowded in and preceding supper in the evening before the family was sleepy. Attended by all in the household, including servants, field workers, and sojourners, as well as the children, they began with a short introductory prayer followed by a psalm and scripture reading. The scripture received a short exposition and the children were questioned concerning it. Then came the larger family prayer in which the concerns of the family were lifted up, "usually most full in giving Thanks for Family-Mercies, confessing Family-Sins, and begging Family-Blessings." [54] Here were offered prayers for the children, any special occasion or event, the sojourner who might be in the household, and so forth. At the close of this prayer the children were dismissed after asking for a blessing from their father and mother.

On Thursday evening the reading of scripture was omitted in order to allow time for catechizing the children and servants, or to examine them "in some other useful Book." [55] Saturday night in Philip Henry's plan brought a review of the scriptures which had been read in the week,

[52] Henry, *Philip Henry*, p. 58 [*CL*, XXVIII, 291]. See also Whateley, *Directions for Married Persons*, p. 49 [*CL*, XII, p. 275]; Robert Bolton, *Walking with God*, p. 255 [*CL*, IV, 389]; *Works*, VII, 77.

[53] Henry, *Philip Henry*, p. 59 [*CL*, XXVIII, 292 ff.]. Cf. Isaac Ambrose, *The Practice of Sanctification*, p. 126 [*CL*, VIII, 74]; Kitchin, "How We Must Reprove," *Morning Exercises*, I, 136 [*CL*, XXI, 435].

[54] Henry, *Philip Henry*, p. 63 [*CL*, XXVIII, 295].

[55] *Ibid.*, p. 64 [*CL*, XXVIII, 296-97]. Catechizing is important but not enough, according to Lewis Stuckley, for he asks, "How seldom do you converse personnally with everyone in your families concerning the practical part of religion?" (Stuckley, *A Gospel-Glass*, p. 221 [*CL*, XIX, 369]. Cf. Alleine, *Vindiciae Pietatis*, p. 353 [*CL*, XVIII, 209].)

with an examination of the children on their meaning, and an explanation of what was not fully understood. Matthew Henry gives credit to these sessions, since they were conducted with "prudence and sweetness," for the instilling of a love and knowledge of the Scriptures in the children.

The Sabbath, however, was the crowning day of worship and on this day, though the regular form was followed, the family prayers were expanded. Psalms were sung after dinner and supper. The evening brought another catechetical session with the children and servants, to which was added a review of the sermons of the day to be sure that all remembered and understood.[56] The prayer of this evening was greatly expanded, with particular notice being given to the role of Henry's family as a minister's family and to the needs and interests of the congregations which he served.

To these daily times and methods of worship Henry added regular instructions for his children in the meaning of their baptism, for which he drew up a form of the Baptismal Covenant, as well as the Lord's Supper. The children were also taught to pray, sometimes as a group without adult supervision, and, of course, to read the Scriptures as early as they were able.[57]

Summarizing the discussion of family worship, Matthew Henry comments:

He managed his daily Family-Worship so as to make it a Pleasure and not a Task to his Children and Servants; for he was seldom long, and never tedious in the Service; the variety of the Duties made it the more pleasant; so, that none who join'd with him had ever any reason to say, Behold what a Weariness is it![58]

And again:

He did not burthen his Children's Memories by imposing upon them the getting of Chapters and Psalms without Book; but endeavored to make the whole Word of God Familiar to them, (ESPECIALLY THE

[56] Henry, Philip Henry, p. 65 [CL, XXVIII, 297]. Stuckley laments the failure of most to follow such a pattern of Sabbath worship. (Stuckley, A Gospel-Glass, pp. 153-58 [CL, XIX, 326-30].)
[57] Henry, Philip Henry, pp. 67-71 [CL, XXVIII, 299-303].
[58] Ibid., p. 64 [CL, XXVIII, 296].

SCRIPTURE STORIES) **and to bring them to understand it and love it,** AND
THEN THEY WOULD EASILY REMEMBER IT.[59]

Such worship was carried on "in the most lively method" to guard it
against becoming a dull formal matter.[60]

From the hints given in Susanna Wesley's own plan for the education
of children, recorded in Wesley's *Journal,* it may be seen that the same
daily pattern of family worship was followed in his childhood home.[61]
Not surprisingly, therefore, Wesley recognizes his affinity with the
Puritan tradition at this point and heartily recommends and insists upon
it as the pattern for his followers.

William Whateley's *Directions for Married Persons* represents another
type of Puritan teaching in the area of family life. According to Whateley it was designed for "good instruction to Young and Unmarried
people" as well as married couples who would "become acquainted" with
the duties of marriage.[62]

Wesley singles out this work for high commendation:

I have seen nothing on the subject in any either ancient or modern tongue,
which is in any degree comparable to it;—it is so full, so deep, so closely, so
strongly written, and yet with the most exquisite decency, even where the
author touches on points of the most delicate nature that are to be found
within the whole compass of divinity. I cannot therefore but earnestly recommend it to the most serious and attentive consideration of all those married
persons, who desire to have a conscience void of offence, and to adorn the gospel
of God our Saviour.[63]

This tract was issued, from the same plates which were used to produce
the edition for *A Christian Library,* as a separate publication in 1753

---

[59] *Ibid.,* pp. 67-68 [*CL,* XXVIII, 300].

[60] *MMC,* p. 53. Bolton comments on family worship in the same vein: "In the discharge
of which maine dutie of Christianitie, utterly neglected by the most, and empoysoned
to many, by their resting onely in the works wrought, take heed of GROWING [Declining]
into [a] forme, [or] customarinesse, PERFORMATORINESSE, which will most certainly
draw the very life-blood and BREATHING [breath] out of those holy businesses." (*Walking with God,* p. 67 [*CL,* IV, 345].)

[61] *Journal,* III, 34 ff.

[62] Whateley, *Directions for Married Persons,* p. 216 [*CL,* XII, 335-36].

[63] *CL,* XII, 253.

and then reprinted again in 1760 and 1768.[64] It would appear that it was widely used by the Methodists for marriage instruction.

The treatise provides a broad and full treatment of the proper relationship between husband and wife; a few of its major features give insight to the Puritan understanding of marriage. To these may be added some comments on the topic by other Puritan divines.

Marriage is, of course, an honorable estate blessed and ordained by God. As such, it is to be kept inviolable, with divorce granted only on the offense of adultery, and the physical relationship is in proper order when it is "sanctified, seasonable, temperate, and willing." [65] Anything less than this threatens the marriage itself.

"Love is the life and soul of marriage, without which, it differs as much from itself, as a carcase from a living body." This statement sounds quite modern and clearly agreeable with many present-day interpretations of marriage, but Whateley's reasoning as to the basis of this love would, indeed, appear archaic to many modern interpreters.

Love must be built CHIEFLY AND principally upon the WILL AND commandment of God, the only sure AND STEADFAST foundation of it . . . . A Christian man must love his wife not only OR PRINCIPALLY, because she is beautiful, wittie, HOUSEWIFELY, dutifull, [and] loving, AND EVERY WAY WEL CONDITIONED; but chiefly, because the Lord of Heaven and earth, TO WHOM ALL HEARTS SHOULD STOOPE, AND ALL AFFECTIONS YIELD, hath said, Husbands, love your wives. The wife also must love her husband, not only or chiefly because he is a PROPER [comely] man of good meanes, and OR GOOD parentage, kind to her, OF GOOD COURAGE, and of good carriage IN EVERY RESPECT; but because he is her husband, and [because] God the soveraigne of all soules hath told women, that they ought to be lovers of their husbands.[66]

[64] *Bibliography,* p. 82. The following appeared as the preface to the separate edition: "I am persuaded, it is not possible for me to write anything so full, so strong, and so clear on this subject, as has been written near an hundred and fifty years ago, by a person of equal sense and piety."

[65] Whateley, *Directions for Married Persons,* p. 15 [*CL,* XII, 262]. These requirements for divorce are based on scripture, but it should be noted that legal divorce in the seventeenth and eighteenth centuries was virtually unobtainable. Only in very rare cases among the aristocracy was it granted.

[66] *Ibid.,* p. 32 [*CL,* XII, 269]; cf. Isaac Ambrose, *The Practice of Sanctification,* p. 131 [*CL,* VIII, 82].

Although love of the partner is "chiefly" because it is commanded, this in no way implies that the mutual love is any less human or that it will not be the closest of human loves. In Bolton's words, it is "a sweet, loving, and tender-powring out of their hearts, with much AFFECTIONATE DEARENESSE [affection], into each others bosomes; in all passages, carriages, and behaviours, one towards another." [67] Such a relation based on the command of God and mutual human love will be characterized by "pleasingness, faithfulness, and helpfulness" in each partner. It will result in the closest of communities which, though cognizant of fault and sins, will not allow these to interfere with the relationship and will be one in which the partners are always looking for the best in each other.[68] It will keep inviolable the secrets and problems shared, while offering all of the help, encouragement, and direction possible. Through all they work together for common piety.

Reflecting the contemporary social forms and understanding of the day, Whateley, along with the other Puritan divines, could not discuss the family without detailing the structure of authority and responsibility in the family. The husband is "head" and sovereign of the wife, master of the household with unquestioned authority.[69] As such, he is responsible for the whole household even though all others have their place and duties to carry out. However, he must learn to exercise his authority with justice, wisdom, and mildness. Abuse of his headship is a gross sin and one from which he cannot escape. "No woman can endure her husband's government with comfort, if gentlenesse does not temper it." [70]

Compassion, LOVE, kindnesse, the declaration of ones sorrow for HER [the] fault [of the person reproved], desire of his good, care of his amendment THAT IS REPROVED; these BE [are] the things that FRAME [dispose] the will to accept of an admonition, and DOE much helpe the kindly working thereof. I am not against the wholesome earnestnesse of reproving, and that sharpnesse of rebuking, which in some cases the Lord

---

[67] Bolton, *Walking with God*, p. 239 [*CL*, IV, 381].

[68] Whateley, *Directions for Married Persons*, pp. 54-60 [*CL*, XII, 278-93]; cf. Stuckley, *A Gospel-Glass*, pp. 224-29 [*CL*, XIX, 371-75].

[69] Whateley, *Directions for Married Persons*, pp. 97 ff. [*CL*, XII, 299 ff.]; cf. Bolton, *Walking with God*, pp. 244-50 [*CL*, IV, 384-87].

[70] Whateley, *Directions for Married Persons*, p. 156 [*CL*, XII, 320].

himselfe commands; but this may well STAND [be] without bitternes, without THE violence of words AND GESTURE, and without THE fiercenesse AGAINST WHICH WE SPEAKE.[71]

Authority can neither be neglected nor abused in the proper Christian household.

Whateley was particularly concerned with the dangers of the household in which the wife was dominant, for, under his pen, her "peculiar duties" include her acknowledgment of her "inferiority" and her recognition that "she must carry herself as an inferior." [72] Isaac Ambrose, while insisting upon the wife's subjection to her husband, also stressed her role as a helper in all areas of the family.[73] Children and servants are under the authority of both husband and wife.

In the choice of a marriage partner the Puritans insist that primary consideration be given to the religious character of the person.

Let pietie be the first mover of thine affection, THE PRIME AND PRINCIPAL PONDERATION IN THIS GREAT AFFAIRE; and then CONCEIVE OF PERSONAGE, PARENTAGE, AND [consider person,] portion, AS THEY SAY, and SUCH *outward* things AND WORLDLY ADDITIONS, AS A COMFORTABLE ACCESSORY, CONSIDERATION onely in a second place.[74]

Wesley also feared the consequences of marrying "unbelievers" and warned against the dangers of attempting to seek "a good match," meaning a worldly good one.[75]

---

[71] *Ibid.*, p. 168 [*CL*, XII, 324]. In the words of Isaac Ambrose, "If he shall have occasion to reprove her, he must keep his words until a convenient time, not [do it] in the presence of others, and then in the spirit of meekness and love." (Ambrose, *The Practice of Sanctification*, p. 132 [*CL*, VIII, 82].)

[72] Whateley, *Directions for Married Persons*, pp. 189-91 [*CL*, XII, 328-30].

[73] Ambrose, *The Practice of Sanctification*, p. 133 [*CL*, VIII, 83]. Ambrose depended upon Bolton's treatise not only for some sections of his outline, in which he treated the family, but also to the extent of duplicating complete sentences and phrases. This is only one example of the common practice of plagiarism in this period. (Cf. *The Practice of Sanctification*, p. 130 [*CL*, VIII, 79]; Bolton, *Walking with God*, p. 239 [*CL*, IV, 381].)

[74] Bolton, *Walking with God*, p. 236 [*CL*, IV, 379]. Herbert Palmer, writing before he was married, desired "that I may never marry with any whom I have reason to judge not to be truly religious, whilst yet I conclude, 'That religion alone is not sufficient to make any match.'" (*Memorials of Godliness and Christianity*, p. 27 [*CL*, XII, 14]. Alleine, *Vindiciae Pietatis*, p. 354 [*CL*, XVIII, 210].)

[75] MMC, p. 483; *Works*, VII, 85.

In relationship to the children the parents are urged to remember their responsibility for them before God and are cautioned to set a good example, since example is the true test of the teaching.[76] Parents are not only responsible for the spiritual nurture of the children but also for their total education and occupation and thereby for their whole demeanor. As a consequence, parental discipline of the family is an important responsibility and one not to be taken lightly. **"Both must discountenance those that MISCARRY [carry] themselves [ill], and both must GIVE COMMENDATION AND GOOD ALLOWANCE TO [commend] them of good behaviour; that so they may both maintaine each others authority to the full."** [77]

From the children's standpoint, they are, of course, first of all, to respect and obey their parents. To maintain their proper relationship there "must be a loving fear, and a fearing love" of the child for the parent, resulting in reverence of speech and carriage, obedience to the "commands, instructions, reproofs, and corrections of their parents," and a true recompense for the care and love they have received from the parent.[78]

Wesley's use and recommendation of William Whateley's work on marriage takes on added significance when we remember Wesley's essentially ascetic attitude toward marriage (even after his own marriage). When he sought instruction in this relationship which he had in some sense depreciated so long, he turned to the Puritan tradition, which held such a high opinion of the blessedness of this state and which was able to make close and meaningful family life a prominent feature of its impact on the community.

Education entails the whole training and not merely the spiritual and academic education of the child. On this education Wesley lays the

---

[76] Whateley, *Directions for Married Persons*, p. 98 [*CL*, XII, 300]; Alleine, *Vindiciae Pietatis*, p. 354 [*CL*, XVIII, 210]; Stuckley, *A Gospel-Glass*, p. 222 [*CL*, XIX, 370]; *The Saints' Everlasting Rest*, in Baxter, *Works*, XXII, 166 [*CL*, XXII, 230].

[77] Whateley, *Directions for Married Persons*, p. 95 [*CL*, XII, 298]; Stuckley, *A Gospel-Glass*, pp. 230-35 [*CL*, XIX, 375-80]; *Works*, VII, 79-80.

[78] Ambrose, *The Practice of Sanctification*, p. 134 [*CL*, VIII, 84-85]; Stuckley, *A Gospel-Glass*, p. 235 [*CL*, XIX, 380]. Wesley extends the obligation for children's obedience even to the grown child and closes with the insight: "Those only who obey their parents when they can live without them and when they neither hope nor fear anything from them, shall have praise from God." (*Works*, VII, 100.)

greatest stress in his sermons on the family. He follows Baxter in pointing out the difficulty of the task of education, mentioning to one of
his followers Baxter's comment that "whoever attempt to profit children will find need of all the understanding God has given them." [79]
This familiar anecdote from his own family expresses it quite well:

I remember to have heard my father asking my mother, "How could you
have the patience to tell that blockhead the same thing twenty times over?"
She answered, "Why, if I had told him but nineteen times, I should have lost
all my labour." What patience indeed, what love, what knowledge is requisite
for this! [80]

But the need for patience and the difficulty of the task in no way negates
its necessity.

Wesley's teachings on education reveal a great similarity to those
given to him by his mother. These instructions portray the household
at Epworth and most likely are those gleaned by Susanna from the
Annesley home. They reveal the stringent discipline tempered with love
which marked the Puritan home. As we shall see, in Wesley's own formulation they are very rigid and almost lose the warmth evident, for instance, in Whateley and Philip Henry.[81] In the materials included in
A Christian Library, Baxter's instructions specifically dealing with
spiritual upbringing of the children are closest to those of Wesley. Both
stress the fact that to train a child in Christianity is to go directly contrary to his nature, which is imbued with love of self, pride, love of the
world, and so forth.[82] To accomplish this, one must, in Baxter's terms,
"rectify their wills." [83] Here Wesley is adamant. For him, as for his
mother, this is the primary task. If the self-will of a child can be broken
and brought under the control of the parent, it is Wesley's logic that
it can more readily be given to God; therefore, "a Wise parent, . . .

[79] Letters, V, 335; cf. The Saints' Everlasting Rest, in Baxter, Works, XXIII, 147 [CL,
XXII, 217].
[80] Minutes (1766), MMC, p. 69; Works, VII, 82-83.
[81] Whateley, Directions for Married Persons, pp. 156 ff. [CL, XII, 320 ff.]; Henry, Philip
Henry, pp. 67-71 [CL, XVIII, 299-303].
[82] The Saints' Everlasting Rest, in Baxter, Works, XXIII, 147 [CL, XXII, 217]; Works,
VII, 89-90.
[83] The Saints' Everlasting Rest, in Baxter, Works, XXIII, 166 [CL, XXII, 230]; Works,
VII, 92; Journal, III, 35.

should begin to break their will the first moment it appears." One should, then, "never, on any account, give a child any thing that it cries for." [84] In order to conquer their natural pride one is not to praise them "to their face." Wesley seems to have been carried away in this admonition for in the next paragraph he tempers this advice by allowing commendation to be given but with the "utmost caution." [85] Such sentiments would naturally cause a modern psychologist to shudder and are obviously open to the charge of endangering the child's development and, if followed strictly, of making the household a regimented prison.[86] Wesley may be excused only if we remember that always in practice such instruction was to be carried out in love. The fact that Wesley himself never actually was faced with the opportunity in a settled household to practice his instruction must also be considered. These instructions appear today impractical and perhaps abusive, but for his own day probably reflect the usual concept of family authority and responsibility.

With Baxter, he insisted that training must be started as soon as the child begins to reason and that instruction of the child must be frequent and with the utmost perseverance.[87] Though Wesley does not follow Baxter in detailing the doctrinal and practical religious matters which must be taught the child,[88] he would have no doubt agreed with Baxter and certainly approved of the manner in which the instructions were to be applied:

And for the manner, you must do all, 1. Betimes, before sin get rooting. 2. Frequently. 3. Seasonable. 4. Seriously and diligently. 5. Affectionately and tenderly. 6. And with authority: compelling, where commanding will not serve; and adding correction, where instruction is frustrate.[89]

[84] *Works*, VII, 92.

[85] *Ibid.*, 93-94.

[86] For a general evaluation and criticism of Wesley's educational system as it was applied outside the home, particularly at Kingswood, see Alfred H. Body, *John Wesley and Education* (London: Epworth Press, 1936). F. C. Pritchard maintains that Wesley's plan for Kingswood was modeled, to some extent, upon the Dissenting academies, particularly as these were proposed by Milton's *Treatise on Education*, to which Wesley refers in his *Plain Account of Kingswood School*. (Pritchard, *Methodist Secondary Education*, pp. 64-65.)

[87] *The Saints' Everlasting Rest*, in Baxter, *Works*, XXIII, 152, 166 [CL, XXII, 219, 230]; *Works*, VII, 81-82.

[88] *The Saints' Everlasting Rest*, in Baxter, *Works*, XXIII, 166-70 [CL, XXII, 230-34].

[89] *Ibid.*, p. 170 [CL, XXII, 234].

In summary, this brief investigation of the teachings relative to the family reveals a close affinity between Wesley and the Puritans and, in the areas of family worship and marriage relationships, actual dependence upon Puritan materials for instruction of his people. To say that he is dependent upon this tradition for his own understanding of these matters is perhaps to go beyond the evidence, although a case might be made for his gaining it through the Epworth household, which served as an expression of the tradition. In any case, in the Puritan tradition he recognizes the expression of essentially his own views and uses this as the pattern for the people called Methodist.

VII

THE SPHERES OF THE CHRISTIAN LIFE: THE CHURCH AND THE WORLD

1. The Church

The church, along with the individual and the family, constituted a signally important area of Christian life for the Puritans and Wesley. As the instituted means God had established on earth to carry out his work, as the community of support and guidance necessary for a full life of faith, and as the normal channel by which one received instruction and through which one usually came to the faith itself, the church is related to all areas of the Christian's life. It is only natural that it receive appropriate attention in the teachings as well as the practice of the Christian believer.

As religion is not merely an outward and formal matter, so the earthly institution of the church must be measured by its spiritual nature as well as its outward form. For the Puritans and for Wesley concern for the church revolved around these dual aspects; consequently, much of the teachings deal with church order and government. The very name of the Puritans signified their interest in bringing the institutional church, as they found it, closer to a "pure" conformity to the church as they understood it to be revealed in the Word of God. It is our purpose in this section to consider the following questions. First, what attitude toward and evaluation of the attempt by the Nonconformists to reform the church is revealed in Wesley's writings? Second, what relationship exists between Puritan practice and understanding and Wesley's own practice in his organization of the Methodist societies, as well as his understanding and use of ordination? Finally, do Wesley's teachings relative to certain aspects of the ministerial office indicate dependence upon Puritan teachings?

Wesley and Nonconformity

It is well to begin by considering Wesley's attitude toward church government or organization and to let him speak for himself. In January, 1746, Wesley read a book which, with other considerations, was to change his whole attitude toward the church and which had momentous repercussions for his movement as it matured, as we shall presently see:

On the road I read over Lord King's *Account of the Primitive Church*. In spite of the vehement prejudice of my education, I was ready to believe that this was a fair and impartial draught; but, if so, it would follow that bishops and presbyters are (essentially) of one order, and that originally every Christian congregation was a church independent on all others! [1]

The Minutes of the 1747 Conference reflect the fruit of this reading:

Q. You profess to obey both the governors and rulers of the Church, yet in many instances you do not obey them; how is this consistent? Upon what

[1] *Journal*, III, 232.

principles do you act, while you sometimes obey and sometimes not?

A. It is entirely consistent. We act at all times on one plain uniform principle —we will obey the rulers and governors of the Church, whenever we can consistently with our duty to God, whenever we cannot, we will quietly obey God rather than man.

Q. But why do you say, you are "thrust out of the churches?" Has not every Minister a right to dispose of his own church?

A. He ought to have, but in fact he has not. A Minister desires I should preach in his church. But the Bishop forbids him. That Bishop then injures him, and thrusts me out of that church.

Q. Does a church in the New Testament mean "a single congregation?"

A. We believe it does. We do not recollect any instance to the contrary.

Q. What instance or ground is there then in the New Testament for a *National* Church?

A. We know none at all. We apprehend it to be a merely political institution.

Q. Are the three orders of Bishop, Priests, and Deacons plainly described in the New Testament?

A. We think they are; and believe they generally obtained in the churches of the apostolic age.

Q. But are you assured that God designed the same plan should obtain in all churches, throughout all ages?

A. We are not assured of this; because we do not know it is asserted in Holy Writ.

Q. If this plan were essential to a Christian church what must become of all the foreign Reformed Churches?

A. It would follow, they are no parts of the church of Christ! A consequence full of shocking absurdity.

Q. In what age was the Divine right of Episcopacy first asserted in England?

A. About the middle of Queen Elizabeth's reign. Till then all the Bishops and Clergy of England continually allowed and joined in the ministrations of those who were not episcopally ordained.

Q. Must there be numberless accidental varieties in the government of various churches?

A. There must, in the nature of things. For, as God variously dispenses His gifts of nature, providence, and grace, both the offices themselves and the officers in each ought to be varied from time to time.

Q. Why is it, that there is no determinate plan of church government appointed in the Scripture?

A. Without doubt, because the wisdom of God had a regard to this necessary variety.[2]

It is clear from these passages that Wesley was willing rather early in his Evangelical career to recognize the validity of various forms of church order. This recognition was not, however, foreign to Anglican divines either in Wesley's own time or during the preceding two centuries, as Norman Sykes has ably shown.[3] Such staunch advocates of episcopacy as Jewel, Hooker, Bancroft, Andrewes, and Laud were willing to recognize that where the necessities of history had deprived a church of the episcopacy, valid ministry and sacraments were present under other forms of ordination even though these were considered to be "defective" forms. Sykes maintains that the early Anglican apologists argued for episcopacy on the grounds of its apostolic lineage, appealing to history and tradition as their authority, but under the pressures of the Puritan advocacy of divine inspiration for Presbyterian order the Anglican position became more rigidly that of divine right.[4] Nevertheless, even in all but the most extreme advocates episcopacy "was held to be not of dominical but of apostolic appointment, and as *divino jure* only in that sense; as necessary where it could be had, but its absence where historical necessity compelled did not deprive a church of valid ministry and sacraments."[5] Wesley's intimation that "foreign Reformed Churches" would necessarily be rejected as "no parts of the church of Christ" under Anglican formulations is evidently unfounded, though it may well have been a common opinion among some of his

---

[2] *MMC*, pp. 35-36. Wesley also credits Edward Stillingfleet's *Irenicon* with providing him with a new opinion of episcopal order, but it is not clear when he read this work. "That it [episcopal order] is prescribed in Scripture I do not believe. This opinion (which I once heartily espoused) I have been heartily ashamed of ever since I read Dr. Stillingfleet's *Irenicon*. I think he has unanswerably proved that neither Christ nor His Apostles prescribed any particular form of Church government, and that the plea for the divine right of Episcopacy was never heard of in the primitive Church." (*Letters*, III, 182.)

[3] Norman Sykes, *Old Priest and New Presbyter* (Cambridge: The University Press, 1956). This is an extended and valuable investigation of the history of the understanding of church order in Anglicanism.

[4] *Ibid.*, p. 60. Wesley is, therefore, substantially correct in noting that from the middle of Elizabeth's reign the divine right argument becomes dominant.

[5] *Ibid.*, p. 81.

contemporaries.[6] This acceptance of the validity of "foreign" church order was not, however, extended to the English Dissenters who, according to Anglican understanding, were under no imperative of necessity and who by their voluntary rejection of episcopacy were in error and had brought upon themselves the condemnation they sustained in England. Wesley was thoroughly Anglican in sharing this view of those who voluntarily dissented,[7] yet he parted from that tradition by distinguishing Nonconformists (those ejected by the Act of Uniformity of 1662) from Dissenters and refusing to reject the validity of the church order established by those Nonconformists.[8] In this he appears to apply the recognition of various forms of church order to England, a step few Anglicans were willing to take.

Wesley's statement quoted above that "both the offices themselves and the officers in each ought to be varied from time to time" also goes beyond what most Anglicans would admit. To admit various forms where necessity demanded is not to admit that such orders "ought" to be. An even more important departure is Wesley's statement of the principle guiding his attitudes toward church governance: "We will obey the rulers and governors of the Church, whenever we can consistently with our duty to God, whenever we cannot, we will quietly obey God rather than man." This express willingness to disobey "the rulers and governors of the Church" where he thought it inconsistent with the will of God was doubtless viewed by Anglicans as undercutting the real authority of the episcopacy and church order as regularly established. The principle is certainly very close, if not identical, to the principle guiding the moderate Puritans in the conflicts over church order when they refused to conform in 1662.

[6] It is just such a recognition of the legitimacy of such churches which allowed the Archbishop of Canterbury to approve the use of the Moravians in a missionary enterprise. When inquiry was made as to "whether anything in their [the Moravians] Doctrines was so far repugnant to those of the Church of England as to make it improper to employ some of the Brethren in instructing the Negroes in Christianity," his opinion was "that he had long been acquainted by Books with the Moravian Brethren, and that they were apostolical and Episcopal, not sustaining any Doctrines repugnant to the thirty-nine Articles of the Church of England; and that he was confirmed in these sentiments of them by the Conferences he had lately had with the Count of Zinzendorf." Peter Böhler was one of the missionaries appointed under this approval. (*Minutes of the Associates of the Late Dr. Bray* [Library of Congress Microfilm No. 665.] III, 13.)

[7] *Works*, VII, 183.

[8] See above p. 37.

At one other point Wesley takes a position in the Minutes of 1745 which may be interpreted as being at variance with episcopal order.

Q.6. Is mutual consent absolutely necessary between the pastor and his flock? A. No question. I cannot guide any soul unless he consent to be guided by me. Neither can any soul force me to guide him if I consent not.

Q.7. Does the ceasing of this consent on either side dissolve this relationship? A. It must, in the very nature of things. If a man no longer consents to be guided by me, I am no longer his guide. I am free. If one will not guide me any longer, I am free to seek one who will.[9]

At the very least, such a sentiment of voluntary association of pastor and parishioners raises some question of the authority and ability of the episcopacy to appoint pastors.[10] Although the comment does seem to raise such a question, Wesley evidently thought mutual consent of pastor and parishioners to be possible within the principles of episcopacy; yet it is interesting that this was very similar to some of the reasoning by the Puritans of congregational persuasion for separation from the Established Church.[11]

Thus, some of Wesley's opinions on church order were in variance with the dominant Anglican interpretations and tended toward those prevalent in the moderate Puritans. However, it should not be assumed that any of these opinions meant that Wesley condoned or encouraged separation from the Church. They were later to bear fruit in his willingness to ordain, but, a true son of the Church of England, he was never to relinquish his opinion that it was "the best constituted National Church in the world" and must be stood by at all costs.[12]

John Wesley's true opinion of the Nonconformists is probably best stated in the following passage. Having commented upon the Quakers and Baptists as having caused much disturbance and trouble by arguing about "opinions and externals," he chastens them for having separated themselves from the Established Church and then continues:

[9] MMC, p. 27.

[10] Colin Williams (John Wesley's Theology Today, p. 220) maintains that Wesley used this argument to justify "his invasion of the parishes of other presbyters on the ground that they had refused to give true guidance to their parishioners, and that therefore the parishioners were no longer obliged to submit to their guidance."

[11] See Geoffrey Nuttall, Visible Saints, pp. 88 ff.

[12] Letters, VII, 239.

The same occasion of offense was, in a smaller degree, given by the Presbyterians and Independents; for they also spent great part of their time and strength in opposing the commonly-received opinions concerning some of the circumstantials of religion; and, for the sake of these, separated from the Church.

But I do not include that venerable man, Mr. Philip Henry, nor any that were of his spirit, in that number. I know they abhorred contending about externals. Neither did they separate themselves from the Church. They continued therein till they were driven out, whether they would or no. I cannot but tenderly sympatize with these; and the more, because this is in part our own case. Warm men spare no pains, at this very day, to drive us out of the Church.[13]

The crux of the matter always lay in separation. Wesley had little sympathy for those who willingly separated; yet he could readily identify himself with those who were forced out. Perhaps the case of Philip Henry and those ejected in 1662 was somewhat more complex than presented here by Wesley and in a sense was also dependent upon "opinions"; yet Wesley's statement reveals the touchstone by which he distinguished between the Puritan factions and indicates the ones he could not readily accept.

His evaluation of early Puritanism is guided by the same principle:

That "the irregularities of Mr. Cartwright did more harm in the course of a century, than all the labours of his life did good," is by no means plain to me. . . . I look upon him, and the body of Puritans of that age, (to whom the German Anabaptists bore small resemblance,) to have been both the most learned and pious men that were then in the English nation. Nor did they separate from the Church; but were driven out, whether they would or no. The vengeance of God which fell on the posterity of their persecutors, I think, is no imputation on Mr. Cartwright or them; but a wonderful scene of divine Providence.[14]

His sympathy for the Nonconformists is further substantiated on several occasions as is seen in this *Journal* entry of April 3, 1754:

[13] *Works*, VIII, 242-43. "We believe it utterly unlawful to separate from the Church unless sinful terms of communion were imposed; just as did Mr. Philip Henry, and most of those holy men that were contemporary with them." (*Letters*, VI, 326.)
[14] *Works*, XII, 88.

In my hours of walking I read Dr. Calamy's "Abridgment of Mr. Baxter's Life." What a scene is opened here! In spite of all the prejudice of education, I could not but see that the poor Nonconformists had been used without either justice or mercy; and that many of the Protestant Bishops of King Charles had neither more religion, nor humanity, than the Popish Bishops of Queen Mary.[15]

"In spite of all prejudice of education" Wesley comes to appreciate the Nonconformists.[16] He was quite conscious of breaking with the traditional pattern set for a minister of the Church of England; nevertheless, he was willing to make the move when convinced of its validity.[17]

In writing against a Dissenter who attempted to defend separation, Wesley comments, "You do not write as did those excellent men, Mr. Baxter, Mr. Howe, Dr. Calamy, who seem always to speak, not laughing, but weeping." [18] Here again is revealed the sympathy for the "reluctant" Nonconformists.

Wesley returns to Philip Henry for an illustration of how the Methodists should look upon their relation to the Church of England:

Should we go to church to hear ourselves abused, by railing, yea, and lying accusations? What said that blessed man Philip Henry when his friend said (after hearing such a sermon), "I hope, sir, you will not go to church any-

---

[15] *Journal*, IV, 93. The same sentiment is expressed, as well as his opinion of the "circumstantials" over which the Puritans argued, in this *Journal* entry: "I snatched a few hours to read *The History of the Puritans*. I stand in amazement: First, at the execrable spirit of persecution which drove those venerable men out of the Church, and with which Queen Elizabeth's clergy were as deeply tinctured as ever Queen Mary's were. Secondly, at the weakness of those holy confessors, many of whom spend so much of their time and strength in disputing about surplices and hoods, or kneeling at the Lord's Supper." (*Journal*, III, 285.)

[16] For Wesley's opinion of the Act of Uniformity and the Act against Conventicles, as well as another expression of his deep sympathy for those who suffered under the strictures of these measures, see his tract, *Thoughts upon Liberty*, in *Works*, XI, 39.

[17] The same "prejudices of education" were not to be repeated in Wesley's own educational enterprises. He included Daniel Neal's *History of the Puritans* among the textbooks of the Kingswood School, where the sons of his preachers were trained. (John Newton, *Methodism and the Puritans*, pp. 8-9.)

[18] *Letters*, III, 251. "I finished the 'Gentleman's Reasons' (who is a Dissenting Minister in Exeter). In how different a spirit does this man write from honest Richard Baxter! The one dipping, as it were, his pen in tears, the other in vinegar and gall. Surely one page of that loving, serious Christian weighs more than volumes of this bitter, sarcastic jester." (*Journal*, IV, 14.)

more"? "Indeed, I will go in the afternoon; if the minister does not know his duty, I bless God I know mine." [19]

The Methodists were to follow Henry in attending and participating in the church, even where unwelcome and persecuted.

What may be said in evaluating these passages? Wesley's acceptance of a broad view of church government distinguished him from the majority of his fellow Church of England ministers. At the same time, his reasoning as to certain aspects of church order brought him close to the moderate Puritan opinions on the topic. He stood, therefore, somewhere between the more rigid Anglican and Puritan positions. Unwilling to make any form of church government exclusive of all others (as had been the case of many moderate men in both parties the century before), he recognized the validity of the type of church government found among the Puritans. This allowed him, while believing the episcopal form to be preferable, to use the Puritan understanding where necessary for his own purposes. The passages above also reveal his genuine sympathy for those more conservative Nonconformists and establish his own willingness to identify himself with their situation. Perhaps the motivation for such identification lay in the fact that he, too, knew the sting of persecution; nevertheless, the identification is present and provides another bond between the two traditions. His use of Philip Henry to indicate the correct attitude toward the church again gives his people instruction patterned after a Puritan example.

Ordination

In view of Wesley's understanding of church order revealed above, discussion is now appropriate concerning Wesley's ordination of some of his preachers to the ministerial office. This much-discussed topic is of interest to the present study, in that it reflects definite similarities to the understanding and form of ordination found in the Presbyterian branch of the Puritan tradition.

---

[19] *Letters*, VII, 333. This evidently was a favorite illustration, for Wesley records it as his own reason to attend church after a poor sermon. (*Journal*, VI, 371.) In *An Account of the Life and Death of Mr. Philip Henry* it is recorded thus: "Once when one of the Curates preached a bitter Sermon against the Dissenters, on a Lord's Day Morning; some wondered that Mr. Henry would go again in the Afternoon, for the second part; *But* (saith he) *if he do not know his Duty, I know mine; and I bless God I can find Honey in a Carcase.*" (Henry, *Philip Henry*, p. 121 [CL, XXVIII, 340].)

Wesley's ordination of others, though legal and valid in his own understanding, was the result "not of choice, but necessity" and would not have been carried out at all had there been any other alternative.[20] In addition, there was no question in Wesley's mind that the practice which he was following was that of the early church and this constituted its justification; therefore, any similarities between his use of ordination and that found in the Presbyterian churches would, in his mind, be only coincidental. Nevertheless, the fact remains that similarities exist and therefore merit our attention.

Wesley's justification and reasoning concerning the original ordinations for America are best expressed in his letter to the American Methodists, in which he applies the understanding seen above:

Lord King's *Account of the Primitive Church* convinced me many years ago that bishops and presbyters are the same order, and consequently have the same right to ordain. For many years, I have been importuned from time to time to exercise this right by ordaining part of our travelling preachers. But I have refused, not only for peace sake, but because I was determined as little as possible to violate the established order of the National Church to which I belonged.

But the case is widely different between England and North America. Here there are bishops who have a legal jurisdiction: in America there are none, neither any parish ministers. So that for some hundred miles together there is none to baptize or to administer the Lord's Supper. Here, therefore, my scruples are at an end; and I conceive myself at full liberty, as I violate no order and invade no man's right by appointing and sending labourers into the harvest.

I have accordingly appointed Dr. Coke and Mr. Francis Asbury to be Joint Superintendents over our brethren in North America; as also Richard Whatcoat and Thomas Vasey to act as elders among them, by baptizing and administering the Lord's Supper.[21]

Here is expressed Wesley's conviction that he is acting both within the form of the primitive church and through the impetus of necessity, the cardinal Anglican criterion for "irregular" ordinations.

Wesley's acceptance of the equation of the orders of bishop and

[20] MMC, p. 192.
[21] *Letters*, VII, 238-39.

presbyter corresponds to the Presbyterian insistence that "presbyter" and "episcopos" were "only different designations for the same church officials." [22] The Presbyterians, following the general Reformed church tradition, had gone the whole way in their implementation of this equation of the bishop and presbyters by eliminating the office of bishop and using only the designation of presbyter to indicate the ministerial office, in which there were no distinctions. Whether or not Wesley also intended to eliminate the office of bishop is a question which led to much contention between various factions within Methodism after Wesley's death and which has been the subject of much Methodist scholarship. It seems most likely that Wesley intended to maintain a modified form of the episcopal system as the normal order, since it was that which "generally obtained in the churches of the apostolic age." [23] However,

[22] James L. Ainslie, *The Doctrines of Ministerial Order in the Reformed Churches of the 16th and 17th Centuries* (Edinburgh: T. & T. Clark, 1940), p. 92.

[23] *MMC*, p. 36. Luke Tyerman expresses the opinion of much of early English Methodism when he states that Wesley, in ordaining Coke, only intended this as a "mere formality to recommend his delegate to the favour of the Methodists in America: Coke, in his ambition, wished and intended it to be considered as an ordination to a bishopric." (*The Life and Times of John Wesley*, III, 434.) This, however, leaves much to be explained, for (1) if Wesley had not intended some form of the episcopacy, why did he participate in the "laying on of hands" for Coke, who was already a presbyter in the Church of England and presumably would have the same powers as Wesley, for whom only an introduction would have been necessary to establish the office of superintendent? (2) Why was it necessary for Wesley in 1788 to consecrate Alexander Mather to the superintendency in England instead of merely appointing him to the office if it was not to be a consecrated office distinct from the other ministers? Even though a bishop or superintendent might not be endowed with extraordinary powers of ordination and is distinguished from a presbyter only in terms of function, this does not mean that this is not a distinct office to which one is installed through consecration. It seems to have been Wesley's intention that Mather be responsible for carrying on the ordinations when that became necessary after Wesley's death. Edgar Thompson quotes Pawson, one of the preachers Wesley ordained for Scotland: "In order, therefore, to preserve all that was valuable in the Church of England among the Methodists, he ordained Mr. Mather and Dr. Coke bishops. These he undoubtedly designed should ordain others. Mr. Mather told us so at the Manchester Conference, but we did not then understand him." ("Episcopacy: John Wesley's View," *LQHR*, 181 [1956], 117.) It should be noted that the term Wesley chose to designate this office (superintendent) was that used in some of the European Reformation churches and in Scotland for a period and is, in fact, the Latin equivalent of the word "bishop." Many early Anglican divines evidently would have preferred this designation and understood the European churches to have retained the office of bishop under a different designation. (Sykes, *Old Priest and New Presbyter*, pp. 14-15, 246.) Wesley perhaps intended to do the same thing. At least, his participation in ordination and the changing of the designation of "bishop" to "superintendent" and that of "presbyter" to "elder" would indicate a modified episcopal form and order. According to Frank Baker, in the case of the two men Wesley ordained besides Mather for work in England, Henry Moore and Thomas Rankin, Wesley uses the term "presbyter" because these ordinations were intended to be valid in England where this term would be more congenial.

his insistence upon the validity of Presbyterian ordination shows his recognition of the authenticity of other forms. He even comments, "Neither Christ nor His apostles prescribe any particular form of church government"; therefore, he never understands the episcopal system to be in any sense the exclusively genuine form.[24] For our purposes it is sufficient to note the similar evaluation of the powers and prerogatives of the presbyter by the Presbyterians and by Wesley.

Along with the rejection of bishops for the Presbyterians went the rejection of any dependence upon a concept of apostolic succession, which meant an unbroken line of consecration. Yet, as James Ainslie points out, the regulation concerning ordination adopted by the Westminster Assembly [25] may be interpreted to mean that some sense of "transmission" or "conveyance" is retained in ordination.[26] Under this understanding the presbyters in ordaining pass on to others what they themselves have received; consequently, the rite is limited to "preaching presbyters"— presumably those who had also received ordination. On the other hand, the regulation may also be interpreted to mean that there will be a regulated form of ordination in which presbyters plead for God to authorize the one they ordain without understanding this to mean "transmission" of authority. In either case, ordination is to be regulated and to be carried out by those who have also received it. Ainslie has shown that, though this restriction was written into the Westminster Form and

("Wesley's Ordinations," *WHSP*, 24 [1943-44], 76.) In any case, a modified episcopacy seems to have been Wesley's intention. This topic is still the subject of much discussion and debate. See Colin Williams, *John Wesley's Theology Today*, pp. 218 ff.; Richard J. Cooke, "Our Methodist Episcopacy," *Methodist Review*, 114 (1931), 206-14. For a recent expression of the opposite viewpoint see J. E. Rattenbury, *The Eucharistic Hymns of John and Charles Wesley*, p. 159.

[24] He continues this statement: "The plea of Divine right, for diocesan episcopacy, was never heard of in the primitive Church." (*Letters*, III, 182.)

[25] "Every minister of the Word is to be ordained by imposition of hands, and prayer, with fasting, by these preaching presbyters to whom it doth belong." (*The Form of Presbyterial Church Government and of Ordination of Ministers Agreed Upon by the Assembly of Divines at Westminster* [Edinburgh: Printed by E. Robertson, 1766], p. 535, cited hereafter as *Westminster Form of Church Government*.)

[26] Ainslie, *The Doctrines of Ministerial Order in the Reformed Churches*, p. 217. Ainslie is rather reluctant to admit this, for he evidently would like to dismiss such a concept of "transmission" when it relates primarily to the office of the minister and his authority to administer the sacraments, although he makes an interesting case for "doctrinal succession," placing the emphasis on the succession of ministers who have taught a "true" doctrine. Norman Sykes (*Old Priest and New Presbyter*, p. 38), credits Bishop Jewell with interpreting apostolic succession "as a succession of doctrine, not of office."

therefore became the common practice, there was widespread difference among the Reformed churches on restrictions as to who might ordain —lay elders sometimes being included. Nevertheless, the assumption behind maintaining competent and standard ordinations indicates the emphasis on unity and some sense of authority.[27]

Wesley also rejected a linear concept of apostolic succession which depended on an uninterrupted succession of bishops since he doubted it could ever be proved and therefore considered it a "fable." [28] This did not, however, entail a rejection of a linear concept of the ministry. Rattenbury points out that his views here were "more akin to those of the Presbyterian Divines." He continues:

It must not be thought that Wesley believed in no apostolic succession because he rejected episcopal succession. What he disbelieved was that bishops and presbyters were of orders inherently different. He thought a presbyter had the rights that a bishop claimed. It is quite evident that he held that orders could only be given by men who had orders. Otherwise, why should he have troubled to give orders himself? He gave them because he believed that ordination, which in the Church of England was only given by bishops was really the function of the whole presbyterate. He held that he, a presbyter, was a New Testament bishop. There is no evidence at all that he thought "orders" could be given by any other persons than bishops and presbyters. He was, in this matter, not a High Church Episcopalian, but a High Church Presbyterian. Whether he taught that there was a special grace bestowed or transmitted by the laying on of hands is undemonstrable, but he obviously thought that authority to administer sacraments could only be transmitted by this method.[29]

Rattenbury's designation of Wesley as a high church Presbyterian in matters of ordination seems a logical one, since it would identify him with those Presbyterians who held a restrictive view of the ministry and of its ordination. According to Ainslie, some of the high church Presbyterians embraced a distinct linear succession doctrine, claiming church power to have descended to them from Christ through the Roman

[27] Ainslie, *The Doctrines of Ministerial Order in the Reformed Churches*, pp. 186-90.
[28] *Letters*, IV, 139-40.
[29] J. Ernest Rattenbury, *Wesley's Legacy to the World* (London: Epworth Press, 1938), p. 193. Probably Williams (*John Wesley's Theology Today*, p. 226) is correct when he says Wesley intends, in his criticism of succession, to reject any concept of a "mechanical succession" but not some form of succession itself.

Church and being no less effective or valid because of this.[30] Rejecting
episcopal succession, they nevertheless claimed a form of ministerial succession. For the Presbyterians and Wesley, the presbyter is able to ordain and in this act conveys authority and thereby maintains unity.

The form followed in the ordination service by Wesley also resem-
bles that of the Presbyterians. Wesley, according to Simon, understood
the presbyters of the church at Alexandria to have joined together in
ordaining a new bishop, chosen from their own number in order to
avoid outside interference from other bishops.[31] When he ordained men
for America he had James Creighton and Thomas Coke, presbyters of
the Church of England, to join with him in order that he might follow
this early church tradition. Where the Presbyterians limited their ordination to that of a presbyter, Wesley, following the early church, extended this to the ordination of a bishop or superintendent. Nevertheless, for the Presbyterians and Wesley no bishop was necessary to give
the ordination validity—under the form of the Church of England the
bishop, even though he is joined by presbyters, must lay on his hands
for the ordination to be valid.

Frederic Platt quotes Richard Whatcoat, one of those ordained on
this occasion, as follows: "Rev. John Wesley, Thomas Coke, and James
Creighton, presbyters of the Church of England, formed a presbytery
and ordained Richard Whatcoat and Thomas Vasey deacons; and the
next day by the same hands they were ordained elders."[32] The similarities between these ordinations and those of the Presbyterians are
obvious. Ordination is a corporate act joined in by more than one
presbyter. It is the action of a presbytery signifying the unified body.[33]
The Presbyterians insisted on ordination as the action of the whole presbytery in order to avoid the problems they saw in the "free" ordinations
of the Independents, but in any case, they took, in general, the same

[30] Ainslie, *The Doctrines of Ministerial Order in the Reformed Churches,* pp. 217-18.
[31] John Simon, *John Wesley, The Last Phase* (London: Epworth Press, 1934), p. 229.
[32] Frederic Platt, "Wesley's Ordinations—A Retrospect," *LQHR,* 160 (1953), 65-66.
[33] "Ordination is the act of a presbytery, the power of ordering the whole work of ordination is in the whole presbytery. . . . The preaching presbyters orderly associated, . . .
are those to whom the imposition of hands doth appertain." (*Westminster Form of Church
Government,* p. 534; cf. Ainslie, *The Doctrines of Ministerial Order in the Reformed Churches,*
pp. 188-89.)

form used by Wesley; and, of course, the Presbyterians could claim with Wesley the precedent of the early church.

Charles Wesley, much to his chagrin, recognized this similarity to the Presbyterian form as is seen in this anguished letter:

I can scarcely believe it, that, in his eighty-second year, my brother, my old, intimate friend and companion, should have assumed the episcopal character, ordained elders, consecrated a bishop, and sent him to ordain our lay preachers in America! . . .

Had they patience a little longer, they would have seen a real bishop in America, consecrated by three Scotch bishops who have their consecration from the English bishops, and are acknowledged by them as the same with themselves. . . . But what are your poor Methodists now? *Only a new sect of presbyterians.*[34]

Though Wesley seemingly intended to establish an episcopal order, even if through the means of an essentially Presbyterian concept of ordination, his followers in England failed to carry out his plan. The Conference of 1794 eliminated ordination by simply ruling that "the distinction between ordained and unordained preachers shall be dropped."[35] Thereafter admission to full connection was considered sufficient ordination. Ordination by the imposition of hands was not resumed until 1836 in England. When it was reinstituted the conference assumed this function with the "President, ex-president, secretary, and three of the other senior ministers" laying on their hands.[36] This form, of

---

[34] Tyerman, *The Life and Times of the Rev. John Wesley*, III, 439-40 (italics mine). As the rest of the letter indicates, Charles sees no future for the Methodists, for they, through "vain janglings" will "like other sects of Dissenters, come to nothing." The dissensions among the Methodists immediately following Wesley's death almost substantiated Charles's prediction. The depth of Charles's bitterness over this action is seen in his quip:

"So easily are Bishops made
By man's, or woman's whim?
Wesley his hands on Coke hath laid,
But who laid hand on Him?"

(Frank Baker, *Representative Verse of Charles Wesley* [Nashville: Abingdon Press, 1962], p. 368.)

[35] George Smith, *History of Wesleyan Methodism* (3 vols.; London: Longman, Green, Longman, and Roberts, 1863), II, 24, cf. 234-35.

[36] *Ibid.*, III, 327.

course, eliminated the necessity of a bishop and made ordination the function of the "presbyters" or "elders" acting for the conference. In British Methodism ordination is still considered to be a function of the conference.[37] In this it is again similar to Presbyterianism, for, as we have seen, Presbyterians always insisted that, though the preaching presbyters are the instruments or conveyors of ordination, it is the Presbytery which ordains.[38] However, other elements of British Methodism are not Presbyterian; thus in the words of Edgar Thompson it has "a constitution which is neither Episcopalian nor Presbyterian, but a unique composition of both." [39]

It has not been the intention of this review of Wesley's ordinations to attempt to prove any dependence upon the Presbyterians but simply to note that in the historical situation as it developed and in Wesley's concept of ordination definite similarities are present which denote further affinities between the two traditions, whether or not they were recognized by Wesley or would have been accepted as such by him.

It should be noted here that, for all of Wesley's vehement denial of separation from the Church of England, he always defined separation in its strictly legal terms,[40] which were not accepted as adequate by the authorities of that church. His establishment of a legal basis for his societies by providing the Methodist Connection with deeds to the property owned by it witnesses to his own unadmitted recognition of the almost certain separation that would come after his death.[41] However, it was the ordinations he performed which finally put him and his movement beyond the pale of the Church of England, for this was a violation of a fundamental Anglican rule of order.[42] To take such

[37]Edgar Thompson, "Episcopacy: John Wesley's View," LQHR, 181 (1956), 117.

[38] Exact correspondence would require that the Presbyterian General Assembly ordain, but in either case those ordaining are acting as instruments of the governing body.

[39] "Episcopacy: John Wesley's View," LQHR, 181 (1956), 117.

[40] Commenting on his ordinations he defines his concept of separation. "If anyone is pleased to call this *separation from the Church*, he may. But the law of England does not call it so; nor can anyone properly be said so to do, unless out of conscience he refuses to join in the service, and partake of the Sacraments administered therein." (MMC, 192.)

[41] Works, VIII, 329-31.

[42] Thompson, "Episcopacy: John Wesley's View," LQHR, 181 (1956), 116. George Eayrs points out that not only did this ordination "dissent from the Church as by law established" but also Wesley's use of extemporaneous prayer, his introduction of "unauthorized" services, and his disregard for parish lines and the authorization of bishops to preach in appointed places,

a step was in reality to separate himself and his society from that church, whether or not he would admit it. In Frank Baker's words, "By his ordinations John Wesley proclaimed himself in deeds if not in words a schismatic, though with the best of intentions and the clearest of consciences." [43]

The Societies

The societal system of Methodism has long been recognized as a key element in its success since it gave the strength of mutual fellowship, as well as providing a structural form peculiarly adapted to the needs of the people. Here it was that the individual believer could gain encouragement and guidance so necessary for continued growth in the faith.

The developed system or "connexion" of Methodist societies firmly and permanently entrenched on the English scene by the late eighteenth century was, of course, the result of more than a half-century of development under the diligent and firm hand of John Wesley, but more than this, it was the expression of his early conviction that *together*— through Christian fellowship—men are able to find, confirm, and grow in their faith.

The formation of the earliest Methodist societies was, like so much of Methodism, a matter of historical circumstance; in both Bristol and London Wesley found himself sought out as a leader by small groups of people, who, under his preaching as well as that of George Whitefield and others, had become interested in improving their faith and Christian life. The organizational structure of such groups or societies was close at hand in both the religious societies of the Established Church, which still existed, particularly in London, and in the Moravian societies, of which Wesley had been an active member since returning from America.

John Simon's first work in his monumental series on Wesley, entitled *John Wesley and the Religious Societies*, contains his persuasive attempt "to show the affinities between the Religious and the Methodist So-

---

as well as his establishment of a conference as the ecclesiastical authority over Methodism may also be considered. These actions established in fact the separateness of Methodism even if Wesley would not recognize it as such. In each of these practices he stands in the Puritan tradition. (Eayrs, "Links Between the Ejected Clergy of 1662, The Wesleys, and Methodism," *The Ejectment of 1662 and the Free Churches*, ed. Alexander Maclaren [London: National Council of Evangelical Free Churches, n.d.], pp. 116-18.)

[43] "John Wesley's Churchmanship," *LQHR*, 185 (1960), 272.

cieties." [44] Here it becomes clear that in many respects Wesley, consciously or unconsciously, was reviving in his own groups some of the principal features of these important Anglican groups. From these groups had arisen such far-reaching work as that carried out by "The Society for Promoting Christian Knowledge," "The Society for the Propagation of the Gospel in Foreign Parts," as well as the controversial "Society for the Reformation of Manners." Simon, while certain that Wesley moves beyond the interest and abilities of these earlier societies, understands him to have preserved their "best characteristics" and to have been at one with their purpose—to promote holiness.[45]

Clifford W. Towlson's study, *Moravian and Methodist,* has done a similar service by investigating Wesley's use of the "bands" within his societies.[46] Wesley's band system of five to ten persons meeting frequently to "confess their faults one to another, and pray one for another, that they may be healed," [47] is convincingly presented as being a direct import from the Moravian practice instituted by Count von Zinzendorf at Herrnhut and followed by Böhler in London. Wesley probably first became acquainted with it among the Moravians of America. Towlson, emphasizing the differences between the English religious societies and the Wesleyan societies, gives more weight to the immediate influence of the Brethren on Wesley in producing the form and character of Methodist societies.[48] He may well be correct since, at the time the societies were begun, Wesley was undoubtedly influenced in all areas by Moravian teaching and practice. However, it is Towlson himself who points out that the Aldersgate Religious Society was an Anglican society rather than Moravian and that "with the growth of the Societies, the bands lost much of their early importance." [49] In this connection it should also be noted that Wesley's early association with the Oxford "Holy Club," resembling as it does the usual religious

[44] John Simon, *John Wesley and the Religious Societies* (London: Epworth Press, 1921), p. 10. See especially chap. I, "The Religious Societies," and chap. XXIII, "A New Society."
[45] *Ibid.,* p. 27.
[46] *Moravian and Methodist,* pp. 184 ff.
[47] *Journal,* II, 50; *Works,* VIII, 272.
[48] *Moravian and Methodist,* p. 192.
[49] *Ibid.,* pp. 184, 194.

society, certainly cannot be discounted as playing its part in the development of the societal form in Wesley's work.[50]

Neither Towlson nor Simon, concerned as they are with a particular aspect of Wesley's societies, discusses another English form of church society which displays striking similarities to Wesley's groups. This is the Puritan "gathered church." Horton Davies has suggested that Wesley's societies may be "an amalgam of two great Puritan concepts namely 'the gathered church' and 'the priesthood of all believers.' "[51] The Methodist application of the great Protestant doctrine of "the priesthood of all believers" in the use of lay preachers, lay leaders of societies, bands, and classes, as well as emphasis upon the individuals' responsibility for one another's spiritual life, requires little comment. However, the similarities between Wesleyan societies and "the gathered church" do merit investigation.

In early Puritanism the distinction between the Presbyterians and the Independents or Congregationalists was principally over the form of church government. The Independents, insisting upon local autonomy whereby those redeemed believers who by their experience of conversion and life of holiness were "gathered" by Christ out of the world, could *voluntarily* join themselves together for mutual fellowship and worship. This principle rejected any "inherited, nominal, birthright type of Christianity,"[52] as well as the Presbyterian form of church organization which might infringe on the voluntary nature as well as local control of each church. Although such a distinction was the principal original difference and the source of much controversy and debate between the two factions, Professor Davies has pointed out that "the ejection of the Puritan divines in 1662 and the failure to comprehend them in 1689 led all the Nonconformists to approximate to the Congregationalist conception of a 'gathered church.' "[53] With the ejection, Puritans of whatever stripe were forced to "gather" their followers into

---

[50] In one of Wesley's accounts of the rise of Methodist societies he traces the societies back to this Holy Club. (*A Short History of Methodism*, in *Works*, VIII, 348.)

[51] Horton Davies, "Epworth's Debt to Geneva—a Field of Research," *The Livingstonian*, 1960, p. 6.

[52] Horton Davies, *Worship and Theology in England: 1690-1850*, p. 25.

[53] *Ibid.*

homes and other meeting places for the functions of fellowship and worship.

While it is not necessary to discuss the general nature of these churches, those features which resemble specific characteristics of Wesley's societies are salient to our study.[54] The understanding of the church as a fellowship of mutually concerned individuals is the first of these features.

As Geoffrey Nuttall points out, a small group consciously separating from a larger body, and often persecuted by such, normally has a real appreciation and demand for fellowship.[55] Such was the case in both Congregationalism and Methodism. More important in this feature of fellowship, however, was the mutual help, encouragement, and support drawn from one another. Speaking of the Congregationalists, Nuttall declares: "This mutual care and 'watchfulness over each other's conversation' are precisely what we find recorded again and again in the church books and histories, from the first day of their formation." [56] Wesley characterizes his societies as "a company of men having the form and seeking the power of godliness, united in order to pray together, to receive the word of exhortation, and to watch over one another in love, that they might help each other to work out their salvation." [57]

Prominent in this fellowship was the sharing of one's religious experience through personal testimonials. Though Wesley did not make the testimonial of one's experience a requirement of admission as had the Congregationalists, the testimonial became a significant feature of the Methodist societies.

Nuttall indicates that the ability of an individual to express his religious views and experiences was not a normal thing in the seventeenth

---

[54] That Wesley recognized that the organization of societies provided an obvious similarity to the Dissenting congregations is indicated by his answer to the question of whether Methodists were not in fact Dissenters, in which he comments, "Although we frequently use extemporary prayer, and unite together in a religious society; yet we are not Dissenters in the only sense our law acknowledges." (*Works,* VIII, 321.)

[55] Nuttall, *Visible Saints,* p. 70. I am largely dependent upon this study for the description of the features of the congregational "gathered church."

[56] *Ibid.,* p. 74. From the Norwich covenant: "We will, in all love, improve our communion as brethren, by watching over one another, and as need shall be, counsel, admonish, reprove, comfort, relieve, assist, and bear with one another." Quoted by Nuttall, p. 81.

[57] *Works,* VIII, 269. See Wesley's "Rules of the Band-Societies" for a description of the intimate inquiry into the spiritual status of one another. *Works,* VIII, 272-73.

century, and, while new for the common man, this requirement of the Congregationalists served to train an articulate laity.[58] The same was true for Methodism, where the small group weekly meeting demanded of the individual an ability of religious self-expression. Lay testimony became an important factor in the spread of the gospel and the training of members where lay leaders were responsible for the spiritual guidance and development of a fledgling convert. It may also be maintained that the discipline and self-expression learned to a significant degree in these small groups in Puritanism and later in Methodism contributed a great deal to the character and self-reliance of the nineteenth-century Englishman.[59]

Along with this mutual consent of the members to share with each other and to be responsible to each other was the mutual consent of the pastor to serve the congregation and of the congregation to accept him. Without an appointive system, such mutual understanding was necessary in the Congregational system, as Nuttall shows. As we have seen, Wesley insisted on voluntary consent between pastor and parishioners. In doing so, he expressed a fundamental Congregational precept and, as Frank Baker asserts, indicated his essential agreement with the Congregational understanding. In the 1745 Minutes either the preacher or a people were allowed to leave the other if "convinced it is for the glory of God and the superior good of their souls." [60] This expression of a Congregational principle did not, however, lead Wesley to reject a comprehensive appointive system. He understood that mutual consent could be present between pastor and parishioners even when the pastor is appointed by an agency other than the local congregation. In the pragmatic application of the theory the principle of an appointive procedure came to a dominant and authoritative position in Methodism.

The second feature to be discussed is the acceptance of holiness as the aim of church life.

---

[58] *Visible Saints*, p. 111.

[59] "The real strength and felicity of the Victorian age lay . . . in the self-discipline and self-reliance of the individual Englishman, derived indeed from many sources, but to a large extent sprung from Puritan traditions to which the Wesleyan and Evangelical movements had given another lease of life." (G. M. Trevelyan, *English Social History* [London: Longmans, Green and Co., 1958], p. 509.). G. P. Gooch, *English Democratic Ideas in the Seventeenth Century* (2nd ed.; New York: Harper & Row, 1957) provides a detailed study of the molding of English political thought and self-reliance by those of the Puritan tradition.

[60] Frank Baker, "John Wesley's Churchmanship," p. 270.

Holiness was of the essence of the Puritan movement, prompted by their appreciation for and insistence upon sanctification. Among the Congregationalists it became a primary category of church membership. Indeed, one must be a "visible saint" to gain admittance, as indicated by this article from the covenant of the church at Altham.

We thus apprehend, that they only are worthy that are Saints visible to the eye of rational charity, or such as, professing faith and repentance, live not in the neglect of any Christian duty or in commission of any known notorious sin; having such a measure of knowledge as to lead Christ into the soul, and the soul to Christ.[61]

If such visible holiness is required for admission, naturally it is expected for continuation in good standing. Wesley's societies, in contrast, are reputed for their openness, requiring only a desire "to flee from the wrath to come, to be saved from their sins." Nevertheless, in his "Rules" for the United Societies he adds that "wherever this is really fixed in the soul, it will be shown by its fruits. It is therefore expected of all who continue therein, that they should continue to evidence their desire of salvation." [62] Such evidence is then detailed and is a chronicle of the holy life, principally, but not exclusively, spelled out here in terms of outward manifestations. His description of *The Character of a Methodist*, on the other hand, emphasizes the inward holiness. In either case, he who was worthy of continuing in the fellowship of the Methodist societies would obviously have qualified as one of the "visible saints." [63]

[61] Quoted by Nuttall, *Visible Saints*, p. 132.
[62] *Works*, VIII, 270.
[63] *Ibid.*, VIII, 340-47. Wesley was early accused of being a Dissenter, partly because of his emphasis on holiness, and his answer merits full quotation since it displays his own understanding of "true" church members, as well as his own relation to the Church of England. "I think it was the next time I was there that the Ordinary of Newgate came to me, and with much vehemence tole me he was sorry that I should turn Dissenter from the Church of England. I told him if it was so I did not know it. . . .

"Our twentieth Article defines a true church, 'a congregation of faithful people, wherein the true word of God is preached and the sacraments duly administered.' According to this account the Church of England is that body of faithful people (or holy believers) in England among whom the pure word of God is preached and the sacraments duly administered. Who, then, are the worst Dissenters from this Church? (1) Unholy men of all kinds; swearers, Sabbath-breakers, drunkards, fighters, whoremongers, liars, revilers, evil-speakers; the passionate, the gay, the lovers of money, the lovers of dress or of praise, the lovers of pleasure more than lovers of God: all these are Dissenters of the highest sort, continually striking at the root of

Holiness was, then, a common object for both Congregationalists and Methodists.[64]

A third feature common to Congregational and Methodist societies was the insistence upon freedom of opinion. This again was a bastion of Congregational thought and polity. Liberty of conscience, or the ability to choose voluntarily their associations without the compulsion of forced belief, was inherent in their whole understanding. It was quite natural that the corollary to this, freedom of opinion or independence of judgment in matters of religion, should also be accepted. Since experience rather than belief was the criterion of membership, the principle by which one was accepted and continued in membership was "Faith in Christ; and Holiness of Life, without regard to this or that circumstance, or opinion in outward, and circumstantiall things." [65] Such liberality led to great variety among the Congregationalists and to many conflicts but was generally upheld.

Wesley's famous statement in his description of a Methodist displays the same general feeling:

The distinguishing marks of a Methodist are not his opinions of any sort. His assenting to this or that scheme of religion, his embracing any particular set of notions, his espousing the judgment of one man or of another, are all quite wide of the point. . . . As to all opinions which do not strike at the root of Christianity, we think and let think.[66]

Wesley's last sentence and the Congregationalist "Faith in Christ" do in fact put restrictions upon their seemingly very liberal sentiments.

---

the Church, and themselves in truth belonging to no church, but to the synagogue of Satan. (2) Men unsound in the faith; those who deny the Scriptures of truth, those who deny the Lord that bought them, those who deny justification by faith alone, or the present salvation which is by faith: these also are Dissenters of a very high kind. . . . Lastly, those who unduly administer the sacraments; who (to instance but in one point) administer the Lord's Supper to such as have neither the power nor the form of godliness. These, too, are gross Dissenters from the Church of England, and should not cast the first stone at others." (*Journal*, II, 335-36.)

[64] It was, of course, also the motivation for the Anglican Religious Societies (Simon, *John Wesley and the Religious Societies*, pp. 10-12) and to some extent for the Moravians, for they were anxious to promote "inward growth" (Towlson, *Moravian and Methodist*, p. 184).

[65] Covenant at Bedford, quoted by Nuttall, *Visible Saints*, p. 114.

[66] *Works*, VIII, 340, 357. For one of Wesley's strongest statements on freedom of conscience see his tract, *Thoughts upon Liberty*, in *Works*, XI, 39-40.

In practice, far greater scrutiny of various "opinions" was practiced by both traditions than these quotations indicate; yet there was a true attempt to allow freedom of opinion in all matters but those relative to the very core of the Christian faith. It is this freedom of opinion, particularly as it applies to church polity, that George Eayrs sees as a principal affinity between the Nonconformists (including, of course, the Congregationalists) and Wesley.[67]

The fourth similarity lies in the covenant and the close discipline required of members. Wesley's use of the personal covenant in a corporate service obviously has a relationship to the Congregational church covenant. The use of covenant for the two groups is different in that for the Congregationalists the covenant constituted the articles of incorporation of their church and must be accepted and usually signed or recited by all members,[68] while Wesley, following Joseph Alleine's variation of this type of covenant, applied it only in terms of a personal covenant, discarding it as the basis of church or societal fellowship. Nevertheless, since he made it a public and corporate service for which real spiritual preparation must be made and which became a major church event, it reflects, at least in part, the church covenants though it cannot be identified with them.

In the Congregational church covenant there was the element of commitment—it was a covenant between God *and* one's fellows—so any transgression of the covenant, usually through the failure to live a holy life and sometimes in matters of belief, constituted grounds for expulsion. In view of the personal nature of the covenant in Methodist societies, it was not understood to imply such obligations, but to enter a Methodist society was to commit one's self to definite societal and personal responsibilities. One must abide by Methodist discipline; attend the class, band, and society meetings; and, most important, lead a holy life. Therefore, expulsion for failure to abide by this pattern was a definite and often-used method of regulation.

[67] George Eayrs, "Links Between the Ejected Clergy of 1662, the Wesleys, and Methodism," *The Ejectment of 1662 and the Free Churches,* p. 114. The passage quoted from Wesley has often been taken to mean that he insisted upon no doctrinal standards and therefore allowed Methodism to be theologically weak. This is a gross misrepresentation of Wesley, although, unfortunately, it may not be of later Methodism.

[68] Nuttall, *Visible Saints,* pp. 74-75.

Article XIX of the Savoy Declaration states the procedure for correction and finally expulsion among the Congregationalists:

Whereas some offenses are or may be known only to some, it is appointed by Christ that those to whom they are so known do first admonish the offender in private (in public offenses where any sin, before all), and in case of non-amendment upon private admonition, the offense being related to the Church, and the offender not manifesting his repentance, he is to be duly admonished in the Name of Christ by the whole Church, by the Ministry of the Elders of the Church; and if this Censure prevail not for his repentance, then he is to be cast out by Excommunication, with the consent of the Church.[69]

A similar procedure was followed by the Moravians, and Wesley recommends it as the legitimate method of clearing the societies of those unwilling to abide by their commitments to the society and to God.[70] Though Wesley used the method in clearing the first societies, later development of the class ticket to "separate the precious from the vile" placed almost total responsibility for judgment in the hands of Wesley or his preachers.[71] In this development, Methodism became autocratic, but as Coomer points out, it had a precedent for this authoritarian nature in Independency, where the "church meeting" could "wield quite as despotic an oversight of the lives of its members." [72]

What is important is the insistence by Congregationalists and Wesley that the church or society must remain holy and diligent in the practice of its faith and that failure of a member to do so would mean severing the bonds of fellowship. No such provision for expulsion, except for nonattendance, was a part of the Anglican religious societies. Perhaps Wesley's insistence upon it explains the close-knit fellowship and responsibility found in the Methodist societies. Later developments in the Methodist societies caused this responsibility for expulsion to lose its

[69] "The Savoy Declaration, 1658," *The Creeds of Christendom*, ed. Philip Schaff (3 vols., 6th ed.; New York: Harper and Brothers, 1931), III, 727. This procedure is, of course, essentially that outlined in Matt. 18:15-17.

[70] Wesley, "The Cure of Evil Speaking," *Sermons*, II, 296-308.

[71] *Works*, VIII, 256.

[72] Duncan Coomer, "The Influence of Puritanism and Dissent on Methodism," *LQHR*, 175 (1950), 349.

nature as a corporate societal action and reflects the autocratic tendencies of Methodism.[73]

A final area of similarity and a most important one is that of the "gathered" nature of the societies and the Congregational churches. Nuttall maintains, and he is supported by Haller, that the earliest Congregationalists attempted to establish their groups in the parochial framework, being in these situations "gathered" communities within the larger group.[74] In the course of time they were forced out or willingly left the Establishment. When this happened the "gathered" community was composed of all those who would come out no matter what their previous affiliations had been. Their separation led them to defend their concepts, and one of the sermons of William Dell included by Wesley in the *Library* expresses this defense of the "gathered" church, as well as its requirement of holiness:

> **There be some that talk much against New Doctrine, which is the old reproach of the Gospel; but surely there was never newer Doctrine than this, *that the Spiritual Church of the New Testament, should be made up of all the People that live in a Kingdom; and that all that are born in such a Nation, should necessarily be stones for the building up of the New Jerusalem.* This is a new Doctrine indeed, which neither the Old nor the New Testament owns; BUT WAS CONVEYED INTO THE WORLD BY THE SPIRIT OF ANTICHRIST. For God doth not now make any People, or Kindred, or Nation his Church; but gathers his church out of every People, and Kindred, and Nation; and none can be stones of this Building, but those that are FIRST Elect, and AFTER MADE precious, through a new Birth, and the gift of the Spirit.[75]**

[73] It should be noted that, though the Methodists developed a strict sense of control among their members which could lead to expulsion, their openness to anyone seeking to "flee from the wrath to come" distinguished them from the Congregationalists, for whom holiness was an entrance requirement rather than a requirement for continuation in good standing. Nuttall credits Wesley with providing the basis for a world church through this openness, while the Congregationalists tended to draw the parish closer and thereby to limit themselves. (Nuttall, *Visible Saints*, p. 159.)

[74] Nuttall, *Visible Saints*, p. 134. "All this [Puritan Reform], we must remember, was done or attempted primarily within the church, and with no admitted intention save to inspire and reform the people through the church. Independency and separation in all their organized forms developed only as the authorities at successive stages placed more and more serious impediments in the way of the reformer's efforts." (William Haller, *The Rise of Puritanism*, p. 53.)

[75] William Dell, *Several Sermons and Discourses* (London: Printed by J. Sowle, 1709), pp. 94-95 [CL, VII, 123].

A major criticism of the Congregationalists by men such as Baxter and Philip Henry was that they disregarded parish lines—"gathering" their members indiscriminately.[76] Wesley's movement had its share of trouble over just such charges. They, like the Congregationalists before them, disregarded parish lines and other ecclesiastical restrictions but not without bringing the stigma of "dissent" upon themselves. Parish churches and some dioceses were declared closed to Methodist preachers over this issue.

When we turn to Wesley's *Advice to the People Called Methodist,* we find that he referred to his own societies as "gathered" communities. "You are just gathered, or (as it seems) gathering rather, out of all other societies or congregations"; "you are gathered out of so many other congregations." [77] Wesley was quite conscious of the reality of his "gathering" from various communions and openly advocated such. Could he have used the term "gathered" during his own time without raising the image of the "gathered churches" so much a part of the English religious scene? It hardly seems possible, and indeed, Wesley himself seems conscious of this very fact, for in this same treatise he carefully distinguishes his societies from the earlier "gathered churches" by pointing out that: "Whereas every other religious set of people, as soon as they were joined to each other, separated themselves from their former societies or congregations; you on the contrary, do not; nay, you absolutely disavow all desire of separation." [78] Wesley, then, seems to recog-

---

[76] Nuttall, *Visible Saints,* p. 108.

[77] *Works,* VIII, 354, 356.

[78] *Works,* VIII, 354. On another occasion, answering the question as to whether his movement was not "gathering churches out of churches," he comments: "If you mean only gathering people out of buildings called churches, it is. But if you mean, dividing Christians from Christians, and so destroying Christian fellowship, it is not." (*Works,* VIII, 251.) It is interesting, however, to note that in expanding this statement he describes the Established churches in such a way as to show that they do not contain Christians nor are they places of Christian fellowship. In this he pointedly gives the reasons which motivated the "gathered church" of the century before and shows that they form his own motivation, but his dedication to the Church of England will not allow him to take the step of separation. No matter how clearly he can enunciate the faults of the Establishment, as well as the reasons which led to previous separations, it does not follow that separation is the only logical step—for himself. He could only be a critical son still respecting and honoring the parent no matter how wayward. Coomer is therefore correct when he says that Wesley never accepted the "gathered church" principle in the sense that he never accepted separation as a part of that principle, but he certainly uses the gathered nature in his own societies. ("The Influence of Puritanism and Dissent on Methodism," *LQHR,* 175 [1950], 349.)

nize the reality of the "gathered" nature of his groups and this affinity with the Congregationalists but vigorously resisted the logical conclusion that this led to separation. As we have seen, his ordinations did in reality constitute such separation, but Wesley never recognized the fact.

He was anxious to maintain the societies within the church—to establish in pietistic fashion "ecclesiolae in ecclesia." Such was also the aim of some early Congregationalists but was abandoned in the face of the reality of nonacceptance. Wesley never abandoned the ideal which he sought; and consequently, though the Methodists remained technically within the Church of England until after Wesley's death, they were eventually forced by circumstance to become "a connection of 'gathered' churches." [79]

In view of these real similarities between the "gathered church" and Wesley's societies, are we able to claim any relationship between the two? It does not appear too bold to assert that Wesley seems to have recognized and accepted some of the more obvious parallels but did not allow any attempt to identify the two movements. Here, of course, he was most concerned with church polity and organization. That he also recognized the other similarities discussed above, such as fellowship, holiness, freedom of opinion, and so forth, seems almost self-evident; yet there is little or no concrete evidence of this unless his willingness to identify himself with and to commend the Puritan tradition, as well as his use of the works of leading advocates of the "gathered church" principle, such as John Owen, William Dell, Lewis Stuckley, and others, be regarded as such. We may, nevertheless, legitimately claim some areas of true affinity, possibly neither as pronounced nor as direct as that exerted by the Anglican religious societies and the Moravians, but still present. Whatever judgment is made as to extent of relationship and affinity, the "gathered church" tradition needs to be considered in any comprehensive study of the background of the Methodist societies.

The Ministry

True to his principle of using profitable material or example wherever he found it, when Wesley turned to the task of instructing his

[79] Davies, *Worship and Theology in England: 1690-1850*, p. 30.

preachers in how to carry out their duties, he relied upon the Puritan tradition for a significant portion of this instruction. Late in 1749 Wesley read *An Account of the Life of the Late Rev. Mr. David Brainerd*, edited by Jonathan Edwards, which had just been published.[80] This account of a Puritan missionary to the Indians was to achieve great popularity, and among the Methodists the popularity was for good reason—an abridgment by Wesley of the account and, more important, the constant recommendation by Mr. Wesley himself.[81]

Throughout his ministry, in dealing with ministers' chafing under the exigencies of their condition or in seeking to point to the dedication required of a minister, Wesley turns to Brainerd.[82] Indeed, the recommendation is written into the handbook of the Methodist ministry—*The Minutes of the Conferences*—and retains its place there throughout the several editions and revisions made during Wesley's lifetime.

Q. What can be done in order to revive the work of God where it is decayed? A. (1) Let every Preacher read carefully over the "Life of David Brainerd." Let us be followers of him, as he was of Christ, in absolute self-devotion, in total deadness to the world, and in fervent love to God and man. Let us but secure this point, and the world and the devil must fall at our feet.[83]

Brainerd's dedication under adverse and discouraging conditions and his ministry spent for others is the example for Wesley's preachers of a dedicated ministry among the people.

---

[80] *Journal*, III, 449. Though Wesley was always to recommend Brainerd, he nevertheless could be critical: "God hath once more 'given to the Gentiles repentance unto life!' Yet amidst so great matter of joy, I could not but grieve at this: that even so good a man as Mr. Brainerd should be 'wise above that is written,' in condemning what the Scripture nowhere condemns; in prescribing to God the way wherein He should work; and (in effect) applauding himself, and magnifying his own work, above that which God wrought in Scotland, or among the English in New England: whereas, in truth, the work among the Indians, great as it was, was not to be compared to that at Cambuslang, Kilsyth, or Northampton."

[81] Wesley's abridgment was to enjoy several printings and editions and became a popular Methodist book. *Bibliography*, p. 143.

[82] *Letters*, VI, 57. "Methodist preachers cannot have always accommodations fit for gentlemen. But let us look upon D. Brainerd, and praise God for what we have." (*Ibid.*, V, 282.)

[83] *Works*, VIII, 328; Wesley helped in raising money for the Indian work and commented on how it can only be effective if preachers can be found "of David Brainerd's spirit." (*Journal*, V, 226.)

Of more consequence, however, is Wesley's inclusion in the Minutes of a substantial section drawn directly from Richard Baxter's *Gildas Salvianus: The Reformed Pastor*. This treatise, written by Baxter at the height of Puritan power and control in the English church, was an appeal to, as well as instruction for, the pastor in "private instruction and catechizing." It was to become the principal work of its kind in the Puritan tradition, serving almost as a manual for the Dissenting ministry. Wesley adopts its main features and methods as those which were to guide the Methodist preacher in the all-important responsibility of house-to-house visitation and instruction.

While he recommends the work as early as 1755, it is in the 1766 revision of the Minutes that he incorporates a succinct abridgment of a large section of the treatise.[84] Though reduced somewhat in later editions, this abridgment was to stand throughout Wesley's lifetime as the standard direction in visitation and private instruction for Methodist preachers.[85]

Clearly, Wesley can completely identify his own interests with the overriding, dynamic emphasis of this treatise, which reveals so well the Puritan demand for the religious cultivation of the whole person in the most intimate and exacting relationship between pastor and parishioner. At this point, the Puritan pattern is the form for the Methodists and constitutes the very instruction itself.

The instructions as included in the Minutes represent some of Wesley's most careful and complete, as well as extensive, abridging. Following his usual pattern, he freely paraphrases and condenses the major points. Because the work is to be used as specific instruction in the execution of

[84] Telford quotes Wesley as recommending the work to the 1755 Conference. (*Letters*, VI, 271.)

[85] The 1766 Minutes serve as the basis of this investigation since they evidently incorporate the original abridgment. In those Minutes the whole abridgment is clearly credited to Baxter, but in the later editions of the Minutes, as recorded in the *Works*, one may be confused as to what is supposedly Baxter and what Wesley. The first paragraph of the 1766 abridgment is enclosed in quotation marks and then the rest incorporated as if it were Wesley speaking. Although it is evidently a printing error, it might easily cause one to mistake the author of the instructions. Such is in fact the case even with the renowned scholar Leslie Church. In his article "The Pastor in the Eighteenth Century" (*LQHR*, 181 [1956], 19-23), he quotes much of Wesley's instructions on visitation as if it were Wesley's own; but it is in reality Wesley's abridgment of Baxter.

the minister's function in the Methodist societies, changes are made to make the instruction applicable to these societies rather than the parish for which they were originally written.[86] Comments relative to the situation of the church in Baxter's own time are eliminated. Wesley's personal preferences are evident in his recommendation that, while each morning is to be spent in study, each afternoon is to be used for house-to-house visitation. Baxter's recommendation had been that two days of the week be given over to visitation. Omitted is a section in which Baxter gives some twenty reasons for the necessity of this work, ranging from justification through scriptural precept to such curious reasons as: if one fails to carry out this responsibility he fails to fulfill the potential of his education, as well as disappointing his parents who set him aside for this work.[87] Evidently Wesley assumed that the necessity was self-evident or that his own requirement for his preachers to carry out such instruction was sufficient justification.

On the whole, however, Wesley is substantially true to Baxter's major instructions, even to the point of including apt illustrations and casual comments. While a detailed account of these instructions is not necessary, a summary of the major points will give insight into the imperative nature of such work, as well as how the Methodists through Puritan instruction were to carry on their visitation.

Wesley's abridgment begins with Baxter's catalog of the hindrances to such work among the people. The ministers will be hampered in the work for they will find themselves lazy and dull; bashful; of a "base, man pleasing temper"; unwilling to jeopardize their own "fleshly" interests, i.e., their tithes or financial support; unskillful in the work; but most important is the minister's own unfaithfulness or weakness, which, of course, means he will have great difficulty convincing others.[88] Among the people one will find an unwillingness to be taught, a dullness which makes it difficult to teach them anything, ignorance to the point of inability to understand the minister, and when "desirable impressions have been made on their hearts" they soon die away without continued

[86] *Gildas Salvianus: The Reformed Pastor*, in Baxter, *Works*, XIV, 316 [*MMC*, p. 66]; cf. p. 278 [*MMC*, p. 65].
[87] *Ibid.*, pp. 276-96 [*MMC*, p. 64].
[88] *Ibid.*, pp. 273-74 [*MMC*, pp. 63-64].

cultivation.[89] Difficult as the task may be under these conditions, it is absolutely necessary, for, as Baxter points out, many of those who have attended services regularly and heard good sermons for many years do not really understand their own condition or the gospel. "**I have found by experience that** [one of these] AN IGNORANT SET THAT HATH BEEN AN IMPROFITABLE HEARER SO LONG, hath GOT [learned] **more** KNOWLEDGE AND REMORSE OF CONSCIENCE **in half an hour's close discourse, than** THEY DID **from ten years' public preaching.**" [90]

Following his usual pattern, Baxter mentions a series of objections which might be raised against this kind of pastoral work and proceeds to answer them in detail. Wesley includes two of the six objections. The first deals with the objection that such intensive private instruction will leave no time for necessary study. Baxter answers by pointing out that "saving of souls" is more important, or in Wesley's version, "gaining knowledge is a good thing, but saving souls is a better." [91] In addition, one will find such work actually to be study in better understanding, and if given the correct amount of time, there will still be time enough for study. But if a choice must be made between the two, "**I would throw by all the libraries in the world, rather than be guilty of the perdition of one soul;** AT LEAST I KNOW THIS IS MY DUTY." [92] Such was the opinion of Baxter and Wesley, who in other circumstances could strongly recommend and require rigid study for the minister. The other objection used by Wesley was Baxter's comment on the supposition that the people would not submit to such a course of instruction. Here Wesley takes

[89] *Ibid.*, pp. 274-75 [*MMC*, p. 64].

[90] *Ibid.*, p. 276 [*MMC*, p. 64].

[91] *Ibid.*, pp. 296-98 [*MMC*, p. 65]. Objections to this type of work omitted by Wesley include the supposition that this course will destroy health in leaving no time for recreation (an objection Baxter and Wesley could make short work of); the understanding that it is not required that ministers "make drudges of themselves," making their lives "a burden and a slavery"; the idea that such instruction is the prerogative and responsibility of the preacher; and the concept that faith comes by hearing the word preached and, therefore, preaching is a far more important aspect of the work. (*Ibid.*, pp. 296-312.)

[92] *Ibid.*, p. 298 [*MMC*, p. 65]. That such a statement expressed Wesley's opinion is seen in a letter to Joseph Benson: "Many persons are in danger of reading too little; you are in danger of reading too much. Wherever you are, take up your cross, and visit all the society from house to house. Do this according to Mr. Baxter's plan, laid down in the Minutes of the Conference: The fruit which will ensue (perhaps in a short time) will abundantly reward your labour." (*Letters*, VI, 65.)

only one of Baxter's several answers, "If some REFUSE OUR HELP [do not], others will ACCEPT IT [gladly]; and the success with them may be so much, as may answer all our labour." [93] Without question, this task will tax all the skill of the minister and is in many ways far harder than study or the preaching of sermons.

To handle correctly a visit or consultation with a family, one should, after speaking with the whole family, "take then the persons one by one, and deal with them as far as you can in private, out of the hearing of the rest." [94] In this private discussion one is to hear what the person knows of the catechism (for Wesley it is what the children know of the "Instructions for Children").[95] This is to be followed by asking them (presumedly the more mature) "some of the weightiest points" of the gospel. Since such a session is to be a learning experience, it is not to be questions alone, but with the questions may be suggested appropriate answers, particularly where they do not seem to understand and/or to be able to answer. Having ascertained what they know of correct religion, one is ready to instruct them "according to their capacities." This is to be accompanied by diligent endeavor to inquire into the actual state of the man's faith—whether he is converted or not. If unconverted, one is to attempt to get him to see his condition. The minister is also to give all persons a "strong exhortation" to duty and to the use of all means to get their souls in right relation to God. Before leaving the house, according to Baxter, one might comment, "I pray you take it not ill that I have put you to this trouble, or dealt thus freely with you! It is as little pleasure to me as to you. If I did not know these things to be true and necessary, I would have spared this labour to myself and you." [96] This must have appeared too much like an apology to Wesley, for it is omitted. One is to close by asking the head of the house to carry on this work of instruction by examining the household at least each Sunday evening.

All of this must be done in the best spirit. One must remember to "speak differently according to the difference of the persons that you

[93] *Ibid.*, p. 309 [MMC, pp. 65-66].
[94] *Ibid.*, p. 319 [MMC, p. 66].
[95] *Ibid.*, p. 320 [MMC, p. 67].
[96] *Ibid.*, p. 333 [MMC, p. 68].

have to deal with." Hence, it must be done in the plainest of language with "Scripture proof for all you say" and with due seriousness.[97]

In later years Wesley adds the comment, "Do this in earnest, and you will soon find what a work you take in hand, in undertaking to be a Travelling Preacher!" [98] Puritan instruction had become the criterion by which a Methodist traveling preacher must measure himself.

Because Wesley's preachers were, for the most part, preachers and pastors without the opportunity of the sacramental functions of the ministry, this pastoral work assumed great importance for them. Supplemented by the societal and class organization, it provided much of the genius of the movement. Wesley's dependence on Puritan precept and teaching in this important pastoral function is, therefore, of major significance.

In summary, this study has revealed that Wesley's teachings and practice relative to the Christian and his church reflect strong affinities between him and the Puritans. While some of these were not consciously recognized, they are nevertheless clearly evident. In the case of the ministerial instruction there is, furthermore, unquestionable dependence. Wesley's understanding of the church, his teachings relative to it, and finally his practice logically carried him toward the Puritan tradition, with separation from the national church the inevitable result. Wesley's tenacious refusal to recognize this fact, though it has been shown he may well have seen the end result, could only retard but not stop this movement toward a closer identity with the Reformed tradition. Only a truly unique mixture of intense dedication to the Church of England and affinity with and sympathy for Reformed precepts expressed in the Puritan tradition could produce one who could so vigorously hold the two together and live with the resultant tensions. Others were not so endowed, and Methodism virtually joined the ranks of Dissent, though there was long found a minority of Methodists to deny this.

[97] *Ibid.*, p. 334 [MMC, p. 68].

[98] *Works*, VIII, 307. "In the afternoon follow Mr. Baxter's plan. Then you will have no time to spare: You will have work enough for all your time. Then, likewise, no Preacher will stay with us who is as salt that has lost its savour. For to such this employment would be mere drudgery. And in order to it, you will have need of all the knowledge you have, or can procure." (*Ibid.*, p. 315.)

2. The World

While the Christian life is begun in personal commitment and reformation of the individual, trained in the family circle and buttressed and matured in the community of believers, its most difficult task is to relate itself to the world, for that world impinges on each of these areas and forms the context for the whole. Instruction in Christian living must therefore include instruction in the proper attitude toward and participation in this world.

For the Puritans and for Wesley the Christian relationship to the world must be viewed from two perspectives. On the one hand, since the ultimate meaning and purpose in life for the Christian comes from relation to God, which produces his final salvation, and not, as in the case of natural man, from the world, a primary concern for the Christian is the transfer of his interests and values from those of the world to those of God. Contamination by the world must be removed. On the other hand, man has been, in the providence of God, placed in a material world which is good if used for its proper purposes, that is, God's glorification. Man must of necessity, therefore, live in relation to the world and, in addition, be responsible for his use of it. This responsibility entails the all-important responsibility to and for his neighbor, both materially and spiritually.

Because the Christian is to be primarily concerned with his relationship to God and not the world, it is no surprise to find one of the dominant Puritan expressions of the Christian relationship to the world in this sentence from John Flavel: "What is a saint, but a stranger and a pilgrim upon earth, a man in a strange country traveling homeward." [99] John Bunyan's *Pilgrim's Progress* was the epitome of this attitude, expressing the Christian's goal and consuming desire to be turned heavenward rather than toward the earth. The traps and snares along the way are principally those connected with the world. Wesley's sympathy with this concept is evident not only in his publication of *Pilgrim's Progress* but also in his own expressions, typified by his comment to his niece

[99] John Flavel, *Husbandry Spiritualized: or, The Heavenly Use of Earthly Things* (Elizabeth Town: Printed by Shepard Killock, 1794), p. 59 [CL, XXVII, 166].

that everything is a blessing "which disengages us from transient things and teaches us to live in eternity." [100] However, his conviction that the blessed life may be lived now in this world would not allow him to put the same stress upon this concept which is sometimes found in Puritan writings.

Such an understanding of the world led the Puritans and Wesley to insist upon the necessity for separation of the Christian from the evil influences of the world, particularly as these were exemplified in those men who, lacking the Christian perspective, were representatives of and apostles for a worldly life. Puritan and Wesleyan teaching relative to a Christian's participating in fellowship or company with a worldly man typifies the concentration on separation from the world.

Bolton advises his congregation concerning company:

That thou never cast thy selfe into wicked company, OR PRESSE AMONGST THE PROPHANE, ESPECIALLY upon choice, VOLUNTARILY AND DE-LIGHTFULLY and abide no longer with them at anytime UPON ANY OC-CASION, then thou hast sound warrant, AND A CALLING THEREUNTO. IT IS UNCOMELY, AND INCOMPATIBLE WITH GOOD CONSCIENCE [to do], It is not for the honour or comfort of Gods children, to KEEPE COMPANY, OR familiarly converse with gracelesse men. . . . There is a strange ATTRAC-TIVE AND IMPERIOUS power in ill company, to empoyson and pervert even the blest dispositions: . . . let a Christian but for a while abandon his HOLY CONFERENCE, AND COMFORTABLE communion with Gods children, and PLUNGE HIMSELFE INTO [stay in] the company of those who are BUT cold and carelesse, LASIE AND LUKE WARME PROFESSORS; and he shall in very short time finde his zeale to be very much cooled, HIS FORWARD-NESSE ABATED, the tenderness of his conscience TOO much qualified with worldly wisdome; much dullness of heart, deadnesse of spirit, drowzi-nesse, and heartlessnesse in his affections to holy things, and a universal decay of his graces insensibly to grow upon him.

In this respect many Christians doe themselves much WRONG, AND AFFLICT THEIR SOULES WITH MANY UNNECESSARY SPIRITUAL MISERIES [injury]. For they DOE sometimes unadvisedly, by reason of kindred, [or] for old acquaintance, ADVANTAGE, AND CARNAL CONTENTMENT, BECAUSE OF WORLDLY WISDOME, IMMUNITY FROM GROSSE SINNES, AND OTHER

[100] *Letters*, VII, 66.

GOOD PARTS OF THE PARTIES, hold A too neare, INTIMATE AND DELIGHTFUL correspondence with such as are BUT [at best] only civill men.[101]

Stuckley expresses the same sentiment and warns that the wicked are not simply the "loose" but also the "formal"—meaning those who are formally Christians but really wicked.[102] Wesley's sermons "On Friendship with the World" and "On Leaving the World" are commentaries upon the dangers inherent in a Christian's necessary contact with men of the world. They express the same concerns as the passage from Bolton, particularly as to the almost unconscious way in which this association with men of the world undercuts resolute concentration upon God. Aware of the particular situations where this danger is greatest, Wesley specifically admonishes one not to marry anyone who lacks religion, for here in the closest of human ties it is almost impossible to live in a situation where "they are subjects, not only of two separate, but of two opposite kingdoms. They act upon quite different principles; they aim at quite different ends." [103] Equally dangerous is association with one's relations or old acquaintances who are not religious. These constitute special danger, for it is "contrary . . . to flesh and blood" to reject such, but to avoid the danger it is nevertheless advisable. One may out of courtesy and natural affection visit such a relative but "it should certainly be as seldom as possible." [104] With Stuckley, Wesley compares such association with the futility and unthinkable act of associating with one who had the plague; it is even more dangerous, for it endangers the soul and not simply the body.[105] Allowance should be made for the fact that in these admonitions Wesley and the Puritans were attempting to guard their followers from the real dangers they saw in the example

[101] Bolton, *Walking with God*, pp. 73-76 [*CL*, IV, 349-50].

[102] Stuckley, *A Gospel-Glass*, p. 325 [*CL*, XIX, 423]. "What brings destruction on God's people, but their joining with the wicked." (*Christ and His Church*, in Sibbes, *Works*, II, 88 [*CL*, VI, 185].

[103] *Works*, VI, 467; *MMC*, p. 158.

[104] *Works*, VI, 474-75. Specific instructions are given by Bolton and Wesley as to how one is to handle the delicate problem of visitation among those who are not Christian. (*Ibid.*, p. 472; Bolton, *Walking with God*, p. 86 [*CL*, IV, 350-51].)

[105] "It had been better we had gone to the pest-house, and eat and drank with persons infected with the plague, EVEN WILST THE SORE AND BETCH WAS RUNNING ON THEM, than to accompany with wicked men; our bodies would have been endangered only by the one; but our souls are by the other." (Stuckley, *A Gospel-Glass*, p. 327 [*CL*, XIX, 424]; *Works*, VI, 459, 470.)

and influence of worldly men and may have therefore overstated the case.[106] However, even in the midst of these teachings concern is displayed for those of the world; the necessary contacts must be made in courtesy, patience, and love.[107]

Due to this common emphasis on separation from the world, there has been a tendency to identify Wesley with the Puritan tradition because of some of the similarities in their teachings which tend to distinguish them from other "worldly" persons—their "preciseness," discipline, and teachings such as sobriety and austerity in dress, criticism of the theater, and their general depreciation of the aesthetic sense of man with its suspicion of beauty and the arts.[108] Undoubtedly, definite similarities between the two traditions are evident in these teachings and may well explain much of the identification of the two movements by Wesley's contemporaries, but it is curious that Wesley includes hardly any of these Puritan teachings and practice in A Christian Library or uses them as examples to be followed. In fact, the two treatises which admonish their readers to sobriety in dress are those of circumspect Anglicans, the anonymous treatise The Whole Duty of Man, and Dr. Cave's Primitive Christianity.[109] Wesley's selections from the Puritans in the Library and otherwise seem to concentrate on the spiritual nature and vitality of the Christian life, on the purity of its holiness rather than instruction in such things as dress, plays, and the arts.

The distinction and separation of the Christian from the world is not, however, the only perspective from which the Christian must view the world. In sharp contrast to the negative attitude expressed above is the recognition that, of necessity, a Christian's active role in everyday life and his responsibility therein involves him inextricably in society and

---

[106] Because of this separatist tendency and the fact that the Christian must be more holy than the worldly man, the Puritans, along with Wesley, recognize the reality that Christians will be persecuted by the world. They take it to be God's providence in order to strengthen them. (Sermons, I, 368, 378; Matthew Hale, Contemplations Moral and Divine, pp. 84-85 [CL, XVII, 219-20]; Christ and His Church, in Sibbes, Works, II, 87 [CL, VI, 182].)

[107] Works, VI, 455; Stuckley, A Gospel-Glass, pp. 331-32 [CL, XIX, 427].

[108] Duncan Coomer, "The Influence of Puritanism and Dissent on Methodism," LQHR, 175 (1950), 349-50. Leslie Stephen, History of English Thought in the Eighteenth Century, II, 433.

[109] The Whole Duty of Man, CL, XII, 106; William Cave, Primitive Christianity, CL, XIX, 69.

social concerns. As a consequence, both Wesley and the Puritans object to an understanding of Christianity which would separate the Christian from the world. Here Wesley parts with both the pietistic tradition and the mystics. He states his position thus: "Christianity is essentially a social religion. . . . It cannot subsist at all, without society,—without living and conversing with other men." [110] How could a Christian do good to *all* men if he associated only with himself or other Christians? How could he be a peacemaker among Christians who presumedly would not need such service? The heart of the matter lies, then, in this: though one should not have any "particular familiarity or any strictness of friendship with them," this does not mean that one is to "renounce all fellowship" with such people.[111]

Edmund Calamy's sermon "On Christian Benevolence," included by Wesley in the *Library,* expresses the Puritan's active concern that the Christian cannot be true to his relationship to the world without real service in the world—without following the command to do good. It is to become the chief business and employment of his life. People are possessed with a

narrow, selfish spirit, when we are concerned for none but ourselves, and regard not how it fares with other men, so it be but well with us; when we follow our own humour, and with great pleasure enjoy the accommodations of our own state; when we think our own happiness the greater, because we have it alone to ourselves; which of all other things is the most directly opposite to that benign and compassionate temper which our Saviour came into the world by his doctrine and example to implant in man.[112]

Calamy, then, like Wesley must object also to those "so taken up with their courses of piety and devotion, that they have no time to do good." [113] Thomas Manton, commenting on Jesus' teaching of the Golden Rule, points out how even Christians so seldom attempt to carry it out.

[110] *Sermons,* I, 382.
[111] *Ibid.,* p. 384.
[112] Edmund Calamy, "On Christian Benevolence," *CL,* XXIII, 277.
[113] *Ibid.,* p. 285.

When your debts are detained, you complain of wrong. Should we not be as CONSCIONABLE FOR [exact in] the speedy payment of others? To buy with a great measure, and sell with a less, is an abomination of the Lord and to men. We judge things done to us thus and thus, and shall we be careless what we do to them? [114]

Wesley's sermons on the Sermon on the Mount raise the same question for the Christian and are particularly concerned with how one is to do good.[115]

In these relationships with others, be they Christians or not, one must always display Christian love. Richard Alleine admonishes his readers to "carry yourselves well towards all men" by being true, thereby eliminating even the lying which is usually allowed in trading with one another; by being just in both thoughts and actions; by being merciful to those in need; by being peaceable so as to possess "an unaptness to be provoked"; and by being "courteous, sweet, and affable in your carriage towards all." [116] Wesley would only add the admonition to be careful and circumspect in judging others.[117] The Christian is to be separated from the world in such a way as to avoid the degrading influence of those of the world, but in no sense is he to be separated from interest in and concern for these men nor is the Christian to attempt to escape from the world.[118] Interest in the worldly man is concern for his condition, both material and spiritual.[119]

[114] Thomas Manton, "Sermon on Matthew vii.12.," in *The Works of Thomas Manton* (22 vols.; London: James Nisbet and Co., 1871), II, 383 [CL, VII, 309]. Cf. Stuckley, *A Gospel-Glass,* pp. 190-94 [CL, XIX, 350-54].

[115] *Sermons,* I, 416; 390 ff.

[116] Alleine, *Vindiciae Pietatis,* pp. 342-46 [CL, XVIII, 202-5].

[117] *Sermons,* I, 518 ff.

[118] Responsibility for those of the world meant not only responsibility for witnessing to them and seeking to bring them to salvation but also a real responsibility for their physical well-being as displayed both in their health and their material status. (See Matthew Pool's sermon "On The Visitation of the Sick," *Morning Exercises,* I, 111 ff. [CL, XXI, 478 ff.]; Wesley's sermon "On Visiting the Sick," *Works,* VII, 117 ff.)

[119] Involved in the Christian's relationship to the world is, of course, the correct use of the material possessions and positions in which he finds himself. Most of the treatises included by Wesley in the *Library* comment upon this, but perhaps Sir Matthew Hale's small treatise on "The Great Audit," in his work *Contemplations Moral and Divine,* in which he treats stewardship, is one of the best examples [CL, XVII, 233-63]. Wesley's sermon on "The Good Steward" (*Sermons,* II, 461-80) is a very similar treatment, both men emphasizing the stewardship not only of material possessions but also of all other abilities and capacities, as well as the privileges of position, education, etc. Wesley's famous comments on the correct use of money also relate to the true stewardship of the Christian (*Sermons,* I, 473 ff.; 309 ff.).

Perhaps examination of an example of a specific teaching related to the Christian's responsibility for his neighbor's spiritual well-being will be instructive as to the proper attitude toward and concern for the world.

Reproof

As was seen in the discussion of Wesley's societies, one of the most important functions of the fellowship was the help and encouragement of the other members, but an equally important role was the duty of calling into question the thoughts or actions of a fellow member where that one appeared to have sinned. The group functioned confessionally and also as a forum of loving and humble criticism. Such groups of frequent and intimate fellowship were ideal for the carrying out of this duty of reprehension, and within this context it is easily understood and appreciated. However, the duty has larger consequences. It is to be applied to the community as a whole and not simply to those of the Christian fold. A Christian cannot comfortably live in a sinful community, nor will his sense of responsibility for others allow him to countenance their sin without at least the attempt to warn and admonish the sinner concerning that sin. A Christian is duty-bound under the command of God to rebuke, admonish, and chastise his fellows, always, of course, with the object of bringing him to the better life of Christian faith in Christ. Naturally, instructions in how to carry out this duty are applicable to both the Christian brother and the secular acquaintance, though the approach may vary according to the condition and status of the one to be admonished.

Wesley identifies his own treatment of the duty of reproof with that of Richard Baxter as found in *The Saints' Everlasting Rest*. While Wesley's reference to Baxter is only to use one of his illustrations, a comparison of their principal teachings, as well as those of John Kitchin, on the nature and method of this duty reveals several points of similarity and affinity.[120]

[120] Wesley's reference to Baxter is as follows: "How striking is Mr. Baxter's reflection on this head, in his 'Saints' Everlasting Rest.' 'Suppose thou wert to meet one in the lower world, to whom thou hadst denied this office of love, when ye were both together under the sun; what answer couldst thou make to his upbraiding? "At such a time and place, while we were under the sun, God delivered me into thy hand: I then did not know the way of salvation, but was seeking death in the error of my life; and therein thou sufferedst me to remain, without

Reproof is naturally directed toward any sin or, for Wesley, toward any error which may lead to sin. It particularly is to be applied to unbelievers where admonishment of outward sin—drunkenness, cursing, sabbath breaking, etc.—will predominate.[121] However, one must be cautious in order not to make a mistake in this matter. Kitchin warns that one must be sure that the accused is truly sinful—he cannot be reproved on supposition or hearsay. It must be a certain sin.[122] In Wesley's words, it should not be "anything of a disputable nature, that will bear much to be said on both sides." [123]

This duty can only be honestly and correctly undertaken in love; therefore, concern for the individual's salvation will characterize it instead of any scorn or pride on the part of the accuser.[124] It follows that it will be done humbly, meekly, compassionately, with a recognition of one's own faults. Nevertheless, it must be done, to use Baxter's terms, "seriously, zealously, and effectually." [125] One cannot mince words in calling attention to the serious nature of the sin but must speak plainly. "A ludicrous reproof makes little impression, and is soon forgot; besides that, many times it is taken ill, as if you ridiculed the person you reprove." [126]

One must also use reproof with prudence and discretion so that it is varied according to the occasion, and according to the relation one has to the accused. For instance, one does not reprove a superior, be he parent or magistrate, in the same manner as one does one's peers, nor is one type

---

once endeavouring to awaken me out of the wrath to come, neither I nor thou need to have come into this place of torment." ' " (*Works*, VI, 298-99.)

[121] Kitchin, "How Must We Reprove," *Morning Exercises*, I, 137 [*CL*, XXI, 436]; *Works*, VI, 298.

[122] Kitchin, "How Must We Reprove," *Morning Exercises*, I, 138-39 [*CL*, XXI, 437-38].

[123] *Works*, VI, 297-98.

[124] *The Saints' Everlasting Rest*, in Baxter, *Works*, XXIII, 78 [*CL*, XXII, 181]; Kitchin, "How Must We Reprove," *Morning Exercises*, I, 141 [*CL*, XXI, 440]; Wesley, *Works*, VI, 300.

[125] "To tell them of sin, or of heaven, or hell, in a dull, easy, careless language, doth make men think you are not in good SADDNESS, NOR DO MEAN AS YOU SPEAK [earnest]; but EITHER YOU scarce think yourselves such things are true, OR ELSE YOU TAKE THEM IN SUCH A SLIGHT AND INDIFFERENT MANNER." (*The Saints' Everlasting Rest*, in Baxter, *Works*, XXIII, 81 [*CL*, XXII, 186]; Kitchin, "How Must We Reprove," *Morning Exercises*, I, 140 [*CL*, XXI, 439].)

[126] *Works*, VI, 301. Wesley allows some exception to this general rule of seriousness, for "a little well-placed raillery will pierce deeper than solid argument" with some "who are strangers to religion." (*Ibid.*)

of reproof as effective for one person as another may be.[127] It must also be seasonable, or when the accused is most likely to accept it. In this matter of occasion, though Wesley accepts the principle, he differs from Baxter and Kitchin, for he asserts that even a drunk man may be justly and compassionately reproved to good effect and, in typical fashion, proceeds to give instances thereof.[128]

One must also let his "reproofs and exhortations be backed with the authority of God. Let the sinner be convinced that you speak not from yourselves, or of your own hand. Show them the very words of Scripture for what you say." [129] Kitchin adds the psychologically sound admonition to take an occasion when you can "commend a man for something, and then RUB [reprove] him UP for his faults." [130] For Wesley the same purpose is served if one prefaces "a reproof with a frank profession of good will." [131] Of course, such a task must be carried out with diligence and patience.

Baxter and Kitchin carefully insist that the one who approaches a brother for the purpose of reproving him must be upright and righteous himself, setting an example in his own life, or the admonition is hypocrisy.[132] Though Wesley fails to note this in his sermon, he doubtlessly sympathized with the caution. In his turn he reminds his readers that the outcome of the reproof or exhortation is finally in the hands of God. Any success in the duty is to be credited to God's action in the life of the person one seeks to help.[133]

Each of these authors is thoroughly convinced that adequate and helpful reproof is the work of a wise and prudent man who can handle the matter without undue offense to his neighbor, yet "none is exempted from this duty for unfitness: No: This ought ye to have done, and not

[127] *The Saints' Everlasting Rest*, in Baxter, *Works*, XXIII, 84 [*CL*, XXII, 186-87]; Kitchin, "How Must We Reprove," *Morning Exercises*, I, 141 [*CL*, XXI, 439-40]; Wesley, *Works*, VI, 302.

[128] *Works*, VI, 302.

[129] *The Saints' Everlasting Rest*, in Baxter, *Works*, XXIII, 85 [*CL*, XXII, 188]; Kitchin, "How Must We Reprove," *Morning Exercises*, I, 142 [*CL*, XXI, 441]; Wesley, *Works*, VI, 301.

[130] Kitchin, "How Must We Reprove," *Morning Exercises*, I, 139 [*CL*, XXI, 439].

[131] *Works*, VI, 301.

[132] *The Saints' Everlasting Rest*, in Baxter, *Works*, XXIII, 87 [*CL*, XXII, 189]; Kitchin, "How Must We Reprove," *Morning Exercises*, I, 137-38 [*CL*, XXI, 437].

[133] *Works*, VI, 300-301.

to have left the other undone." [134] By this method and in the context of these cautions one must take up the task. Wesley ends his sermon with this impassioned plea to his followers, which testifies to his own emphasis on the duty:

I have now only a few words to add unto you, my brethren, who are vulgarly called Methodists. I never heard or read of any considerable revival of religion which was not attended with a spirit of reproving. I believe it cannot be otherwise; for what is faith, unless it worketh by love? Thus it was in every part of England when the present revival of religion began about fifty years ago: All the subjects of that revival,—all the Methodists, so called, in every place, were reprovers of outward sin. . . . Come, brethren, in the name of God, let us begin again! Rich or poor, let us all arise as one man; and in anywise let every man "rebuke his neighbor, and not suffer sin upon him!" Then shall all Great Britain and Ireland know that we do not "go a warfare at our own cost:" Yea, "God shall bless us, and all the ends of the world shall fear him." [135]

Wesley's affinity with this Puritan emphasis, seen in his reference to Baxter on the subject but more concretely in the almost identical directions for practicing the duty, provides another area of relationship in their teachings on the Christian life.

If one wonders why the "duty of reproof" has received this rather extended treatment when it is only one among many duties, it is well to remember that this duty as carried out in the community was probably the one which most vividly revived in the eyes of Wesley's contemporaries the image of the earlier Puritans. As he expresses it, the charge against Christians—understanding here his own movement—is that they would not "keep their religion to themselves." [136] So it had been with the Puritans, and the identification of the two traditions out of their application of this duty expresses their common view of one aspect of the Christian's relationship to the world around him.

Social Awareness

This brief examination of the similarities between the Puritan and Wesleyan understanding of a Christian's position in the world reveals

[134] Kitchin, "How Must We Reprove," *Morning Exercises*, I, 138 [*CL*, XXI, 437]; *The Saints' Everlasting Rest*, in Baxter, *Works*, XXIII, 85 [*CL*, XXII, 195]; Wesley, *Works*, VI, 299.
[135] *Works*, VI, 303-4.
[136] *Sermons*, I, 369.

areas of affinity. These are found in their concept of a Christian's separateness from the world in order not to be contaminated by the world, and at the same time their immense concern for and responsibility in the world. The emphasis in both traditions upon the necessity for the Christian to call the worldly neighbor into question through reproof, and at the same time to present the gospel to him, stresses the religious character of the individual. The concern for man's physical well-being, as displayed in an interest in everything from his health to correct treatment in business relations, witnesses to the social awareness of the Puritans and Wesley. The political perspectives of the two traditions as they relate to the Christian's participating in the world are not discussed above because Wesley does not include any of this material in the *Library,* or his other abridgments, except for a few statements which reflect the Christian's responsibility to understand and support the constituted authority.[137] Conservative Tory that he was, Wesley would hardly have approved of the republicanism of some of the Puritans nor of their involvement in the revolution and change of governmental form.[138]

In evaluation of the Methodist understanding of the Christian's relationship to the world, J. H. Nichols offers some suggestive possibilities. Nichols understands pietism and Puritanism to have a very close relationship in their beginnings and emphases, but he also suggests that only after the failure to succeed in shaping the national community through Cromwell did the individualistic and introspective features so dominant in pietism come to the fore in Puritanism.[139] He sees Wesley's movement, even where it makes a major contribution to the humanitarian reforms of the eighteenth and nineteenth centuries, as carrying "still further the individualistic tendency of late Puritanism," so that "attention was concentrated on personal rather than social morals, and sensual-

---

[137] See Samuel Annesley's sermon "God's Sovereignty Our Support in All Worldly Distractions," in which the purpose and duties of the political order are discussed. (*CL,* XXIV, 6-9.)

[138] His series of tracts on the American Revolution display his political understanding and are suggestive as to the responsibility of the Christian in these affairs. (*Works,* XI, 80-155.) Certainly, Wesley was neither unaware of the political implications of the Christian faith nor did he fail to express himself on these matters, but his sympathies would not have led him to any form of republicanism. The political spectrum of the Puritans was, of course, extremely broad, and the more conservative would have been close to Wesley's own position.

[139] James H. Nichols, *History of Christianity: 1650-1950* (New York: The Ronald Press, 1956), pp. 81-82.

ity was more feared than selfishness." [140] While this evaluation is suggestive since it is, in part, true and does offer an interesting explanation of the connection between Wesley and Puritanism, it places so much emphasis upon concern for the individual in the teachings of Wesley and Methodism that it is in danger of overlooking the immense social concern generated by the Wesleyan revival.

It is true that the dominating concern for the salvation of the individual was a hallmark of Wesley's movement. In addition, Methodism was not concerned with the type of community reform sought by the early Puritans, wherein a theocratic state would result in social reformation.[141] Nevertheless, it is precisely the concern for the salvation of the individual which formed the basis of Methodism's social concern. Raymond Cowherd, discussing the background of political and social reforms of the nineteenth century, asserts: "The resurgence of Protestantism during the eighteenth century, chiefly as a result of John Wesley's preaching, convinced many that all the obstacles to individual salvation, whether ignorance, slavery, or plenty should be removed." [142] Cowherd gives credit to the heirs of the Wesleyan and Evangelical revivals for the principal work of humanitarian social reform in the century following.[143] Concern for the individual carried with it concern for his social condition. J. E. Rattenbury, responding to a charge of excessive individualism in Wesley, makes it clear that such an analysis simply overlooks Wesley's statements and actions on social questions of his day.

He [Wesley] states his opinion on the questions of population, the increase of the great towns, the depletion of the rural districts, unemployment, the causes of unemployment, the remedies for unemployment, the land question, small holdings, agriculture, fisheries, taxation, the National Debt, East India stock, the legitimacy of speculation, the accumulation and the distribution of wealth, luxury, dress, money, intemperance, smuggling, and the production of

[140] *Ibid.*, p. 92.
[141] Although Nichols may be correct in discerning a strengthening of the pietistic and individualistic tendencies of Puritanism after their ejection, the emphasis upon this type of understanding was certainly very strong in many of the early writings of the Puritans, and perhaps was more influential in the earlier period than Nichols seems to indicate here.
[142] Raymond G. Cowherd, *The Politics of English Dissent* (New York: New York University Press, 1956), pp. 7-8.
[143] *Ibid.* This is particularly true in the areas of education, slavery, and factory work laws. (See Cowherd, 36 ff., 46 ff., 141 ff.)

useful and useless articles, the evil of pensions, and kindred themes. He was interested in electricity, medicine, and law, and particularly at such points as they bore on the social life of the poor. His writings abound with allusions to the social conditions of the people, and are not wanting in most drastic suggestions for the removal of wrongs and injustices under which he thought they suffered, and he created the simple social organizations which were the model and framework of the labour organizations of a succeeding age.[144]

Rattenbury's insight is supported by Robert Wearmouth's and Maldwyn Edwards' analyses of what effect Methodism had on the common people of the eighteenth century, particularly in terms of their social condition.[145] To be concerned with personal morals does not preclude a valid and strong concern with social morals.

Wesley's social awareness and concern produced social change even if this was primarily on an individualistic basis supported by the corporate discipline of the societies. The next century was to see the full flower of the social reform movements with a large share of the leadership coming from the Evangelical members of the Church of England. The Methodists, as Cowherd shows, were forced by their concern for the individual to take an active role in these humanitarian social reform crusades, which of their very nature demanded political action.[146] The independent Methodist bodies which split from the Wesleyan Methodists after John Wesley's death tended to more liberal political sentiments and took a much more active role in politics, most often in league with the Dissenters. The Wesleyan Methodists continued in sympathy with Wesley's conservative Toryism, only taking active political roles where necessary to accomplish social reform.[147]

The Dissenters, heirs of seventeenth-century Puritanism, found them-

[144] J. E. Rattenbury, *Wesley's Legacy to the World*, pp. 228-29. Rattenbury's section dealing with this question is a thorough analysis of the social aspects of Wesley's teachings as well as an attempt to show influence of Methodism in the social reforms of the nineteenth century, which saw the transfer of the political allegiance of much of Methodism to the liberal rather than the conservative party. Cf. Élie Halévy, *A History of the English People in 1815*, trans. by E. I. Watkin and D. A. Barker (3 vols.; London: T. Fisher Unwin, 1924), I, 359-74.

[145] Robert F. Wearmouth, *Methodism and the Common People of the Eighteenth Century* (London: Epworth Press, 1945), pp. 202 ff., 299 ff.; Maldwyn Edwards, *John Wesley and the Eighteenth Century* (London: Epworth Press, 1955), 146 ff.

[146] Raymond Cowherd, *The Politics of English Dissent*, p. 17.

[147] *Ibid.*, pp. 17, 31, 135.

selves at one with the Methodists in working for social reform, but their concern for religious independence also carried them into the cause of political reform, particularly the democratic reform of Parliament. Cowherd's suggestion that the Wesleyan tradition issued in humanitarian social reform, while that of the Puritans issued in social and political reform is, then, instructive in understanding the emphases of the two religious traditions.

Nichols' identification of Wesley with the more pietistic characteristics of the Puritans may then be correct and, in fact, may offer some explanation for the joint concern of their heirs with humanitarian reform. To suggest, however, that this pietistic bent means an excessive concern for the person rather than the society fails to consider adequately the social awareness in Wesley's thinking or the activities of the Methodists in the area. It might be maintained that Wesley's emphasis on personal salvation and personal morals tended to give more weight to these concerns than to those of social questions, but such an evaluation separates into two aspects or elements what, in Wesley's thinking, was one concern—the most fruitful use of the whole man in God's service.

SUMMARY OF
PART III: THE CHRISTIAN LIFE

In the area of instruction in Christian living the relationship between Wesley and the Puritan divines becomes even more evident than in those affinities discernible in the theological foundations of these teachings. Wesley clearly is dependent upon the Puritan tradition in several teachings relative to Christian living, and close affinities are present elsewhere, in both teaching and practice.

First, Wesley's use of the works of Joseph Alleine and Richard Baxter in his plan to reach the unconverted with the Christian message, as well as with instruction in Christian living, witnesses to his appropriation from the Puritan tradition of both a pattern for and practical instructions in this work.

Second, the agreements between Wesley and the Puritan tradition in their understanding of sanctification and its importance quite naturally produced affinities in their teachings relative to the purpose and final destiny to which Christian life leads. Holiness is such a dominant feature of both traditions that affinities here are almost inevitable and clearly evident. It is, however, Wesley's dependence on his grandfather's exposition of conscience which again introduces his dependence upon the Puritan pattern. Here the significant relationship is undeniable. Wesley's use of and recommendation of the treatises dealing with afflicted consciences strengthen this relationship.

Third, Wesley's recognition of the Puritans' peculiar ability to make such interests as self-examination, self-denial, and growth in grace applicable to the personal life of the common man guided his use of their works in this area. Through recommendation of Bishop Hall's and Baxter's guidance in meditation, he identifies himself with Puritan instructions for the individual.

Fourth, there can be little question of the influence of the Puritan tradition upon Wesley in his understanding of and instruction in a Christian's participation in family life and religion. His high recommendation of Whateley's understanding of marriage, his use of Philip Henry as giving the pattern for family worship, and the similarities between his own teachings and those of Puritans, relative to education, make this influence clear. To claim Puritan influence in this important field is not to eliminate the influence of other traditions, but Puritanism must be considered as one prominent source for Wesley's understanding, and in the case of family worship it is the pattern.

Fifth, in the area of the Christian teachings relative to the church Wesley's recognition of similarities and actual affinities between his own teachings and practice and those of the Puritans is manifested by his practice in his Methodist societies, but his attachment to the Church of England will not allow him consciously to stress this. His clear sympathy for the Nonconformists, while not a recommendation of separation, would nevertheless distinguish him from many of his contemporary Anglican brethren. While both he and the Presbyterians could and did trace their interpretation of church order and ordination to the early church without any recognition of contemporary dependence, the affinities in their teachings on this subject are obvious. Wesley's use of the "gathered" principle in organizing the societies, while reflecting Moravian influence, undoubtedly in the eyes of his contemporaries suggested the Independents, and affinities with that tradition are evident even if Wesley for other reasons could not emphasize them.

Dependence upon the Puritan tradition in terms of instruction and example for his preachers is clearly evident in Wesley's recommendation of Brainerd and his virtual requirement that his preachers follow Baxter's pattern of visitation. A closer tie is hardly possible than that represented by the incorporation of Baxter's own instruction to the Reformed pastorate into the manual of instruction for Methodist preachers.

Sixth, Wesley's rejection of the asceticism of his mystic mentors and the quietistic tendencies of the Moravians led him closer to the Puritan attitudes toward the world. Recognizing the inadequacy of this world to give meaning to life, and looking beyond this world for true purpose in life, Wesley and the Puritans took seriously the necessity of a Christian's participation in and responsibility for the world. Serious responsibility for one's neighbor entails not only concern for his spiritual life but also his moral, physical, and social well-being, as the Puritans and Wesley clearly understood.

In this all-important area of instruction in Christian living Wesley's dependence upon the Puritan tradition for both precept and pattern in certain teachings, as well as his identification with others through his own practice, clearly evidences the vital, living relationship between his own teachings and those of the Puritans.

Conclusion

This study has investigated the varied types of evidence available concerning John Wesley's relationship to Puritan expressions of the Christian life in thought, teaching, and practice. A deliberate effort has been made to avoid the identification of Wesley with the Puritan tradition on the basis of those outward similarities which may be found in both traditions in the teaching and practice of an austere, circumspect, holy life. While such identification merely on the basis of similarity is not to be depended upon for evidence of any distinctive relationship, it is not without its value, for it does mark the broad area of Christian life as that which most obviously connects the two traditions. For Wesley's contemporaries, as well as many of his commentators since, it was this similarity which brought immediate identification. Similarity of expression concerning Christian living points to a dominating emphasis in each tradition on the Christian life. Behind the obvious similarities is substantial evidence of significant interconnection of the two traditions, largely arising out of this concern. On the basis of our investigation several conclusions may be drawn.

First, the use of Puritan writings, properly abridged and edited, was, to a large extent, motivated by Wesley's desire to make use of expressions of truth as he understood it no matter what the source, yet the incidence of such materials in *A Christian Library* and in his other publications clearly indicates that Wesley, led by the natural affinities between his own understanding and that of the Puritans, allows these expressions to predominate. Wesley's selection is not at random; therefore, we may assume that this preponderance indicates that he found these presentations most congenial to his own interests and thus makes this tradition a major source of his teaching on the Christian life.

Second, correlations between the two traditions are principally to be found in their interpretations of particular doctrines, specific teachings, and actual practice. In these Wesley does not necessarily gain his own insights from Puritan writers but he does, on the whole, recognize his agreement with them, consciously commend them, and establish them as valid interpretations and practice for his own followers. This allows these presentations to become the conveyors of these particular insights to his people. Although they may not have been the source of these insights for Wesley, used as instructive pieces they become this among his followers. These agreements provide avenues of even closer identification between his followers and the Puritan tradition.

Third, correlation is most definite and distinct in those areas in which Wesley's use of Puritan precept and example becomes the very pattern and manual of practice for Methodists. In these cases there is a far more definite dependence upon the tradition for the shaping of the character of his own movement.

Fourth, it is with the "moderate" Puritans that Wesley most closely identifies himself; even more notable are his comments commending their positions and his defense of and sympathy for the Nonconformists (understanding here those Puritan ministers ejected in 1662). Richard Baxter's name and teachings have run like a thread throughout this study. Baxter is a prime example of this moderate position and it is with him that Wesley most closely identifies himself. Although Baxter's theology, particularly in its Arminianism, is not typical of the majority of Puritans, he nevertheless represents the very best elements of the spirit and character of the tradition and is perhaps their foremost apologist, as well as a leading systematician of the teachings on Christian life.

Wesley's alignment with the moderate Puritans did not, however, blind him to the contributions of the more radical among them. Both his request for guidance from Philip Doddridge and his familiarity with all factions testify to his willingness to use the insights of the tradition at a time when to do so was to disregard the "prejudices" of his education and to run counter to the dominant theology and practice of his contemporaries in the Established Church.

Fifth, Wesley's attitude toward the Puritans showed evidences of growing appreciation as early as 1737-38 when he began to read some of their major works. His inclusion of a wide array of these authors in *A Christian Library* also testifies to his conviction that their teachings were reliable and of real value. Later use of their presentation as support for some of his own theological teachings, particularly as these were molded by conflicts of his own day, witnesses to his occasional dependence on Puritan formulation. In view of these facts it is possible to affirm that, while Wesley's chief relationship to the Puritans is his use of their teachings, Puritan theology does in fact contribute in certain areas to Wesley's mature theological position.

Sixth, joint concerns in church polity and practice are evident in the stance both Wesley and the Puritans of 1662 were forced to take toward the Church of England. Wesley's concern with an ecclesiology for reinforcing the Christian life led him to embrace in his societal system the "gathered church" principle of the Puritan tradition. The same is true for his principles of ordination. These considerations, combined with the emphasis on the Christian life, distinguished him from what he considered to be the "formalized" religion of his contemporaries and identified him with the Puritan tradition. They also led his movement to a *de facto* separation from the Church of England, and such understanding and practice placed his followers in the "free church" tradition. As with the Puritans of 1662, such a development was the result of the practical situation in which the people called Methodists, including Wesley himself, found themselves. It was not a choice one would want to make but conscience allowed no other.

Seventh, the similarity between the spirit, theology, and practice of Wesley and the Puritans, the real relationship evident in theology and teachings, and his definite dependence upon that tradition for instances of precept and pattern make it possible to affirm a conscious, distinct, and significant connection of Wesley with the Puritans in their interpretation of, and compulsive concern for, the Christian life. Joined to the affinities evident in his liturgical indebtedness, his educational theory, his biblical concern, and the Puritan character of his family background and home training, John Wesley's Puritan heritage was clearly a prominent feature in the expression of his own thought and practice and, to some extent, helped mold both thought and practice. Considering the numerous aspects of this relationship and their aggregate impact on Wesley, we may affirm with Gordon Wakefield that "the Puritan influence upon him [Wesley] is incalculable." [1] Once again, we need to be warned against overemphasis at this point and to recognize each of the other distinctive and significant influences upon him, but Puritanism is not to be discounted when this is done.

Recognizing the valid and important relationship between Wesley and the Puritans and giving full weight to it, what may be said in evaluating their joint concerns? It is abundantly clear that for the Puritans, as well as for Wesley, the concern to express the relevance of the Christian gospel to every motivation and action of human life was the result of their own experience. Out of their relationship to God, made possible through his grace and their faith in Jesus Christ, came a dynamic awareness of the new possibilities for meaningful life—life which is transformed in word and deed because it has a new center providing its impetus and continuity. The dynamic energy of this experience demanded expression in both precept and example in daily living and also in order that others might be presented with the possibilities of this new life. Definitive teachings in Christian living are, for the Puritans and Wesley, the irresistible consequence of personal ex-

---

[1] Gordon Wakefield, "Puritanism, Its Necessity, Dangers and Future," *Methodist Sacramental Fellowship Bulletin,* Summer, 1961, p. 2.

perience. It is not surprising, therefore, that they play such a dominant role in both movements.

This acute awareness of personal experience and of its ramifications permits a disproportionate emphasis on the experience itself. Wesley is open to the criticism that Wakefield levels at Puritanism on this point: "The Puritan stress on the moment and process of conversion and the agonized search for assurance tended to give the spiritual life a perpetual squint of self-regard. It too ruthlessly schematized the struggles of certain rare men of spiritual genius and made them the pattern for the many." [2] Such self-regard is carried by Wesley and the Puritans to the point of intense introspection of daily life and, of course, may become demonic in itself. Although self-regard is balanced to some degree by concern for the neighbor and the world, the dangers of concentration on experience, assurance, and regimented daily action are still present, and caused much of the reaction against these emphases among their more serious critics. Wesley is also guilty of the same systematic exploitation of certain men as examples, valid as this approach may be within its limits. Recognizing these dangers and understanding the limitation which they place on the expressions found in Wesley and the Puritans, it is still necessary to affirm that their discovery for their respective periods of the reality and validity of personal experience is a major key to their revolutionary effect on the religious life of their time. The discovery that "I, even I" have the possibility and promise of relationship to God is the existential confrontation that lies at the core of meaningful religious life, be it personal or corporate. For their neighbors Wesley and the Puritans recaptured this essential truth, with all of its pitfalls.

The reality of this experience necessitates the attempt to translate into specific teaching what it will mean in the life of the believer. Any endeavor to do this carries with it the dangers of understanding the teachings themselves as authoritative, rigid, and unchangeable. When explained as the correct mode of Christian life, particularly as they relate to specific situations, they tend to be understood in this authoritative manner. As a result, they may be understood as legalistic. Puritan and

[2] Ibid., p. 4.

Conclusion

Methodist teachings are often subjected to this criticism and, to some extent, it is legitimate. As Nuttall points out in speaking of the Congregationalists, Puritan teachings so stress piety of practice that they appear to be "hard and unloving." [3] Perhaps Wesley's dominant emphasis on the motivation of love and his openness to all persons tempers this, but to many his teachings could hardly appear more rigid and hard. Their narrowness toward many of the common pleasures of life, their distrust of the arts, and their glorification of serious-mindedness most often brought such charges from contemporaries against Wesley and the Puritans. While one would want to admit the real danger of these teachings and would not want to defend the extremes to which they were occasionally carried, particularly in their depreciation of the aesthetic, they must be judged by their intention to speak a relevant and commanding word to those who would make of the world, whether consciously or unconsciously, that which gives meaning and purpose to life. The historical situation to which Wesley spoke makes these teachings, with all of their legalistic and ascetic trappings, particularly meaningful. He was attempting to restore purposeful modes of discipline in an era when social, moral, and religious complacency at the best and debauchery at the worst were stock responses to life. The strength with which both the Puritans and Wesley stressed their teachings of Christian life may tend to allow a degeneration into pious legalism, but such is not their intent. Their intent is always that "singleness of mind" which seeks the experience of relationship to, and glorification of, God in daily life.

This same motivation explains the centrality of Wesley's doctrine of perfection. Purity of heart and mind as one seeks God and his manifestation in Christian living is the goal. Without question the doctrine is idealistic and by human standards impossible and unrealistic. The inconsistencies present in Wesley's doctrine, i.e., an imperfect perfection wherein some elements of sin are still present and a perfection wherein moral improvement must continue, tend to discount any real meaning in the term "perfection." Though the Puritan teaching of perfection as expressed by John Preston is free from some of these problems, it is

[3] Nuttall, *Visible Saints*, p. 162.

still idealistic. Nevertheless, in this doctrine it is the intention of both the Puritans and Wesley to take seriously the reality of God's active work in the present world and to establish in unequivocal terms the unlimited possibilities which this gives to man. Recognizing its deficiencies and problems, we may still affirm of the Wesleyan and Puritan expressions what Gordon Rupp maintains is the contribution of Wesley's doctrine: "Here . . . is a confident reliance on the will and power of God to work the signs and wonders of redeeming grace in this present evil age." [4] It is a lesson often unheeded in the days of the Puritans and Wesley, as well as our own.

The Puritan involvement in the political and social life of the community of their time kept them from the quietistic tendencies of the Continental Pietism to which they appear to be closely related in emphasis and spirit. Their conviction that God actively works to transform all spheres of life, including "life in the world" with all its ramifications, always stands behind their insistence upon involvement in the world. Wesley's early asceticism is mitigated by this same conviction and it keeps him from embracing the quietistic and separatist tendencies of Pietism. This insistence upon involvement in the world is at least a partial explanation of the phenomenal success of Puritanism and Methodism as popular religious movements. Asceticism is by its nature individualistic and "otherworldly," while quietistic pietism most often finds expression in separation from the world to create the ideal Christian community. Neither of these have much possibility of appealing to the masses since these masses of necessity must remain in the world. A major strength of Puritanism and Methodism lay in their acceptance and affirmation of the world with all the possibilities of its corrosion and corruption of the gospel message. One must admit that in both traditions are found attitudes and statements which may be construed to mean that they sought separation from the world. Their extreme condemnation of "evil men" and their admonition to avoid friendship with these appear to suggest that the Christian must separate from them. But to avoid fellowship with these persons is neither to avoid contact with them nor to assuage true Christian concern and love for them, for to love a

[4] Gordon Rupp, *Principalities and Powers* (Nashville: Abingdon-Cokesbury Press, 1952), p. 99.

person is not to embrace all his ways. In this they are clear. While we reject the implications of some of the more extreme expressions and even question whether they allow the possibility of true Christian concern and love, we must see that the intent of such statements is always to insulate the believer from the temptations embodied in his neighbor and not the rejection or condemnation of that neighbor himself.

The strength of the popular appeal of the Puritan and Methodist movements was also dependent upon the fact that each embodied within itself methods by which individual believers were supported in their faith through active fellowship with other believers. Such fellowship found its strength in the willingness of its participants to be committed unequivocally to the gospel and to be as honest as humanly possible in their relations with other members of the fellowship, as well as to be dedicated to a life of discipline typified by their covenants. Here they could expect to be confronted with their successes and failures to live the life of faith, but most important, here they could always expect the support and encouragement of those fellow seekers who in love were willing to call them into question. Whether these groups were the family "house churches," the small congregation, or Wesley's system of societies and classes, they provided the constant encounter so necessary to the continuation and development of faith. The most frequent expression of the communal nature of the faith has been in the form of religious communities separated from the world, e.g., monastic and pietistic communities. It was the ability of the Puritans and Wesley to foster this communal aspect of fellowship among persons who remain in the world which accounts in part for their appeal and their tenacious ability to weather the storms of controversy which surrounded each movement. Perhaps the genius of these groups is being rediscovered in our day.[5]

Wesley's dream that these societies of Christian fellowship should become true "ecclesiolae in ecclesia" did not finally materialize. As a result, there is a tension present in his doctrine of the church. His insistence on the unity of the church which would not allow him to

---

[5] Recent representative commentators on the subject are Robert A. Raines, *New Life in the Church* (New York: Harper & Row, 1961); Elton Trueblood, *The Company of the Committed* (Harper & Row, 1961); George Webber, *God's Colony in Man's World* (Nashville: Abingdon Press, 1960).

separate is matched by his awareness of the failure of the church to exemplify in its doctrines and practice the truth of the gospel, an awareness which forces him to attempt the renewal of the church through "ecclesiolae." Although these two concepts perhaps need not always be in opposition, the historical situation in which Wesley found himself created a tension between them. His preparedness, albeit reluctantly, to take the steps which allowed separation indicates that in the final analysis he would not allow church order to stand in the way of what he considered to be the proclamation of the truth. By his refusal to separate himself he held tenaciously to church unity, but in acting to make separation possible he embraced a position in extreme tension with this very unity.

The tension found here in Wesley's position is, of course, not peculiar to him but is perhaps evident throughout the history of the church. It is partially grounded in the tension which normally exists in every ecclesiology between unity and holiness. Those who insist on unity must be willing to embrace all believers without particular regard to their individual exemplification of holiness, while those who insist on universal holiness have tended to separate and withdraw in order to attain it. The catholic tradition, so often embodied in empirical or majority churches, has in the name of catholicity, doctrine, and order been unwilling to sacrifice unity and has embraced holiness in particular saints and perfectionist communities rather than demanding it in the same degree for all communicants. Protestantism, while separating on the basis of the primacy of faith and the priesthood of all believers, has, particularly in its free church manifestations of Puritanism and Pietism, also insisted on a universal application of holiness to minister and congregation alike, even at the expense of church unity. The unity of the *one* church is, then, often in tension with the *holy* church, and Wesley's position embraced both aspects.

Unable to maintain the tension and to hold together the elements of unity and holiness, Wesley's followers were forced to separate. As a result, they were left with, at best, a mixed understanding and interpretation of church order, since as separatists they still held an intense appreciation for the importance of this order itself. In England this resulted in an appointive system based on an essentially Presbyterian form

252

of ordination. In America it allowed a modified form of episcopal ordination but also incorporated Presbyterian forms of church government
in which conferences became equivalent to synods and assemblies. Viewed
in one way this allowed Methodism to embrace the better elements of
both forms of church polity; yet, as will happen in any mixture, the
basic principles lose some of their distinctiveness and force, resulting
in at least a partial loss of an adequate understanding of the importance
of the doctrine of the church. In the current ecumenical discussions
Methodism must recover Wesley's intense concern for an adequate doctrine of the church and, to be true to its heritage, must with Wesley
affirm the proclamation of the gospel to have precedence over matters
of church order without losing its real appreciation for the place and
importance of this order itself.

The impact of Puritanism and the Wesleyan Revival on the religious
thought and life of England in their respective centuries must be judged
from various perspectives, taking into account the religious, social, and
political aspects. Even then the true consequences are incalculable. At
the heart of this impact are the changed lives of individuals who committed themselves to Christ through these movements. Presenting a
view of the Christian faith which made it meaningful, relevant, and
vital to each life, both the Puritans and Wesley were able to convey an
effective and intense appreciation for the disciplined life. Unafraid to
proclaim what this meant in specific teachings covering every aspect
of one's daily life, they offered the people a meaningful pattern for
living which could be embraced even with all its dangers of legalism and
idealism. Puritan casuistry and Wesleyan emphasis on ethical instruction
helped fill the void left by the removal of the elaborate Roman Catholic
system of ethical teaching. In doing so, they provided both the rationale
and theology for such a life, while pointing to the norms by which
Christian living should be judged. Perhaps the heirs of these two great
English religious movements need to recapture the vital concern for
Christian living. Few would want to attempt to reintroduce specific
teachings, which, in many cases, arose out of cultural problems of
their own period, but much would be gained by a new awareness that
Christian belief issues in Christian action. Differences in church order,
polity, and institutional integrity might again become subservient to

the demand for the proclamation of the gospel and its transforming power in the present world, just as these matters were subservient to this demand for our forefathers. As it was this dominant concern for the Christian life which established affinities and relationships between Wesley and the Puritans, perhaps it may also be a basis for drawing together their heirs in the present day.

If such endeavors are forthcoming, they will need to consider the breadth of the relationship of Wesley and his forefathers, the Puritans. Wesley's recognition and adoption of Puritan teachings and patterns as his own make it quite clear that an adequate evaluation of the sources of Methodist teaching and practice must give full weight to the significant contribution of that peculiarly influential pattern of Christian living—English Puritanism.

Appendix I

  The following is a complete list of the authors in the order they appear in the first edition of *A Christian Library*. The works of the Puritan authors are also indicated.

The initials used in this Appendix indicate bibliographies of the period and the author list given to Wesley by Philip Doddridge. Wesley's list of authors is compared to these works to ascertain the general usage of the works included in the *Library* and to discover how closely Wesley followed book lists which particularly emphasized Puritan materials. Doddridge's "Letter to Mr. Wesley" is indicated by the initial (D). As shown here, Wesley included some of Doddridge's suggestions as to authors from both the Puritan and Established Church traditions. However, Doddridge had also suggested many of his own contemporaries whom Wesley chose not to consider; he used practically no literature of his own period in the *Library*. Wesley obviously depended upon the list for guidance but went beyond it for his authors; only eight of Wesley's thirty-one authors from Puritans are found in Doddridge's list.

Comparison is also made with the bibliographies of John Wilkins and Richard Baxter and indicated by the initials (W) and (B). Like Bishop

Hall, Wilkins (1614-1672), Bishop of Chester, had Puritan sympathies. His work, *Ecclesiastes, or, A Discourse Concerning the Gift of Preaching*, republished in 1651, contained a systematic catalog of English religious literature, including most of the important Puritan writings of the period.[1] In all, a third of the Puritan writings Wesley used are recommended in this early list. Baxter's bibliography, contained in his work *A Christian Directory*, might also have served Wesley as a source list, for it includes recommendations of more than a third of the Established Church authors and more than half of the Puritans used by Wesley.[2] These comparisons show that Wesley, to a large extent, used well-recognized writers who had been authoritative and reliable spokesmen of the tradition.

Several of the treatises included by Wesley in the *Library* bear no indication of their authorship in either the first or the second edition. Wesley may have considered some of them so well known that to indicate an author was unnecessary; e.g., *The Whole Duty of Man*, usually credited to Richard Allestree (d. 1681) enjoyed from its first printing in 1658 at least twenty printings or editions by 1700.[3] In the majority of the cases, however, it is more likely that Wesley did not know the authors, since the tracts were presumably published as anonymous works during his time. Most of the authors of these tracts have since been identified.[4] Where identification has been possible, the tracts are listed by author and bracketed. Identifying information may be found in the footnotes.

Ancient Fathers

Clement of Rome	(B)	(W)
Polycarp		(W)

---

[1] John Wilkins, *Ecclesiastes, or, A Discourse Concerning the Gift of Preaching* (London: Printed by T. R. and E. M. for Samuel Gellibrand, 1651), ii; *DNB*, LXI, 266.

[2] Richard Baxter, *A Christian Directory*, pp. 917-29.

[3] For a summary of the question of authorship of this work and a discussion of its influence on Wesley, see G. Thompson Blake, "The Whole Duty of Man," *LQHR*, 183 (1958), 293-97.

[4] Later scholarship has made identification possible through extremely helpful bibliographical studies such as *The Dictionary of Anonymous and Pseudonymous English Literature*, ed. James Kennedy (8 vols.; London: Oliver and Boyd, 1926); Donald Wing, *Short Title Catalogue of Books Printed in England, Scotland, Ireland and Wales* (3 vols.; New York: For Index Society by Columbia University Press, 1945); Douglas Bush, *English Literature in the Earlier Seventeenth Century: 1600-1660*; and others.

Ignatius .... (B)   (W)
Macarius

Foreign Authors

John Arndt (German)
Blaise Pascal (French)
Anthoniette Bourignon (French)
Don Juan D'Avila (Spanish)
Miguel de Molinos (Spanish)
(Devotional Tracts Translated from the French)

Anonymous Materials

Devotional Tracts Translated from the French
A Collection of Prayers for Families
A Country Parson's Advice to His Parishioners

Church of England Authors

Jeremy Taylor (1613-1667) .... (B)   (W)
Ralph Cudworth (1617-1688)
Nathanael Culverwell (d. 1651)[5]
John Smith (1618-1652)
[Richard Allestree (1619-1681), An Extract
    from the Whole Duty of Man][6] .... (B)
Robert Sanderson (1587-1663) .... (B)   (W)
[James Garden (n.d.), A Discourse Concerning
    Comparative Religion][7]
John Worthington (1618-1671)
Seth Ward (1617-1689) .... (B)
Thomas Ken (1637-1711)

---

[5] Nathanael Culverwell is listed by John Newton, *Methodism and the Puritans* (p. 8), as a Puritan. However, since Culverwell was one of the Cambridge Platonists and conformed to the Established Church in 1662, he is considered in this study a Church of England author. (*DNB*, XIII, 288.)

[6] Also included in the *Library* is another work credited to Allestree, *Private Devotions for Several Occasions*. Both are works of the 1660 period and, though published anonymously, are now generally attributed to Allestree, who served as a confidant of Charles II during his exile. (Douglas Bush, *English Literature in the Earlier Seventeenth Century*, p. 295; Donald Wing, *Short Title Catalogue*, I, 29; *DNB*, I, 324-25.)

[7] This tract bears the exact title of a university discourse published anonymously by James Garden in both English and Latin. Garden was deposed from his professorship at Aberdeen for refusing to sign the Westminster Confession of Faith. (*Dictionary of Anonymous and Pseudonymous English Literature*, I, 387; Donald Wing, *Short Title Catalogue*, II, 96; *DNB*, XX, 409.)

[Nicholas Horsman (d. 1683), The Spiritual Bee] [8]

Anthony Horneck (1641-1697)	(D)		
William Cave (1637-1713)			(W)
Simon Patrick (1626-1717)			
Abraham Cowley (n.d.)			
John Goodman (1640-1675)			
Robert Leighton (1611-1684)			
Isaac Barrow (1630-1677)	(D)	(B)	(W)
Henry More (1614-1687)		(B)	
Richard Lucas (1648-1715)	(D)		
Edward Reynolds (1599-1676)			(W)

[Susannah Hopton, Devotions for Every Day of
   the Week] [9]

Robert South (1634-1716)			
Henry Scougal (1650-1678)	(D)		
John Tillotson (1630-1694)	(D)	(B)	
Edward Young (1643-1705)		(B)	(W)
Charles Howe (1661-1742)			
William Beveridge (1637-1708)			

Puritan Authors

John Fox (1516-1587)   (B)   (W)
   Extracts from the Acts and Monuments of the
      Christian Martyrs
Samuel Clarke (1599-1683)   (B)   (W)
   Supplement of Mr. Fox's Acts and Monuments
      Extracted from Mr. Samuel Clarke's General
      Martyrology
   The Lives of Various Eminent Persons
Joseph Hall (1574-1656)   (D)   (B)   (W)
   Meditations and Vows, Divine and Moral
   Heaven Upon Earth, or Of True Peace of Mind
   Letters on Several Occasions

---

[8] This work is now credited to Horsman, a fellow of Corpus Christi College, Oxford, who was a supporter of the Church of England throughout his life. (*Dictionary of Anonymous and Pseudonymous English Literature*, V, 347; *DNB*, XXVII, 388.)

[9] This title covers a work commonly known as *Hickes's Reformed Devotions*. Originally written by the Roman Catholic John Austin, around 1668, it was "reformed" under the pen of Mrs. Susannah Hopton for use in the Church of England and issued anonymously with a preface by Dr. George Hickes, from which it drew its popular name. (*Bibliography*, p. 93; *Dictionary of Anonymous and Pseudonymous English Literature*, II, 49.)

A Passion Sermon, preached on Good Friday,
   1609
Holy Observations
Solomon's Song Paraphrased
Robert Bolton (1572-1631) [10]   (D)   (B)   (W)
A Discourse on True Happiness
General Directions for a Comfortable Walking
   with God
Instructions for Comforting Afflicted Con-
   sciences
A Treatise Concerning the Word of God
A Treatise on Self-Examination
A Treatise on Fasting
John Preston (1587-1628)   (B)   (W)
The Breast Plate of Faith and Love
The New Covenant, or The Saint's Portion
Richard Sibbes (1577-1635)   (D)   (B)   (W)
A Fountain Opened; or The Mystery of God-
   liness Revealed
The Nativity of Christ Celebrated by Angels
A Discovery of the Near Union and Com-
   munion betwixt Christ and The Church
Thomas Goodwin (1600-1680)   (D)   (W)
A Child of Light Walking in Darkness
Christ the Object and Support of Faith
The Heart of Christ in Heaven towards Sin-
   ners on Earth
The Return of Prayers
The Trial of a Christian's Growth
Sir Matthew Hale (1609-1676)
Contemplations, Moral and Divine
Richard Alleine (1611-1681)   (B)
Vindiciae Pietatis; or, A Vindication of Godliness
A Rebuke to Backsliders, and A Spur for
   Loiterers
The Nature and Necessity of Godly Fear

[10] Along with the treatises, Wesley included brief biographies of several of the authors:
Robert Bolton, John Preston, Richard Sibbes, Thomas Goodwin, Matthew Hale, John Howe,
Isaac Ambrose, John Owen, Joseph Alleine, Hugh Binning, and Samuel Shaw.

John Bunyan (1628-1688)

A Relation of the Holy War

[Lewis Stuckley (1622-1687)

A Gospel-Glass: or, A Call from Heaven, to
Sinners and Saints by Repentance and Reformation, to Prepare to Meet God] [11]

John Brown (1610-1679)

Christ the Way, the Truth, and the Life

Samuel Annesley (1620?-1696)

How We May be Universally and Exactly
Conscientious [12]

God's Sovereignty Our Support in all Worldly
Distractions

The Hindrance and Helps to a Good Memory
of Spiritual Things

The Adherent Vanity of Every Condition Is
Most Effectually Abated by Serious Godliness

John Kitchin (d. 1662?)

How Must We Reprove, that We May Not

---

[11] Stuckley's work was a popular Puritan treatise. Stuckley was ejected from his position as a
preacher in Exeter Cathedral in 1662, where he had gathered a Congregational church which
met alongside the dominant Presbyterian congregation. (Donald Wing, *Short Title Catalogue*,
III, 310; *Journal*, IV, 189 n.; A. G. Matthews, *Calamy Revised*, 469.)

[12] The first edition of *A Christian Library* includes six sermons credited to Samuel Annesley
which purport to have been preached by him at Cripplegate during his pastorate there. Thomas
Jackson in editing the second edition, however, credits one of these, "How Must We Reprove,
that We May Not Partake of Other Men's Sins," to the Rev. Mr. John Kitchin (d. 1662?). Two
others, "The Visitation of the Sick" and "How We May be Universally and Exactly Conscientious," he credits to the Rev. Matthew Pool (d. 1679). The discrepancy occurs because
these three sermons were published in the first volume of a series of four volumes of sermons
by eminent Puritans, edited by Samuel Annesley between 1661 and 1690. Annesley wrote a
prefatory letter and the first sermon of each of these volumes. The first edition of the first
volume, entitled *The Morning Exercises at Cripplegate* (London: Printed for J. Kirton and
N. Webb, 1661), designated no authors of the various sermons, but the fourth edition (London:
Printed by A. Maxwell and R. Roberts for Tho. Cockerill, 1677) does give the authors of each
sermon. Since this edition appeared in Annesley's own lifetime, it is assumed that the author
listings are reliable. According to the list in the fourth edition, Jackson was correct in designating Pool as the author of the sermon on visitation and Kitchin as the author of the sermon on
reproving. He is incorrect, however, in crediting "How We May be Universally and Exactly
Conscientious" to Pool. This is Annesley's work. It is so designated in the fourth edition and
it is the first sermon in the volume. Annesley carries out the pattern of including one of his
own sermons as the first in each volume of the series. Wesley most likely was working from an
early edition in his preparation of *A Christian Library* and did not have the designation of
authors before him. Pool and Kitchin were ejected in 1662. (A. G. Matthews, *Calamy Revised*,
pp. 310, 394.)

Appendix I

Partake of Other Men's Sins

Matthew Pool (1624-1679)

How Ministers or Christian Friends May and Ought to Apply Themselves to Sick Persons, for Their Good, and the Discharge of Their Own Conscience

Richard Baxter (1615-1691)   (D)   (W)

The Saints' Everlasting Rest

[Thomas Crane (1631-1714)

A Prospect of Divine Providence][13]

Stephen Charnock (1628-1680)

Of the Knowledge of God

Of the Knowledge of God in Christ

Edmund Calamy (1600-1666)

On Christian Benevolence

On the Wickedness of the Heart

On the Resurrection

John Flavel (1630-1691)   (D)

A New Compass for Seamen: or, Navigation Spiritualized

Husbandry Spiritualized: or, the Heavenly Use of Earthly Things

The Causes and Cures of Mental Error

John Howe (1630-1705)   (D)   (B)

The Living Temple

William Dell (d. 1664)

Christ's Spirit, A Christian's Strength

The Building, Beauty, Teaching, and Establishment of the Truly Christian Church

The Stumbling-Stone

Thomas Manton (1620-1677)   (B)

Sermons on Several Subjects

Isaac Ambrose (1604-1663)

The Doctrine of Regeneration

The Practice of Sanctification: Exemplified in the Believer's Privileges and Duties

[13] Thomas Crane, author of this tract, had been given a church and its living by Cromwell and was ejected upon the restoration. (*Dictionary of Anonymous and Pseudonymous English Literature*, IV, 748; Donald Wing, *Short Title Catalogue*, I, 393; *DNB*, XIII, 12.)

Looking unto Jesus: or, the Soul's Eying of
Jesus, as Carrying on the Great Work of
Man's Salvation
Francis Rous (1579-1659)
Academia Coelestis: The Heavenly University
John Owen (1616-1683)   (D)   (B)   (W)
The Mortification of Sin in Believers, the Neces-
sity, Nature, and Means of it
The Nature, Power, Deceit, and Prevalency of
the Remainders of Indwelling Sin in Believers
Of Temptation, the Nature and Power of it
ΧΡΙΣΤΟΛΟΓΙΑ or, A Declaration of the
Glorious Mystery of the Person of Christ,
God, and Man
Of Communion with God the Father, Son, and
Holy Ghost
Herbert Palmer (1601-1647)   (B)
Memorials of Godliness and Christianity
Of Making Religion One's Business
An Appendix, Applied to the Calling of a
Minister
William Whateley (1583-1639)   (B)   (W)
Directions for Married Persons
Joseph Alleine (1634-1668)   (B)
An Alarm to Unconverted Sinners
A Counsel for Personal and Family Godliness
Two Practical Cases of Conscience Resolved
Samuel Shaw (1635-1696)   (B)
Immanuel: or, A Discourse of True Religion
Communion With God
An Extract from The Assembly's Shorter
Catechism; with the Proofs thereof out of the
Scriptures   (B)
Samuel Rutherford (1600-1661)   (B)   (W)
Extracts from The Letters of Mr. Samuel
Rutherford
Hugh Binning (1627-1653)
Fellowship with God: or, Sermons on the First
Epistle of St. John

262

Appendix II

The following is a complete list of the men whose lives are recounted in *A Christian Library* as examples of Christian faith and piety. Those Puritan lives which are noted in Appendix I, note 10, are not listed here. The Puritan bibliographies to which Wesley's list of authors is compared (see p. 256) are indicated as: (B) Baxter, *A Christian Directory*; (W) Wilkins, *Ecclesiastes, or a Discourse Concerning the Gift of Preaching*.

Foreign Leaders

Philip Melanchthon	(B)	(W)
John Calvin	(B)	(W)
Galeacius Caracciolus		
Philip de Mornay	(B)	(W)
Henry Atling		
Frederick Spanheim		

Gregory Lopez
Peter Martyr   (B)   (W)

Church of England Leaders
Bernard Gilpin (1517-1583)
Richard Hooker (1554-1600)   (B)   (W)
Henry Wotton (1568-1639)   (B)
John Donne (1573-1631)   (W)
George Herbert (1593-1633)
William Bedell (1571-1642)
Henry Ussher (1550?-1613)   (B)   (W)
Henry Hammond (1605-1660)   (B)   (W)

Puritan Leaders
William Whitaker (1548-1595)   (B)   (W)
John Bruen (1560-1625)
Richard Blackerby (1574-1648)
Philip Sidney (1619-1698)
Richard Mather (1596-1669)   (W)
John Rowe (1588-1662)
Joseph Woodward (?-1660)
Nicholas Leverton (1660-1662)
Nathanael Barnardiston (1588-1653)
Samuel Fairclough (1594-1677)
James Fraser (1639-1699)
Thomas Tregoss (?-1671)
Samuel Winter (1603-1666)
Scottish Divines (Hugh Kennedy, Patrick Simp-
    son, Andrew Steward, Mr. Davidson, Robert
    Bruce, Robert Blair, John Welsh)
Thomas Cawton (1605-1659)
Philip Henry (1631-1696)
George Trosse (1631-1713)
Thomas Wilson (1601-1653)   (W)
John Eliot (1604-1690)

Select Bibliography

Primary Sources

Wesley's Works

Wesley, John. *A Christian Library: Consisting of Extracts from and Abridgments of the Choicest Pieces of Practical Divinity which have been Published in the English Tongue.* 2nd ed. 30 vols. London: Printed by T. Cordeux, for T. Blanshard, 1819-26.

————. *A Concise Ecclesiastical History.* 4 vols. London: J. Paramore, 1781.

————. *A Concise History of England.* 4 vols. London: R. Hawes, 1776.

————. *Directions for Renewing Our Covenant with God.* London: Printed by J. Paramore, 1780.

————. *Explanatory Notes upon the New Testament.* London: Epworth Press, 1958.

————. *Explanatory Notes upon the Old Testament.* 3 vols. Bristol: Printed by William Pine, 1765.

————. *An Extract of The Rev. Mr. Baxter's Aphorisms of Justification.* 4th ed. London: Printed for G. Whitfield, 1797.

————. *The Journal of the Rev. John Wesley, A.M.* Ed. by Nehemiah Curnock. 8 vols. London: Epworth Press, 1909.

————. *The Letters of the Rev. John Wesley, A.M.* Ed. by John Telford. 8 vols. London: Epworth Press, 1931.

————. *The Sunday Service of the Methodists in North America with Other Occasional Services.* London: 1784.

————. *Wesley's Standard Sermons.* Ed. and Annotated by Edward H. Sugden. 2 vols. London: Epworth Press, 1921.

————. *The Works of the Reverend John Wesley.* Ed. by Thomas Jackson. 3rd ed. 14 vols. London: Wesleyan Conference Office, 1872.

————. *An Alarm to Unconverted Sinners.* By Joseph Alleine. Abridged by John Wesley. 2nd ed. Dublin: Printed by Robert Napper, 1794.

————. *Christian Letters.* By Joseph Alleine. Abridged by John Wesley. 2nd ed. Bristol: Printed by William Pine, 1767.

————. *A Call to the Unconverted.* By Richard Baxter. Abridged by John Wesley. 2nd ed. Dublin: Printed by Robert Napper, 1795.

Puritan Works

Alleine, Joseph. *An Alarm to Unconverted Sinners.* London: Printed by Nevil Simmons, 1672.

————. *Christian Letters.* London: Printed by J. Darby for Nevil Simmons, 1672.

————. *Divers Practical Cases of Conscience Satisfactorily Resolved.* London: Printed for Nevil Simmons, 1672.

Alleine, Richard. *Vindiciae Pietatis: or, A Vindication of Godliness.* London: 1664.

Ambrose, Isaac. *The Works of Isaac Ambrose.* 1 vol. London: Printed by Henry Fisher, n.d.

Ames, William. *The Marrow of Sacred Divinity.* London: Edward Griffin, 1642.

Annesley, Samuel (ed.). *The Morning Exercises at Cripplegate or, Several Cases of Conscience Practically Resolved, by Sundry Ministers, September, 1661.* London: Printed for Joshua Kirton and Nathaniel Webb, 1661.

————. *The Morning Exercises at Cripplegate, St. Giles in the Fields, and in Southwark.* Ed. by James Nichols. 6 vols. London: Printed for Thomas Tegg, 1844.

Baxter, Richard. *Aphorisms on Justification.* London: Printed for Francis Tyton, 1644.

————. *A Call to the Unconverted to turn and live and accept the Mercy while Mercy may be had, as ever they would find Mercy in the day of Their Extremity.* London: Printed by R. W. for N. Simmons, 1669.

———. *A Christian Directory: or, A Summ of Practical Theologie, and Cases of Conscience.* London: By Robert White for Nevil Simmons, 1673.

———. *Gildas Salvianus: The Reformed Pastor.* Vol. XIV of *Works.*

———. *The Practical Works of Richard Baxter.* Introduction and Life by William Orme. 23 vols. London: James Duncan, 1830.

———. *Reliquiae Baxterianae, or Mr. Richard Baxter's Narrative of His Life and Times.* Published from his own manuscript by Matthew Sylvester. London: 1696.

———. *Richard Baxter's Confession of His Faith, Especially Concerning the Interest of Repentance and Sincere Obedience to Christ, in our Justification and Sanctification.* London: Printed by R. W. for Tho. Underhil, 1655.

———. *The Saints' Everlasting Rest.* Vols. XXII and XXIII of *Works.*

Binning, Hugh. *The Works of Hugh Binning.* London: A. Fullarton and Co., 1851.

Bolton, Robert. *A Discourse About the State of True Happiness.* London: Printed by Felix Kyngston for Thomas Weaver, 1631.

———. *General Directions for a Comfortable Walking with God.* London: 1641.

———. *Instructions for a Right Comforting of Afflicted Consciences.* London: Printed by Felix Kyngston for Thomas Weaver, 1631.

———. *The Saints' Selfe-enriching Examination.* London: Printed by Anne Griffin for Rapha Harford, 1634.

Burnett, Gilbert. *The Life and Death of Sir Matthew Hale.* London: Printed for William Shrowsbury, 1682.

Calamy, Edmund. *An Abridgement of Mr. Baxter's History of His Life and Times with an Account of the Ministers, etc. who were Ejected after the Restoration of King Charles II and their History to the Year 1691.* London: Printed for John Lawrence, 1713.

———. *An Account of the Ministers, Lecturers, Masters and Fellows of Colleges and Schoolmasters who were Ejected or Silenced after the Restoration in 1660 by the Act of Uniformity.* London: Printed for John Lawrence, 1713.

———. *A Continuation of the Account of the Ministers, Lecturers, Masters and Fellows of Colleges and Schoolmasters who were Ejected or Silenced after the Restoration in 1660 by the Act of Uniformity.* 2 vols. London: Printed for John Lawrence, 1713.

———. *The Nonconformist's Memorial.* Ed. by Samuel Palmer. 2 vols. London: Printed for W. Harris, 1775.

Clarke, Samuel. *A General Martyrology containing a Collection of all the Greatest Persecutions which have befalled the Church of Christ from the Creation to our present times; Where is given exact an Account of the Protestant Sufferings in Queen Mary's Reign. Together, with a large Collection of Lives of great Persons, eminent Divines, and singular Christians, famous in their generations for Learning and Piety; and most of them sufferers for the Cause of Christ.* Glasgow: J. Galbraith and Co., 1770.

The Confession of Faith of the Assembly of Divines at Westminster, from the Original Manuscript written by Cornelius Burges. Ed. by S. W. Carruthers. London: Presbyterian Church of England, 1946.

Dell, William. *Several Sermons and Discourses.* London: Printed by J. Sowle, 1709.

Doddridge, Philip. "Letter to Mr. Wesley: A Scheme of Study for a Clergyman," *The Arminian Magazine*, I (1778), 419-25.

Flavel, John. *Husbandry Spiritualized: or, The Heavenly Use of Earthly Things.* Elizabeth Town: Printed by Shepard Killock, 1794.

The Form of Presbyterial Church Government and of Ordination of Ministers Agreed Upon by the Assembly of Divines at Westminster. Edinburgh: Printed by E. Robertson, 1766.

Foxe, John. *Acts and Monuments of the Christian Martyrs, and Matters Ecclesiasticall passed in the Church of Christ, from the Primitive beginning to these our daies.* 4 vols. London: Printed for the Company of Stationers, 1641.

Goodwin, John. *Imputatio Fidei, or a Treatise on Justification.* London: Printed by P. O. and G. D., 1642.

Goodwin, Thomas. *A Child of Light Walking in Darkness: or A Treatise Shewing the Causes, by which, the Cases, wherein, and the Ends, for which God Leaves His Children to Distresses of Conscience. Together with Directions How to Walk, so as to Come Forth of Such Condition.* London: Printed by F. G. for R. Dawlman, 1659.

———. *The Tryall of a Christian's Growth.* London: Printed for R. Dawlman, 1643.

Hale, Sir Matthew. *Contemplations, Moral and Divine.* London: Printed by William Godbid for William Shrowsbury, 1676.

Hall, Joseph. *The Works of Joseph Hall.* Ed. by Josiah Pratt. 10 vols. London: Printed by C. Whittingham, 1808.

Henry, Matthew. *An Account of the Life and Death of Mr. Philip Henry.* 3rd ed. London: Printed for J. Lawrence, J. Nicholson, J. and B. Sprint, N. Cliffe, and D. Jackson, 1712.

Select Bibliography

Kitchin, John. "How Must We Reprove That We May Not Partake of Other Men's Sins," *The Morning Exercises at Cripplegate, St. Giles in the Fields, and in Southwark,* Vol. I. Ed. by James Nichols. 6 vols. London: Printed for Thomas Tegg, 1844.

Manton, Thomas. *Twenty Sermons.* Vol. II in *The Works of Thomas Manton.* 22 vols. London: James Nisbet and Co., 1871.

Owen, John. *Concerning the Holy Spirit.* Vols. II and III of *Works.*

————. *The Doctrine of Justification by Faith Through the Imputation of the Righteousness of Christ Explained, Confirmed, and Vindicated.* London: Printed for R. Boulter, 1677.

————. *On Communion with God the Father, Son, and Holy Spirit.* Vol. X of *Works.*

————. *The Works of John Owen.* Ed. by Thomas Russell. 28 vols. London: Printed for Richard Baynes, 1826.

Palmer, Herbert. *Memorials of Godliness and Christianity in a Discourse of Making Religion Ones Business.* London: Printed for Samuel Crouch, 1681.

Perkins, William. *The Works of William Perkins.* 3 vols. London: John Legatt, 1616.

Preston, John. *The Breast Plate of Faith and Love.* London: Printed by W. I. for Nicholas Bourne, 1630.

————. *The New Covenant, or The Saints' Portion. A Treatise Unfolding the All-Sufficiencie of God, Man's uprightness, and the Covenant of Grace, delivered in fourteen Sermons upon Gen. 17:1.2.* London: Printed by I. D. for Nicholas Bourne, 1630.

Shaw, Samuel. *Communion with God.* Glasgow: Printed by R. Urio, 1749. Reprinted 1829, Glasgow: For William Collins.

————. *Immanuel: or a Discovery of True Religion; as it Imports a Living Principle in the Minds of Men.* Glasgow: Printed by R. Urio, 1749.

The Shorter Catechism of the Westminster Divines: Being a facsimile of the First Edition "with the Proofs thereof out of the Scriptures;" which was ordered to be Printed by the House of Commons, 14th April 1648. Ed. by J. H. Cotton and J. C. Pears, Jr. Nashville: Printed for Presbyterian Theological Seminary, Chicago, 1943.

Sibbes, Richard. *Bowels Opened: or A Discovery of the Neere and Deere Love. Union and Communion betwixt Christ and the Church.* Vol. II of *Works.*

————. *A Description of Christ.* In Vol. I of *Works.*

————. *A Fountain Opened.* In Vol. V of *Works.*

————. *A Fountain Sealed: or the Duty of the Sealed to the Spirit, and the*

Worke of the Spirit in Sealing. London: Printed by T. Harper for L. Chapman, 1637.

————. *Light From Heaven.* London: E. Purstow, 1638.

————. *The Nativity of Christ.* In Vol. V of *Works.*

————. *Salvation Applied.* In Vol. V of *Works.*

————. *The Works of Richard Sibbes.* Ed. by A. B. Grossart. 7 vols. Edinburgh: James Nichol, 1862.

Stuckley, Lewis. *A Gospel-Glass: Representing the Miscarriages of English Professors or, A Call from Heaven to Sinners and Saints, by Repentance And Reformation to Prepare to Meet God.* London: Printed by R. Edwards, 1809.

Whateley, William. *A Bride-Bush: or, A Direction for Married Persons.* London: Printed by Bernard Alsop for Beniamin Fisher, 1623.

Wilkins, John. *Ecclesiastes, or, A Discourse Concerning the Gift of Preaching.* 3rd ed. London: Printed by T. R. and E. M. for Samuel Gellibrand, 1651.

Other Works

Church, Stephen. "Letter to the Rev. Mr. Wesley," *The London Magazine,* XXIX (1760), 587-90.

The Country Parson's Advice to His Parishioners. London: For Benjamin Tooke, 1680.

Fletcher, John. *Checks to Antinomianism.* 4 vols. New York: J. Soule and T. Mason, 1820.

————. *Works of John Fletcher.* 4 vols. New York: Carlton and Lanahan, n.d.

Fuller, Thomas. *The History of the Worthies of England.* London: By J. G. W. L. and W. G., 1662.

Hill, Richard. *A Review of all the Doctrines taught by the Rev. Mr. John Wesley; Containing, A Full and Particular Answer to a Book entitled, "A Second Check to Antinomianism." In Six Letters of the Rev. Mr. F - - - - r. Wherein the Doctrines of A twofold Justification, Free Will, Man's Merit, Sinless Perfection, Finished Salvation, and Real Antinomianism, Are Particularly Discussed: and The Puritan Divines and Protestant Churches Vindicated from the Charges brought against them of holding Mr. Wesley's Doctrines. To which are added A Farrago; and Some Remarks on the "Third Check to Antinomianism."* London: E. and C. Dilly, 1772.

Neal, Daniel. *History of the Puritans, or Protestant Non-Conformists from the Reformation to the Toleration Act of King William and Queen Mary.* 4 vols. Dublin: Printed for Brice Edmond, 1755.

Owen, T. E. *Methodism Unmasked; or the Progress of Puritanism from the Sixteenth to the Nineteenth Century.* London: Printed for J. Hatchard, 1802.

Walton, Isaac. *The Lives of Donne, Wotton, Hooker, Herbert, and Sanderson.* Cambridge: Brown, Shattuck, and Co., 1832.

Secondary Sources

Articles and Periodicals

Baker, Frank. "The Beginnings of the Methodist Covenant Service," *LQHR*, 180 (1955), 215-20.

––––––. *"A Study of John Wesley's Readings,"* *LQHR*, 168 (1943), 140-45.

––––––. "John Wesley's Churchmanship," *LQHR*, 185 (1960), 210-15, 269-74.

––––––. "Wesley's Ordinations," *WHSP*, XXIV (1944), 76-80, 101-3.

––––––. "Wesley's Puritan Ancestry," *LQHR*, 187 (1962), 180-86.

Betz, Ernst. "Pietist and Puritan Sources of Early Protestant World Missions," *Church History*, XX (1951), 28-51.

"A Bibliographical Catalogue of Books Mentioned in John Wesley's Journals," *WHSP*, IV (1903-4), 17-19, 47-51, 74-81, 107-111, 134-40, 173-76, 203-10, 232-38.

Blake, G. Thompson. "The Whole Duty of Man," *LQHR*, 183 (1958), 293-97.

Bowmer, John C. "Wesley's Revision of the Communion Service in *The Sunday Service of the Methodists*," *LQHR*, 176 (1951), 230-37.

Brauer, Jerald C. "Reflections on the Nature of English Puritanism," *Church History*, XXIII (1954), 99-108.

Brown, W. Adams. "Covenant Theology," *Encyclopedia of Religion and Ethics*, Vol. IV. Ed. by James Hastings. 13 vols. Edinburgh: T. & T. Clark, 1912.

Butterworth, R. "Wesley and the Dissenters," *WHSP*, VIII (1911-12), 25-29.

Cameron, Richard M. "John Wesley's Aldersgate Street Experience," *Drew Gateway*, XXV (1955), 210-19.

Cannon, William R. "John Wesley's Doctrine of Sanctification and Perfection," *The Mennonite Quarterly Review*, XXXV (1961), 91-95.

Chiles, Robert E. "Methodist Apostasy: From Free Grace to Free Will," *Religion in Life*, XXVII (1957), 438-49.

Church, Leslie. "The Pastor in the Eighteenth Century," *LQHR*, 181 (1956), 19-23.

Cooke, Richard J. "Our Methodist Episcopacy," *Methodist Review*, 114 (March, 1931), 206-14.

Coomer, Duncan. "The Influence of Puritanism and Dissent on Methodism," *LQHR*, 175 (1950), 346-50.

Cushman, Robert E. "Theological Landmarks in the Revival Under Wesley," *Religion in Life*, XXVII (1957), 105-18.

Davies, Horton. "Epworth's Debt to Geneva—A Field for Research," *The Livingstonian* (1960), pp. 5-6.

["Didymus"]. "Mr. Wesley's *Christian Library*," *The Wesleyan-Methodist Magazine*, VI (1827), 310-16.

Fortney, Edward L. "The Literature of the History of Methodism," *Religion in Life*, XXIV (1955), 443-51.

Halévy, Élie. "La Naissance du Methodisme en Angleterre," *La Revue de Paris*, IV (1906), 519-40, 841-67.

Harrison, A. W. "Fifty Years of Studies in Methodist History," *WHSP*, XXIV (1943-44), 17-26.

[H.R.O.]. "Tract Societies," *The Wesleyan Methodist Magazine*, LXX (1847), 269-70.

Hunter, Frederick. "The Origins of Wesley's Covenant Service," *LQHR*, 164 (1939), 78-87. Also found in *WHSP*, XXII (1940), 126-30.

———. "Sources of Wesley's Revision of the Prayer Book in 1784-88," *WHSP*, XXIII (1941-42), 123-33.

Jackson, George. "John Wesley as a Bookman," *LQHR*, 160 (1935), 294-305.

Joy, James R. "Wesley: Man of a Thousand Books and a Book," *Religion in Life*, VIII (1939), 71-84.

Lawton, George. "Notes on Early Methodism in Northampton," *WHSP*, XXV (1945-46), 88-90.

Lindström, Harald. "The Message of John Wesley and the Modern Man," *Drew Gateway*, XXV (1955), 186-95.

Lloyd, A. Kingsley. "Charles Wesley's Debt to Matthew Henry," *LQHR*, 171 (1946), 330-37.

Martin, E. "The Christian Library," *WHSP*, II (1899-1900), 190-92.

Mumford, Norman W. "The Organization of the Methodist Church in the time of John Wesley," *LQHR*, 171 (1946), 35-40, 128-35.

Norwood, Frederick A. "Methodist Historical Studies, 1930-1959," *Church History*, XXVIII (1959), 391-417; XXIX (1960), 74-88.

Outler, Albert. "Towards a Re-Appraisal of John Wesley as a Theologian," *The Perkins School of Theology Journal*, XIV (1961), 5-14.

Platt, Frederic. "Wesley's 'Ordinations'—A Retrospect," *LQHR*, 160 (1935), 63-73.

Rattenbury, J. Ernest. "Note on Article on 'Sources of Wesley's Revision of the Prayer Book of 1784-88,' " WHSP, XXIII (1941-42), 173-75.

"Remarks on John Arndt's True Christianity," The Methodist Magazine, XLII (1819), 427-34.

"Review of the Christian Library," The Methodist Magazine, I, (1821), 306-8.

Rupp, E. Gordon. "Some Reflections on the Origin and Development of the English Methodist Tradition," LQHR, 179 (1953), 166-75.

Sanders, Paul S. "What God Hath Joined Together," Religion in Life, XXIX (1960), 491-500.

Sangster, W. E. "Wesley and Sanctification," LQHR, 171 (1946), 214-20.

Shipley, David C. "Wesley and Some Calvinistic Controversies," Drew Gateway, XXV (1955), 195-210.

Swift, Wesley. "Methodism and the Prayer Book," WHSP, XXVII (1949-50), 33-41.

————"The Sunday Service of the Methodists," WHSP, XXIX (1953-54), 12-20.

Thompson, Edgar. "Episcopacy: John Wesley's View," LQHR, 181 (1956), 113-18.

Trinterud, Leonard J. "The Origins of Puritanism," Church History, XX (1951), 37-57.

Wakefield, Gordon. "Puritanism, Its Necessity, Dangers, and Future," Methodist Sacramental Fellowship Bulletin (Summer, 1961), pp. 2-5.

Books

Ainslie, James L. The Doctrines of Ministerial Order in the Reformed Churches of the 16th and 17th Centuries. Edinburgh: T. & T. Clark, 1940.

Anderson, William K., ed. Methodism. Nashville: The Methodist Publishing House, 1947.

Augustine. Basic Writings of St. Augustine. Ed. by Whitney J. Oates. 2 vols. New York: Random House, 1948.

Baines-Griffiths, David. Wesley the Anglican. London: MacMillan and Co., 1919.

Baker, Eric. The Faith of a Methodist. Nashville: Abingdon Press, 1958.

Baker, Frank. Representative Verse of Charles Wesley. Nashville: Abingdon Press, 1962.

Beal, William. The Fathers of the Wesley Family. London: T. Mason, 1833.

Belden, Albert D. George Whitefield—The Awakener. London: Sampson Low, Marston, Co., 1930.

Bett, Henry. The Spirit of Methodism. London: Epworth Press, 1943.

Bishop, John. Methodist Worship: In Relation to Free Church Worship. London: Epworth Press, 1950.

Body, Alfred H. John Wesley and Education. London: Epworth Press, 1936.

Brailsford, Mabel R. *A Tale of Two Brothers: John and Charles Wesley*. London: Rupert Hart-Davis, 1954.

Bready, J. Wesley. *England Before and After Wesley*. New York: Harper and Brothers, 1938.

Brook, Benjamin. *The Lives of the Puritans*. 3 vols. London: Printed for James Black, 1813.

Burtner, Robert W., and Chiles, Robert E., eds. *A Compend of Wesley's Theology*. Nashville: Abingdon Press, 1954.

Bush, Douglas. *English Literature in the Earlier Seventeenth Century: 1600–1660*. Oxford: Clarendon Press, 1945.

Cannon, William R. *The Theology of John Wesley*. Nashville: Abingdon Press, 1946.

Carter, Henry. *The Methodist Heritage*. Nashville: Abingdon Press, 1951.

Cell, George Croft. *The Rediscovery of John Wesley*. New York: Henry Holt and Co., 1935.

Church, Leslie. *The Early Methodist People*. London: Epworth Press, 1948.

————. *More About the Early Methodist People*. London: Epworth Press, 1949.

Clarke, Adam. *Memoirs of the Wesley Family*. London: Printed by J. and T. Clarke, 1823.

Coke, Thomas, and Moore, Henry. *Life of the Reverend John Wesley Including an Account of the Great Revival of Religion in Europe and America of which he was the First and Chief Instrument*. London: G. Paramore, 1792.

Cowherd, Raymond G. *The Politics of English Dissent*. New York: New York University Press, 1956.

Crowther, Jonathan. *The History of the Wesleyan Methodists*. 2nd ed. London: Richard Edwards, 1815.

Dargan, E. C. *The History of Preaching*. 2 vols. London: Hodder and Stoughton, 1905.

Davies, Horton. *The English Free Churches*. London: Oxford University Press, 1952.

————. *The Worship of the English Puritans*. London: Dacre Press, 1948.

————. *Worship and Theology in England: From Watts and Wesley to Maurice, 1690-1850*. Princeton: Princeton University Press, 1961.

Deschner, John. *Wesley's Christology*. Dallas: Southern Methodist University Press, 1960.

The Dictionary of Anonymous and Pseudonymous English Literature. Ed. by James Kennedy. 8 vols. London: Oliver and Boyd, 1926.

Dictionary of National Biography. Ed. by Leslie Stephen. 59 vols. London: Smith, Elder and Co., 1885.

DuBose, H. M. *The Symbol of Methodism*. Nashville: Publishing House of the M. E. Church, South, 1907.

Edwards, Maldwyn. *Family Circle: A Study of the Epworth Household in Relation to John and Charles Wesley*. London: Epworth Press, 1949.

————. *Methodism and England*. London: Epworth Press, 1943.

————. *John Wesley and the Eighteenth Century*. London: Epworth Press, 1955.

Emory, John. *History of the Discipline of the Methodist Episcopal Church*. New York: Lane and Scott, 1851.

Flew, R. Newton. *The Idea of Perfection in Christian Theology*. London: Oxford University Press, 1934.

Green, John R. *Short History of the English People*. New York: Harper and Brothers, 1898.

Green, Richard. *John Wesley: Evangelist*. London: The Religious Tract Society, 1905.

————. *The Works of John and Charles Wesley: A Bibliography*. London: Methodist Publishing House, 1906.

Green, V. H. H. *The Young Mr. Wesley*. New York: St. Martin's Press, 1961.

Halévy, Élie. *A History of the English People in 1815*. Trans. by E. I. Watkin and D. A. Barker. 3 vols. London: T. Fisher Unwin, 1924.

Haller, William. *The Rise of Puritanism*. New York: Harper and Row, 1957.

Harmon, Nolan B. *The Rites and Rituals of Episcopal Methodism*. Nashville: Publishing House of the M. E. Church, South, 1926.

Herbert, Thomas W. *John Wesley as Editor and Author*. Princeton: Princeton University Press, 1940.

Hilderbrandt, Franz. *Christianity According to the Wesleys*. London: Epworth Press, 1956.

Huehns, Gertrude. *Antinomianism in English History*. London: Cresset Press, 1951.

Hunt, John. *Religious Thought in England From the Reformation to the End of Last Century*. 3 vols. London: Strahan and Co., 1870-73.

Kirk, K. E. *The Vision of God*. London: Longmans, Green, and Co., 1931.

Lawson, John. *Notes on Wesley's Forty-Four Sermons*. London: Epworth Press, 1952.

Lee, Umphrey. *John Wesley and Modern Religion*. Nashville: Cokesbury Press, 1936.

Legg, J. Wickham. *English Church Life: From the Restoration to the Tractarian Movement*. London: Longmans, Green and Co., 1914.

Lindström, Harald. *Wesley and Sanctification*. London: Epworth Press, 1950.

MacDonald, James A. *Wesley's Revision of the Shorter Catechism Showing the Connection of Methodist Doctrine with that of the Reformed Church, the Ancient Faith, and the Word of God.* Edinburgh: Geo. A. Morton, 1906.

Maclaren, Alexander, ed. *The Ejectment of 1662 and the Free Church.* London: The National Council of Evangelical Free Churches, n.d.

Macphail, Andrew. *Essays in Puritanism.* London: T. Fisher Unwin, 1905.

Matthews, A. G. *Calamy Revised: being a Revision of Edmund Calamy's Account of the Ministers and Others Ejected and Silenced, 1660-1662.* Oxford: Clarendon Press, 1934.

McConnell, Francis J. *John Wesley.* Nashville: Abingdon Press, 1939.

Miller, Perry. *The New England Mind: The Seventeenth Century.* New York: The Macmillan Company, 1939.

Minutes of the Methodist Conferences, 1744-1798. London: John Mason, 1862.

Molland, Einor. *Christendom: The Christian Churches, Their Doctrines, Constitutional Forms and Ways of Worship.* New York: Philosophical Library, 1959.

Neely, T. B. *Doctrinal Standards of Methodism.* New York: Fleming H. Revell Co., 1918.

A New History of Methodism. Ed. by W. J. Townsend, H. B. Workman, George Eayrs. London: Hodder and Stoughton. 1909.

Newton, John. *Methodism and the Puritans.* London: Dr. William's Trust, 1964.

Nichols, James H. *History of Christianity: 1650-1950.* New York: Ronald Press, 1956.

Nuttall, Geoffrey F. *The Holy Spirit in Puritan Faith and Experience.* Oxford: Basil Blackwell, 1947.

————. *Visible Saints: The Congregational Way 1640-1660.* Oxford: Basil Blackwell, 1957.

Outler, Albert, ed. *John Wesley.* New York: Oxford University Press, 1964.

Overton, J. H. *The Evangelical Revival in the Eighteenth Century.* London: Longmans, Green and Co., 1886.

Peters, John L. *Christian Perfection and American Methodism.* Nashville: Abingdon Press, 1956.

Phillips, James M. "Between Conscience and the Law: The Ethics of Richard Baxter (1615-1691)." Unpublished Ph.D. dissertation, Princeton University, 1959.

Piette, Maximin. *John Wesley in the Evolution of Protestantism.* Trans. by J. B. Howard. New York: Sheed and Ward, 1937.

Pritchard, F. C. *Methodist Secondary Education.* London: Epworth Press, 1949.

Rattenbury, J. Ernest. *The Eucharistic Hymns of John and Charles Wesley.* London: Epworth Press, 1948.

————. *Wesley's Legacy to the World.* London: Epworth Press, 1928.

Rees, Thomas. *The Holy Spirit in Thought and Experience.* New York: Charles Scribner's Sons, 1915.

Rupp, E. Gordon. *Six Makers of English Religion, 1500-1700.* London: Hodder and Stoughton, 1957.

Schaff, Philip, ed. *The Creeds of Christendom.* 6th ed. 3 vols. New York: Harper and Brothers, 1931.

Schmidt, Martin. *John Wesley, A Theological Biography.* Nashville: Abingdon Press, 1962.

Shilling, S. Paul. *Methodism and Society in Theological Perspective.* Nashville: Abingdon Press, 1960.

Shipley, David C. "Methodist Arminianism in the Theology of John Fletcher." Unpublished Ph.D. dissertation, Yale University, 1942.

Simon, John S. *John Wesley and the Religious Societies.* London: Epworth Press, 1921.

————. *John Wesley and the Methodist Societies.* London: Epworth Press, 1923.

————. *John Wesley and Advance of Methodism.* London: Epworth Press, 1925.

————. *John Wesley, the Master Builder.* London: Epworth Press, 1927.

————. *John Wesley, the Last Phase.* London: Epworth Press, 1934.

Smith, George. *History of Wesleyan Methodism.* 3 vols. London: Longman, Green, Longman, and Roberts, 1863.

Southey, Robert. *The Life of Wesley and the Rise and Progress of Methodism.* New York: Wm. B. Gilley, 1820.

Starkey, Lycurgus M., Jr., *The Work of the Holy Spirit.* Nashville: Abingdon Press, 1962.

Stephen, Leslie. *History of English Thought in the Eighteenth Century.* 2 vols. London: Smith, Elder, and Co., 1881.

Stevenson, George J. *Memorials of the Wesley Family.* London: S. W. Partridge and Co., 1876.

Sykes, Norman. *Church and State in England in the Eighteenth Century.* Cambridge: The University Press, 1934.

————. *Old Priest and New Presbyter.* Cambridge: The University Press, 1956.

Todd, John M. *John Wesley and the Catholic Church.* London: Hodder and Stoughton, 1958.

Towlson, Clifford W. *Moravian and Methodist.* London: Epworth Press, 1957.

Trevelyan, G. M. *English Social History.* London: Longmans, Green and Co., 1958.

Tyerman, Luke. *The Life and Times of the Rev. John Wesley, A.M.* 3 vols. New York: Harper and Brothers, 1872.

————. *The Life and Times of the Rev. Samuel Wesley, A.M., Rector of Epworth.* London: Simpkin, Marshall and Co., 1866.

Valliamy, C. E. *John Wesley.* London: Epworth Press, 1958.

Wakefield, Gordon Stevens. *Puritan Devotion: Its Place in the Development of Christian Piety.* London: Epworth Press, 1957.

Watkin-Jones, Howard. *The Holy Spirit from Arminius to Wesley.* London: Epworth Press, 1929.

Watt, Robert. *Bibliotheca Britannica.* 4 vols. Edinburgh: Archibald Constable and Co., 1824.

Wearmouth, Robert F. *Methodism and the Common People of the Eighteenth Century.* London: Epworth Press, 1945.

Webber, F. R. *A History of Preaching in Britain and America.* 3 vols. Milwaukee: Northwest Publishing House, 1952.

Wesley Bicentennial, 1703-1903. Various authors. Middletown, Conn.: Wesleyan University, 1904.

Whitefield, George. *Journals.* London: Banner of Truth Trust, 1960.

Whitehead, John. *The Life of The Rev. John Wesley.* 2 vols. London: Printed by Stephen Couchman, 1793.

Willey, Basil. *The Eighteenth Century Background.* London: Chatto and Windus, 1940.

Williams, Colin W. *John Wesley's Theology Today.* Nashville: Abingdon Press, 1960.

Wing, Donald. *Short Title Catalogue of Books Printed in England, Scotland, Ireland and Wales, 1640-1700.* 3 vols. New York: For Index Society by Columbia University Press, 1945.

Yates, Arthur. *The Doctrine of Assurance.* London: Epworth Press, 1952.

INDEX

279

Index

/